# The Peace Corps

# The Peace Corps

## ROBERT G. CAREY

FOREWORD BY
JOSEPH H. BLATCHFORD

PRAEGER PUBLISHERS

New York · Washington · London

To my wife, Helen, and my sons,

Rob, Tim, and Christopher

PRAEGER PUBLISHERS
111 Fourth Avenue, New York, N.Y. 10003, U.S.A.
5, Cromwell Place, London S.W.7, England

Published in the United States of America in 1970
by Praeger Publishers, Inc.

Library of Congress Catalog Card Number: 75–81192

This book is No. 22 in the series
    *Praeger Library of U.S. Government Departments and Agencies*

Printed in the United States of America

# Foreword

by JOSEPH H. BLATCHFORD
*Director of the Peace Corps*

This book by Robert Carey takes a serious, in-depth look at the nature, history, and prospects of the Peace Corps.

The author points to the central truism that the strength of the Peace Corps is with the individual volunteers who have answered the call from overseas for help to till the soil, build the bridges, and teach the children. Mr. Carey correctly sees the Peace Corps staff, from Director to an associate director of a small country, as existing to support the volunteer. The only reason for any staff member's work is to encourage and help guide the volunteers.

In the new directions looked to by the Peace Corps, we are committed to bringing host-country men and women onto Peace Corps staffs. We are also determined to add to the volunteer-"mix" more mid-career Americans with the specific skills so needed overseas.

As Mr. Carey points out, the work we do today is built upon the successes of thousands of volunteers who have served before. The changes we are making are designed to make more effective the work of the volunteers of today and tomorrow.

Brotherhood cannot simply be a fuzzy, romantic hope. Careful planning and evaluation of what we are doing and how we can do it better must occupy the Peace Corps in the

1970's. This book brings together developments that are past and many of those that are current. And it depicts our plans and hopes for the further building of the Peace Corps as a force for understanding.

# Preface

Anyone who has the temerity to write about the Peace Corps must have patience and fortitude. The research, writing, and modification of early drafts of this book took many more months than I had anticipated. Daily—sometimes hourly—a change took place within either the Peace Corps or a host country. This mutability made both the original writing and revision doubly difficult. Even as this preface is being written, the Peace Corps world is changing: India is beset by political power struggles and religious strife; an uneasy peace exists between two major racial groups in Malaysia; the Middle East faces new turmoil; Kenya and the Somali Republic are recovering from the assassination of national leaders; a new regime has taken over in Bolivia. And the struggle in Vietnam continues to hang like a dark cloud over the entire world, with economic development in Southeast Asia but one of the hopes it shadows.

In addition to constant change, there is another set of odds against which an author must work. For every volunteer and for every staff member, there is a different shade of opinion about what the Peace Corps has been, is, and ought to be.

This book, therefore, is not a definitive work on the Peace Corps. It cannot be. That task remains for one who has lived his own Peace Corps experience and can undertake such a reporting venture in a more stable time.

To further complicate my own task, a change in Peace Corps leadership took place at a time when the manuscript for this work should have been finished and ready for typesetting. The original final chapter was written under the assumption that Jack Vaughn would continue as Director at least until March 1, 1971, when, by law, he would have had to step down. But, on March 17, 1969, a new Director was appointed. It saddened me to watch Vaughn leave the agency he loved so well and served with such dignity and compassion. Fortunately, as U. S. Ambassador to Colombia he will not be out of touch with Peace Corps volunteers.

The new Director, Joseph Blatchford, possesses some of the personal characteristics of both his predecessors. Like Sargent Shriver, he is outgoing, confident, his own man, and respectful but not afraid of Congress. Like Jack Vaughn, he is compassionate, intensely committed, impatient with the official trappings of Washington, and volunteer-oriented. Unlike either, however, Blatchford sees the Peace Corps as the catalyst for an international volunteer movement in which the agency can maintain its identity and independence but do more than convey a person-to-person message of love from the United States. To the traditional spirit of the Peace Corps, he would like to add an ingredient for which he has been soundly damned by some past and present volunteers and staff members (who have a way of being possessive about the agency and its mystique). That ingredient is technical assistance. He explained why in hearings before the House Foreign Affairs Committee in July, 1969: "Requests for outside aid, particularly those bringing people instead of money, today reflect higher priorities and call for higher skills both because the problems are increasingly sophisticated and because of the almost universal yearning to be free of outside dependence."

Blatchford has also indicated that he is ready to accede to congressional requests to find ways of measuring Peace Corps effectiveness. In this endeavor he may find a rocky road. There seems to be no accurate, meaningful method for measuring Peace Corps "success," despite the American proclivity for measurable results. There is little about the Peace Corps that is either standardized or scientific. It is an agency nearly devoid of artificial and calculated orthodoxy.

The Corps has a litany, to be sure, but it is the litany of the explorer and the frontiersman, not the organization man. It may be that, in the final analysis, its impact can be measured only in the thousands of personal relationships and experiences of volunteers and their hosts, and they defy a pollster's tabulations.

So many persons have contributed to this book that reference to the entire Peace Corps does not seem unreasonable. The former volunteers who were interviewed both overseas and in the United States are too numerous to name. Some present and former staff members deserve special mention for their unstinting help and patience with what one of them called "the longest one-man sit-in in Peace Corps history." They are Robert Hatch, Stuart Awbrey, Ann Anderson, Susan Biddle, Paul Reed, William Hintz, Rachel Singer, Douglas Stafford, Bruce Potter, Buster Lewis, Robert Steiner, Leon Cox, James Hooper, Alberto Ibarguen, Richard Laird, Aubrey Owen, Robert Semmler, Henry Wheatley, Henry Norman, Michael Furst, and Peter Larson. I extend a special word of appreciation to Jack Vaughn and Joseph Blatchford, and to C. Payne Lucas, who personifies the commitment that characterizes the Corps.

*Adelphi, Maryland*
*October, 1969*

# Contents

# List of Charts and Tables

# Maps

# The Peace Corps

# I

# A Bold Proposal

---

It was two o'clock in the morning, and the mid-October chill held a hint of winter. Indifferent to both the late hour and the cold, a crowd of ten thousand University of Michigan students gathered to listen to the junior Senator from Massachusetts giving an unscheduled campaign speech. Characteristically hatless and without a topcoat, the young man, who in less than a month was to be elected thirty-fifth President of the United States, stood on the steps of the Michigan Union Building and spoke without a prepared text. Casually and somewhat tentatively, John Fitzgerald Kennedy suggested the creation of a volunteer corps of Americans to serve the cause of freedom by helping to fight poverty, disease, hunger, and ignorance in the developing nations of the world.

It was his way of sampling reaction to an idea that had been debated within the Kennedy camp for months and that had won strong endorsement from many of the candidate's strategists. Nine days before this unscheduled appearance, in a press release entitled "Message of Senator John F. Kennedy to the Nation's New Voters," Kennedy had said that, if elected President, he would

> explore thoroughly the possibility of utilizing the services of the very best of our trained and qualified young people to give of from three to five years of their lives to the cause of world peace by forming themselves into a Youth Peace Corps, going to the places that really need them and doing the jobs

that need to be done. . . . Such service would be considered service in the national interest.

Members of the Young Democrats, with the help of Students-for-Kennedy clubs, began distributing copies of the message on campuses throughout the country, and student newspapers gave the idea strong coverage.

It had been assumed at campaign headquarters that Kennedy would propose the idea in person at a time and place calculated to give the plan full benefit of the widest possible exposure to the general public. The occasion chosen caught all but a small number of his lieutenants by surprise, and not even Kennedy was prepared for the response to his spur-of-the-moment Michigan speech. The students met the idea with sustained applause and began to discuss ways of promoting the proposal before they returned to their rooms and dormitories. Several days later, while campaigning in Toledo, Ohio, Kennedy was greeted by a delegation of University of Michigan students who handed him a petition signed by several hundred volunteers for Peace Corps service.

Perhaps because the Michigan speech was spontaneous and was made at two o'clock in the morning, press coverage of the event was meager. Not until November 2, 1960—almost the eve of the election—did the rest of the nation learn of Kennedy's proposal for a Peace Corps, when the candidate enlarged on the idea during a speech at the Cow Palace in San Francisco. In a number of magazine and newspaper articles, in testimony before congressional committees, in Peace Corps publications, and in newspaper stories where he was directly quoted on the subject, the first Peace Corps Director, R. Sargent Shriver, Jr., repeatedly referred to November 2, 1960, and the Cow Palace as the date and place of the Peace Corps's birth. To a large, live audience, with national television exposure and maximum press and radio coverage, Kennedy for the first time explained how he proposed to implement the idea:

I . . . propose . . . a peace corps of talented young men and women, willing and able to serve their country . . . for three years as an alternative or as a supplement to peacetime selective service, well qualified through rigorous standards, well trained in the language, skills, and customs they will need to know, and directed and paid by the ICA point four agencies. We cannot discontinue training our young men as soldiers of war, but we also want them to be ambassadors of peace. . . .

This would be a volunteer corps, and volunteers would be sought among not only talented young men and women, but all Americans, of whatever age, who wished to serve the great Republic and serve the cause of freedom.

To most Republicans, the proposal seemed a political gimmick. Using terms such as "cult of escapism," Republican candidate Richard M. Nixon said the Corps would be a "haven for draft dodgers." Calling it a "juvenile experiment," President Dwight D. Eisenhower suggested that Peace Corps volunteers be sent to the moon because it was an "underdeveloped area."

To some Democrats, it appeared that Kennedy had stumbled onto the idea as a last-minute inspiration in a campaign that had brought forth few real issues and in which the role of the television make-up man had become as important as that of the speech-writer. But Kennedy's introduction of the Peace Corps proposal into the campaign at the eleventh hour was not without purpose. He needed an issue that might catch his opponent napping and throw him off stride. He also needed as much support as he could get from the followers of Hubert Humphrey and Adlai Stevenson and believed that the idealism of the proposal might help to woo some of them, as well as some Rockefeller Republicans, into his camp.

Ironically, early in the campaign, Nixon had been given an outline of a study on a youth peace corps by one of his advisers, a specialist on African affairs, but he had shelved the plan. Although he liked it, he thought it contained too many risks. In focusing his rebuttal on the draft-deferment issue, Nixon did not help his cause among students of voting age.

Beyond the political strategy, however, Kennedy had approached the Peace Corps idea cautiously and, in fact, had had to be convinced of its merits. He knew the country would have to reach maturity in its international attitudes before it could accept and support a Peace Corps. During his campaign, he sensed a widespread interest in relations between the United States and other nations. He noted that many of the citizens he met complained that the nation displayed little imagination in handling its foreign affairs. When it became evident to him that he had hold of an idea whose time had come, he planted it where, if it were to grow and flourish, it might receive its best nourishment—in the minds of young Americans. He chose well.

## AN IDEA FROM THE PAST

Millions of words have been written about the Peace Corps since it was first proposed by John Kennedy. Much of the early writing pointed out that the idea was not new but had existed in one form or another for many years. Since its creation, the Peace Corps has given more publicity to the American philosopher William James and his essay "The Moral Equivalent of War" than the author or the essay received while James was alive. At the Universal Peace Conference in Boston in 1904, James suggested that "draft-age young men be put to work building, not destroying"; his essay appeared in pamphlet form six years later, under the auspices of the Association of International Conciliation.

James had counterparts both before and after his time.* In 1901, two American troopships dropped anchor in the Philippines. On board were fourteen hundred American teachers who had answered President William McKinley's call to help teach the Filipinos, in the words of the teachers,

* For a thorough treatment of the subject, see Charles J. Wetzel, "The Peace Corps in Our Past," *The Annals of the American Academy of Political and Social Science,* Vol. 345 (May, 1966), pp. 1–11.

"self-reliance," the "dignity of labor," and "democracy." McKinley's plea was made after the United States had taken the islands by military force in the wake of the Spanish-American War. One of the troop carriers was the U.S. Army transport *Thomas,* from which the name given the teachers, Thomasites, was derived. There were 540 teachers aboard the *Thomas*—most scarcely past the age of twenty. During their first two years in the Philippines, 27 of them died of tropical diseases or were killed by bandits. Although some left for home because they were unable to adapt to a foreign environment and culture, most of the original fourteen hundred teachers stayed at least two years. By 1902, over one-third of the primary-school teachers in the Philippines were Thomasites.

Congressman Henry S. Reuss of Wisconsin, who has been called the "father of the Peace Corps" because of his early interest in the idea, takes delight in pointing out that Saint Benedict led missions of young men from the wealthy society of Rome to work in the underdeveloped areas of northern Europe more than fifteen hundred years ago. Indeed, many religious and other private organizations have been conducting programs similar to those of the Peace Corps for years.

The work of private groups has taken on special significance since the mid-1950's. As new nations emerged under the leadership of men who had been educated in mission schools or had been helped during their youth by private, nonprofit organizations, the impact of these groups on the rise of nationalism in Africa and Asia became evident. Their significance was recognized by Sargent Shriver when, in his plan for the Peace Corps, he proposed to make volunteers available to developing nations through "private voluntary agencies carrying on international assistance programs."

RECENT FORERUNNERS

The International Voluntary Services (IVS) may be as much the prototype of the Peace Corps as any other organization. It was formed in 1953 by church leaders seeking, in part, to provide direction for American missionary programs. Although representatives of Roman Catholic and Protestant churches are on the governing board, the IVS is nondenominational and not formally religious. Its volunteers overseas do not proselytize. Legislation submitted by President Eisenhower and passed by Congress in 1953 permitted the International Cooperation Administration (ICA), forerunner of the Agency for International Development (AID), to sign contracts for program administration with such groups as the IVS. The organization now has contracts with both the Peace Corps and AID, as well as with private foundations.

The IVS agricultural program in Egypt received wide acclaim in the mid-1950's when two young IVS workers who had been managing a 33-acre experimental farm had to be evacuated during the Suez crisis. Describing the event to the Senate in the summer of 1960, Senator Hubert H. Humphrey related that "one of the first requests that the Egyptian Government made of ours after the crisis had subsided was 'Get those two men back there, and give us ten more just like them. Their fame has spread up and down the Nile.'"

Still another private organization has been compared to the Peace Corps. In 1962, President Kennedy told a delegation of visitors to the White House that the group they represented "really were the progenitors of the Peace Corps." He was referring to Operation Crossroads Africa, founded in 1957 to promote interracial as well as international understanding by the Reverend James H. Robinson, a Harlem minister. Participants in the program, primarily students who help finance their tours, spend a summer working and traveling in Africa.

In the 1930's, the American Friends Service Committee (AFSC) established short-term work camps in the United States in which young Americans worked alongside young people from other countries. In 1960, the AFSC extended the Quaker concept of work camps and field training to overseas sites through a Voluntary International Service Assignments (VISA) program. The first VISA camps were set up in India and Tanganyika (now Tanzania).

A private organization that has worked closely with the Peace Corps is the Experiment in International Living (EIL), founded in 1932 by Dr. Donald B. Watt. Experimenters spend the summer months touring and living with families in foreign nations. The EIL program had a strong influence on the creation of the Peace Corps because of its philosophy and because of the individuals who had been a part of it. Sargent Shriver led EIL groups overseas when he was in college. Both the wife and the daughter of Congressman Reuss were experimenters, and so was Harlan Cleveland, co-author of *The Overseas Americans* and former assistant secretary of State for International Organizations Affairs. As chairman of the Committee on Education Interchange Policy of the Institute of International Education, Cleveland helped prepare a report that Shriver used to develop a Peace Corps proposal for President Kennedy.

The United States was not the first nation to sponsor volunteer technical assistance programs. Since 1954, the Netherlands's Bureau for International Technical Assistance has sent young specialists to work with the U.N. Expanded Technical Assistance Program. The volunteers work from one to three years without salary but receive an allowance of $25 per month, paid at the end of their tours. The British Volunteer Service Overseas, founded through private means in 1958 but now government-supported, sends volunteers overseas to serve one year, without salary, before entering a university. The Volunteer Graduate Association for Indonesia, founded by the National Union of Australian University Students, sends university graduates to work for the Indonesian Government for two or three years at local rates of pay. The Roman Catholic Church sponsors the Council for Developing Aid, formed in West Germany in 1959 to provide overseas technical assistance. Its volunteers are given food, lodging, and medical care at Catholic missions abroad and serve three years.

A CALL FOR ACTION

In July, 1958—at the same time that Congressman Reuss began his drive for a volunteer corps—a book was published that aroused public interest in sending overseas Americans who were willing to work directly with the people of less-developed lands. *The Ugly American,* by Eugene Burdick and William J. Lederer, may have given the Peace Corps its greatest single impetus. Its title has been widely misunderstood and misused.

The authors, who became consultants for the Peace Corps's program in the Philippines, made clear their belief that the United States needed more ugly Americans like Homer Atkins representing it overseas. Atkins was a wealthy engineer whose fingernails were black with grease and whose hands bore scars from a lifetime of work. His language was salty, and he wasted little time with most of the American technicians and diplomats he met in Southeast Asia. His way of conducting technical assistance programs in foreign countries was simple and direct: Get out in the "boondocks" and find out what the needs of the people are. Burdick and Lederer's approach was not original; diplomats from other nations, particularly the Soviet Union, had been using this technique for years.

Other Americans recognized the need for more than mere financial aid to developing nations. In 1950, leaders of the United Automobile Workers recommended that President Harry Truman create a government-sponsored technical aid program. Professor Charles J. Wetzel, in an article in the *Annals of the American Academy of Political and Social Science,* May, 1966, wrote:

> Walter Reuther, the union's president, speaking to the Indian Council on World Affairs in New Delhi in 1956, urged adoption of a scholarship program to prepare young Americans for a United Nations Technical Task Force. Victor Reuther, director of the union's international affairs program, substantially suggested a Peace Corps to the Senate Foreign Relations Committee in May 1959, calling for "technical missionaries with

slide rules, with medical kits, and textbooks, to fight communism on a positive basis." The laborites urged candidate Kennedy to make the youth corps one of his campaign issues.

## EARLY LEGISLATIVE PROPOSALS

On June 5, 1958, the late Senator Richard L. Neuberger of Oregon addressed the Senate during debate on mutual security authorizations for the fiscal year beginning July 1, 1958. He said, "I desire to invite to the attention of my colleagues some of the most convincing reasons I have ever heard for the continuation and maintenance of mutual security as recommended by the President and supported by the Senate Committee on Foreign Relations." He was referring to the program for training teachers in Nepal, administered by the University of Oregon through an ICA contract. He announced that the university was about to negotiate a new contract and expressed hope that funds would be appropriated for this and similar programs, stressing that they are as necessary as military and financial assistance to nations outside the Iron Curtain.

Senator Neuberger was one of the first members of Congress to urge that the United States help provide education for the citizens of less-developed nations. He was soon joined by Congressman Reuss, who had proposed the establishment of a volunteer corps during a lecture at Cornell University in 1958. In a speech on the floor of the House and in several magazine articles, Reuss described the "electric" response among college students to his proposal and suggested the establishment of a "Point Four Youth Corps," a plan he continued to promote for the next year and a half.

Congressman Reuss's proposal was significant in the development of the Peace Corps. He had linked a volunteer corps with the nation's foreign aid program and had suggested that its organization and administration be handled by the federal government. In addition, his plan had been supported by the Organization of Young Democrats and the

National Student Association, both of which promoted the idea on campuses across the country and helped generate the favorable response that greeted Kennedy's proposal.

In 1960, Congressman Reuss and Senator Neuberger each sponsored a bill calling for a study of the feasibility of a youth corps. The bills were combined into an amendment to the Mutual Security Act of 1960, which authorized the President to arrange for a "nongovernmental" study of the "advisability and practicability of a Point Four Youth Corps, under which young U.S. citizens would be trained to serve abroad in programs of technical cooperation." An appropriation of $10,000 was made to finance the study, which the Colorado State University Research Foundation subsequently conducted under a contract with the ICA. The Foundation submitted a favorable preliminary report in February, 1961. In the final report, submitted to Congress on June 5, 1961, the Foundation endorsed the Peace Corps as "advisable and practicable" and recommended that legislation be passed to make it a permanent agency. )

## THE HUMPHREY BILL

(In June, 1960, Senator Hubert Humphrey spoke against the Reuss-Neuberger amendment to the Mutual Security Act —not because he opposed the idea, but because he thought the time had come for direct action. Consequently, he submitted a bill proposing the immediate establishment of a "Peace Corps of American young men to assist the peoples of the underdeveloped areas of the world to learn the basic skills necessary to combat poverty, disease, illiteracy, and hunger." In his argument, Humphrey stressed the need for a moral rearming of American foreign policy. His bill was submitted four months to the day prior to Presidential candidate Kennedy's first public mention of a similar proposal.)

Humphrey's bill proposed the creation of a separate agency that would "work in the closest cooperation with the Department of State, the U.S. Information Agency, and especially the International Cooperation Administration," and would "allow the President flexibility in the administration of our overall foreign aid program." He suggested a three-year term of service and a draft deferment for volunteers during their tours.

## THE PEACE CORPS IS BORN

( In February, 1961, when he had received the preliminary report from the Colorado State University Research Foundation, President Kennedy asked Sargent Shriver to form a task force to study and organize a Peace Corps program) Shriver described that hectic month in which the original guidelines for the Corps were developed in *National Geographic* of September, 1964:

> To keep from getting fired by my brother-in-law, I needed help badly. Working out of a room in Washington's Mayflower Hotel, I started rounding up friends who had some knowledge of international student exchange and education programs, plus practical experience in managing them. They, in turn, called friends of theirs, and pure chance brought me other splendid people.
>
> From early each morning until late at night all through February of 1961, some 15 to 20 of us argued, wrangled, suggested, proposed, until finally we had completed the outline of an organization. We were none too soon. President Kennedy wanted to know what was taking us so long—a whole month! I replied weakly that no one had ever tried to put together a Peace Corps before.

One of the men who caught Shriver's attention during February's dawn-to-dusk schedule was Warren W. Wiggins. Wiggins, a deputy director with the International Cooperation Administration, had written a paper entitled "The Towering Task," which had outlined the pitfalls to be avoided in organizing a peace corps. Shriver made the paper required reading for those working with him at the Mayflower Hotel.

Late one night, Shriver sent a telegram to Wiggins at his suburban Virginia home, asking that he come to the Mayflower at dawn the next morning. Wiggins complied, and the event became known in Peace Corps legend as "the midnight ride of Warren W. Wiggins."

The task force report, completed by Shriver and his associates in less than a month, was submitted on February 28. In the report, Shriver concluded:

> I am satisfied that we have sufficient answers to justify your going ahead. But since the Peace Corps is a new experiment in international cooperation many of the questions considered below will only be finally answered in action, by trial and error. . . .
>
> The Peace Corps can either begin in very low gear, with only preparatory work undertaken now and when Congress finally appropriates special funds for it—or it can be launched now and in earnest by executive action, with sufficient funds made available from existing Mutual Security Appropriations to permit a number of substantial projects to start this summer. . . . I recommend that the Peace Corps should be launched soon so that the opportunity to recruit the most qualified people from this year's graduating classes will not be lost. Nor should we lose the opportunity to use this summer for training on university campuses.

On the day after the submission of Shriver's report, March 1, 1961, President Kennedy created the Peace Corps by executive order "on a temporary pilot basis" as a separate agency within the State Department. Three days later, he named Sargent Shriver Peace Corps Director.

In the report, Shriver had recommended that the Peace Corps be attached to the State Department but be given independent status. He argued, as had Humphrey, that the President would need this flexibility to assure healthy development of the Corps. In the executive order that temporarily set up the agency, Kennedy placed the Peace Corps within the Department of State. As the legislation proposing its permanent establishment began to take shape, however, Kennedy and his White House advisers agreed that the Peace Corps should be placed under the new Agency for International Development. Shriver, on a world tour to sample the attitudes of national leaders toward the proposed program, learned of the decision while visiting India. In desperation, he cabled two of his lieutenants to seek the help of Vice-President Lyndon B. Johnson, who immediately went to see the President and spent an animated half-hour outlining the advantages of giving the Corps its independence. The President finally agreed. It was a crucial victory for the development of the agency.

In creating the Peace Corps by executive order, the President took a calculated political risk. He had been elected by only 49.7 per cent of the popular vote—certainly not a mandate. In addition, he was the first President elected in this century whose party failed to gain in Congress at the same time. Although a respectful relationship with Congress seemed essential, Kennedy chose to create the Peace Corps before the agency had received official congressional approval. There were few precedents for his action. Franklin D. Roosevelt had established an agency simply by issuing a press release, but the circumstances surrounding Kennedy's first months in office were not comparable with those of FDR's first one hundred days. Kennedy did not act without assurances that his program would have congressional blessing, however. He conferred with members of Congress in advance and was promised support. When the draft legislation was sent to Congress, he chose Sargent Shriver and Lyndon Johnson to run interference for the measure.

In addition, Kennedy was careful to stay within the limits of public law. The executive order was issued under the authority of the Mutual Security Act of 1954, as amended. The authority of the Director of the Peace Corps and his relationship to the Secretary of State was traced from that Act, and the agency was temporarily financed by contingency funds authorized under it. By linking the Peace Corps to the

Mutual Security Act, President Kennedy officially made the agency a part of the U.S. foreign assistance program and of the nation's foreign policy in general. )

## A BILL GOES TO CONGRESS

On May 30, 1961, Kennedy submitted draft legislation to Congress for the permanent establishment of the Peace Corps. The measure requested $40 million for fiscal year 1962 to enable the Corps to have 500 to 1,000 volunteers abroad by the end of 1961 and 2,700 volunteers overseas or in training by June, 1962. Few who had been connected with the study and creation of the Peace Corps anticipated how rapidly it would begin and grow.

On June 1, 1961, Hubert Humphrey introduced the draft legislation in the Senate, announcing that he was submitting the bill for himself and for Senator J. William Fulbright. Joint sponsorship came from Senators Claiborne Pell, Joseph S. Clark, Benjamin A. Smith, II, Gale W. McGee, Philip A. Hart, Albert Gore, Jacob K. Javits, John Sherman Cooper, Robert S. Kerr, Prescott Bush, Paul Douglas, Frank E. Moss, and Maurine B. Neuberger.* The draft legislation was introduced in the House by Congressman Thomas E. Morgan of Pennsylvania, chairman of the House Foreign Affairs Committee. Identical bills were introduced by thirteen of his colleagues, including Congressman Reuss.

Sponsorship by Congressman Morgan and Senators Humphrey and Fulbright lent ample prestige to the bills. Fulbright was, and still is, chairman of the Senate Foreign Relations Committee; Humphrey, the committee's third-ranking Democrat, enjoyed national prestige from the primary campaigns of the previous year. And it was convenient to have the chairman of the House Foreign Affairs Committee act as the bill's floor manager in the House.

The legislative history of the Peace Corps Act is brief. The

---

* Senator Maurine B. Neuberger was elected in November, 1960, to the seat left vacant by the death of her husband.

Senate Foreign Relations Committee held hearings on June 22 and 23, 1961, and the bill was reported favorably on August 10. The House Foreign Affairs Committee held hearings early in August; the bill was reported favorably on September 5, 1961. Following debate, the House amended and passed the bill, H.R. 7500, by a roll-call vote of 287 to 97. The bill was modified by the Senate and sent to conference. On September 19, the conference version of the legislation was reported favorably. Two days later, H.R. 7500, as reported by the conference committee, was passed in the House by a roll-call vote of 253 to 79 and in the Senate by a voice vote. The President signed the Act into law on September 22, 1961, and the Peace Corps came into being under Public Law 87–293. Kennedy announced when he signed the Act that more than thirteen thousand applications for the Peace Corps had already been received.

## CONFERENCE COMMITTEE ACTION

The major provision added to H.R. 7500 by the conference committee permitted the Peace Corps to employ thirty persons in high-level administrative positions at salaries not determined by the Civil Service Classification Act of 1949, as amended. The salaries of twenty of these persons could be above $15,030 per year, the level of civil service supergrade jobs. The Senate bill, without regard to the Classification Act, would have permitted the hiring of thirty-five persons, of whom twenty-five could have been paid supergrade salaries. The House bill, incorporating the recommendation of the Manpower Subcommittee of the House Post Office and Civil Service Committee, included no such provision. The Peace Corps was to apply to the Civil Service Commission for all personnel, and high-level administrators would be assigned to the Corps from the Commission's supergrade pool. The conference committee report stated, "It was recognized that sound management was essential to the success of this new program. The managers on the part of the House, therefore, receded from their position and agreed to thirty excepted positions, of which twenty could be compensated at rates above GS–15."

This compromise was important for Shriver's plans. He hoped to recruit the best administrators he could find and did not want to rely on civil service registers. Shriver preferred persons without government experience and avoided consultation with the Civil Service Commission whenever possible.

### THE PEACE CORPS ACT

(The Congress of the United States declares that it is the policy of the United States and the purpose of this Act to promote world peace and friendship through a Peace Corps, which shall make available to interested countries and areas men and women of the United States qualified for service abroad and willing to serve, under conditions of hardship if necessary, to help the peoples of such countries and areas in meeting their needs for trained manpower, and to help promote a better understanding of the American people on the part of the peoples served and a better understanding of other peoples on the part of the American people.)

When former Peace Corps Director Jack Vaughn quoted this passage from the Peace Corps Act, he sometimes added, "I cite this sentence not for its elegant syntax, its rich imagery or its lyrical flow of language—in case you were wondering. I cite it because, for all its bulk, it is a serviceable carry-all for the ideas that have animated the Peace Corps for eight years."

(The three goals of Peace Corps service are outlined in this brief passage. Volunteers are not only to provide skilled manpower to the countries in which they serve but also to foster a better understanding of the United States among their hosts and promote a better understanding of the peoples and cultures in other parts of the world among Americans.) Any judgment of the success of the Peace Corps must be measured against all three goals.

(The rest of the Peace Corps Act, as passed by Congress in 1961, is relatively uncomplicated. Some of its provisions have been modified over the years, but the major points remain unchanged. The Director and deputy director of the Peace Corps are appointed by the President with the approval of the Senate. The Secretary of State is given responsibility "for the continuous supervision and general direction" of programs administered by the Peace Corps.

Peace Corps activities in each host country are to be coordinated with those of other U.S. Government agencies "under the leadership of the chief of the United States diplomatic mission." The Peace Corps is "not to be assigned to perform services which could more usefully be performed by other available agencies of the United States Government in the country concerned," except with the approval of the Secretary of State.

Peace Corps volunteers are not to be considered employees or officers of the U.S. Government. However, they are protected against civil suits under the Federal Tort Claims Act "and any other Federal tort liability statute" and are given certain privileges enjoyed by federal civilian employees, such as compensation for disability and credit toward retirement from federal service.

Volunteers are to be provided "with such living, travel, and leave allowances, and such housing, transportation, supplies, equipment, subsistence, and clothing as the President may determine to be necessary for their maintenance and to insure their health and their capacity to serve effectively."

Service as a Peace Corps volunteer "shall not in any way exempt such volunteer from the performance of any obligations or duties under the provisions of the Universal Military Training and Service Act.")

## PROBLEMS RAISED IN DEBATE

Congressional debate on the Peace Corps legislation was lively. Proponents cited the idealistic and humanitarian values the Corps embodied. Opponents, led by Congressman Harold R. Gross and Senator Bourke B. Hickenlooper, both of Iowa, expressed fears that sending unseasoned youngsters overseas would lead to nothing but trouble. Senator Hickenlooper even suggested that Congress had "bought a pig in a poke."

There were more serious objections raised in the debate, as well. Congressman August E. Johansen of Michigan announced his opposition to the Peace Corps and questioned the legality of its creation. He stated that "it was an unconstitutional act to initiate this program without Congressional authorization. . . . I deeply resent statements made by spokesmen for the Peace Corps as to the moral obligation which Congress now has to continue the agency."

The Congressman also raised a question about the relationship of the Peace Corps to the nation's foreign policy—a point that has never been clear. Johansen cited two statements made by Peace Corps representatives during the hearings. The first, quoted from the record, stated that the Corps "is to be a part of the total foreign policy of the United States, and is to work in harmony with the policy objectives of the Government of the United States as expressed by the Secretary of State." The second said, "If the Peace Corps appears as an arm of American foreign policy, it cannot make its maximum contribution to our national interest." Johansen was disturbed by an "obviously unresolved conflict among the most ardent supporters of the Peace Corps program as to whether or not this agency is an instrument of American foreign policy." He concluded:

> Indeed, it is even suggested that a certain number of the Peace Corps volunteers be assigned to operate "within a clearly international framework" because "there are, unfortunately, countries in which any activity which lies purely within the auspices of the U.S. Government is the object of grave suspicion and in which the effectiveness of any Peace Corps activity would thus be seriously reduced." I cannot possibly support an agency with respect to which its own most ardent supporters entertain such completely opposite, fundamental policy views.

The question Johansen raised continues to be debated. The role of the Peace Corps in national foreign policy is ambiguous, and the agency must redefine its position with every major change in U.S. foreign policy. However, both the State Department and the Peace Corps affirm that the volunteer is an independent agent overseas. In his presentation to Congress in 1967, Jack Vaughn succinctly explained the Corps's position:

. . . a Volunteer is on his own, and we won't have it any other way. He is not an instrument of American foreign policy. Rather he is a living token of the human aspirations and good wishes of the American people. What we are about in the Peace Corps is not to assure the future, our way; it is to assure a future, any way at all.

# II

# The Formative Period

---

(The Peace Corps got off to a fast start. President Kennedy signed the executive order creating the agency less than six weeks after taking the oath of office. Sargent Shriver was named Director three days later and immediately began to draw talented and dedicated young men to Washington to staff the new agency.)

From the day of his confirmation as Peace Corps Director, Shriver became a familiar figure on Capitol Hill. His notes and records indicate that he talked to 363 members of the House and Senate in support of the agency. The overwhelming vote of approval given the legislation surprised even President Kennedy and prompted him at the time he signed the Peace Corps Act into law to "express my esteem for the most effective lobbyist on the Washington scene, Mr. Sargent Shriver."

The early days at Peace Corps headquarters, located northwest of Lafayette Park, just a block from the White House, were chaotic. To the visitor, the activity appeared to be barely under control. The writer will never forget going into an office to inquire about applying for a staff position and emerging two hours later, after having helped move file cabinets, office furniture, and office supplies into place. He left, convinced that the first volunteers would not be overseas for years.

But events proved him wrong. Within six months, the initial organization of the Peace Corps had been set up, the Washington staff numbered 362, and more than six hundred volunteers were at work in eight countries.)

## SETTING UP THE STAFF

Shriver established and presided over what his biographer, Robert A. Liston, has described as "a fast-paced, highly-charged, loosely-run operation." He chose men for top-level staff positions who were unimpressed with bureaucratic conventions and not interested in the Corps as a career and who made the Peace Corps work by breaking, at one time or another, every rule accepted by professional public administrators.

To find the sort of men he wanted, Shriver set up an operation known as Talent Search. Immediately after the election, Kennedy had asked Shriver to look for the best available men for Cabinet and sub-Cabinet posts. Shriver had put together a small but efficient staff under the direction of two of Kennedy's top campaign aides, and with their help had presented the President-elect with a list of names that included, among others, Robert McNamara, Dean Rusk, and David Bell. Shriver took the list of contacts developed during this search to the Peace Corps, where it was expanded by the staff of Talent Search to include two hundred leaders from business, universities, foundations, and government whose careers and experience made them ideal consultants. Each individual was told of the Peace Corps's needs and was asked to suggest the names of those they recommended for staff positions. They were not to include men from within their own organization or to consult those they recommended. The response was impressive. More than one thousand names were suggested in the first year. Shriver personally interviewed each candidate, including every physician and secretary sent abroad.

The men Shriver hired were generally young, highly competent, and dedicated to the concept of the Peace Corps. There were journalists, lawyers, academicians, experienced political campaigners, and federal civil servants. All but a handful of them have now left the agency. Some have gone into private consulting work, some to universities, and others to new government jobs, but they continue to keep in touch with one another. In an interview early in 1966, a former staff member reminisced about the early years:

> There was continuous staff turnover under Sarge, because that is the way he wanted it. He sought an infusion of new ideas—constantly—and a lot of people went away bitter because of this. But I think Shriver was the kind of fellow who was needed to get the program off the ground. He drove everyone including himself to the limits of his physical and mental capacities. He called in everybody and his brother to get at problems. He made a fetish of this, often assigning two or three persons the same problem without any of them knowing it. This often did not sit well. It caused a lot of thought and hard work to go down the drain.
>
> I will say, though, that he listened well, and he always made us feel as though we were right in the palace. He had a capacity to jack people up by their boot straps. You came away feeling as though you had just made a real point with him. Later on, you tried to remember what conclusions had been reached during the conversation and sometimes you discovered there were none. A well-known Shriverism was: "Don't bug me with details—go get the job done."
>
> After Kennedy's death, the agency's arteries began to harden. The assassination had robbed the Corps of some of its glitter, and we seemed to be going the way of all other bureaucracies.

Not only insiders, but outsiders as well, have commented on Shriver's special effectiveness in the formative period of the Peace Corps. A retired U.S. Civil Service Commission bureau chief, who helped set up the testing program for volunteer applicants, described his initial response to the Peace Corps in an interview:

> Without revealing my personal reactions to Shriver as an administrator, I have to say that his performance during those early months was truly amazing. I have never seen Congress react so strongly and so swiftly to a one-man campaign like that. I believe other old Washington hands would agree with me when I say that I have never seen a new agency get off the

ground and moving as soundly and as effectively as did the Peace Corps.

When the idea was first suggested, few of us ever had much hope that it would result in anything but complete chaos. We had visions of being overrun by long-haired kooks from all parts of the country. Instead, we keep seeing droves of just nice-looking, eager American kids. He made real believers of us.

## ORGANIZATION UNDER SHRIVER

⟨One of the first jobs facing Shriver and his staff was to set up the minimal structure necessary even for an agency that was to take pride in calling itself unstructured⟩ The task of designing the organization fell to Shriver and to experienced men like Warren Wiggins, Bradley Patterson, Jr., who had helped set up the first Cabinet Secretariat and then served as assistant secretary to the Cabinet under President Eisenhower, and Jack Young, who had just returned to government service after eight years with the management consultant firm of McKinsey & Company. Young, on loan from the National Aeronautics and Space Administration (NASA), where he had been serving as director of Management Analysis, joined the Peace Corps on the day President Kennedy signed the executive order creating the agency. Within three months, he had set up the Office of Management and enrolled the agency's charter staff. He then returned to NASA.

⟨Providing volunteers and overseas staff with medical support was a major problem for Shriver, who admits that he spent sleepless nights looking for a solution during February, 1961⟩ "In retrospect," Shriver once said, "it seems only a lucky chance that someone mentioned to me that the Coast Guard has no medical service of its own. The Public Health Service takes care of the health of Coast Guardsmen. I put in a call to Dr. Luther Terry, who was then Surgeon General of the United States and head of the Public Health Service. To my huge relief, Dr. Terry said, 'Yes, we would like to take on the Peace Corps.' "

# CHART I

## Organization of the Peace Corps Under Sargent Shriver

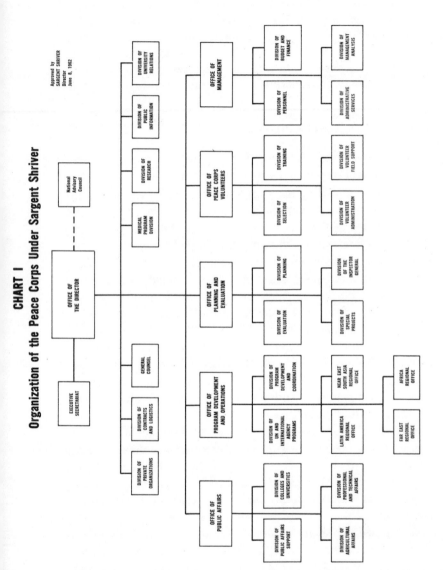

Approved by
SARGENT SHRIVER
Director
June 8, 1962

⌐The organization of the Peace Corps changed little during Shriver's tenure. Under the Office of the Director, five major offices—Public Affairs, Program Development and Operations, Planning and Evaluation, the Peace Corps Volunteer, and Management—were set up, each headed by an associate director⌐ (See Chart I.)

Program Development and Operations, the programing arm, quickly became the hub of the agency under the leadership of Warren Wiggins. The office included a division for program development and coordination, regional offices for Latin America, Africa, Near East/South Asia, and the Far East, and a liaison office for the United Nations and other international agencies.

⌐Public Affairs, initially headed by Bill D. Moyers, who later became deputy director of the Corps, was responsible for recruiting volunteers, answering inquiries, and coordinating relations with Congress. Planning and Evaluation, conceived and organized by William Haddad and Charles Peters, sent evaluators to training sites and host countries to discover weaknesses and foster continual improvement of the Corps. The selection, training, and support of volunteers overseas was handled by the Office of Peace Corps Volunteers, under the direction of Lawrence E. Dennis, a member of Shriver's original planning team.⌐

⌐Smaller divisions, reporting to the Director, provided general support for overall Peace Corps operations. The Division of Private Organizations encouraged and coordinated the sponsorship and administration of Peace Corps programs by such groups as the Experiment in International Living, CARE, the YMCA, and the YWCA. Contracts and Logistics conducted final negotiations on all Peace Corps contracts and supplied volunteers with such items as teaching aids, agricultural tools, books, and surveying equipment. The Research Division studied the information that began to come into the Washington offices as soon as the first volunteers arrived in their host countries. The Medical Program Division evaluated health problems in proposed overseas projects, conducted physical and psychiatric examinations of volunteers, provided health care and instructions during training and overseas service, and offered technical advice on the development of public health programs overseas. Public Information handled publicity and other press services; University Relations negotiated with universities and colleges for the administration of programs overseas; and the General Counsel provided legal assistance on official matters.)

In the early months, the agency functioned as a continuous staff meeting. The initial group shared ideas and worked informally. As the staff grew and this system became impractical, Shriver established a communication system built around "big" Tuesday and Thursday meetings and "little" Monday, Wednesday, and Friday sessions. The Tuesday-Thursday meetings included the entire professional staff; the "little" sessions were devoted to division or area responsibilities. The agenda of these meetings ranged from discussions of policy to reports on new programs.

Although Shriver attempted to keep the agency from becoming bureaucratic, he fought a losing battle. The competition that he deliberately encouraged led to power struggles among the staff, which he arbitrated with considerable skill. During 1965, when he divided his attention between the Peace Corps and the Office of Economic Opportunity (OEO), he lost control of the situation. Within the agency, this period became known as the "year of the long knives." Offices or divisions that had direct command of a budget or control of project authorization often absorbed those which did not.

## The First Programs

(In the early months of 1961, the men who had gathered to help Shriver with his task force report concluded that the Corps should begin with a pilot program of from 300 to 500 Peace Corps volunteers (PCV's). In April and May of that year, Shriver, Special Assistant to the President Harris Wofford, and Peace Corps Associate Directors Franklin Williams and Edwin Bayley went to Africa and Asia to talk with national leaders about the Corps. The overwhelming interest in the program abroad, combined with the favorable response at home, led Shriver and his staff to revise their initial estimate. They now sought to have from 500 to 1,000 volunteers overseas by December 31, 1961, and 2,700 PCV's overseas or in training by June 30, 1962. The first request for volunteers came from the government of Ghana in June, 1961. Former President Kwame Nkrumah asked for as many teachers as the Peace Corps could provide for the fall term. The governments of Nigeria, Tanganyika, India, Pakistan, Malaya (now the Federation of Malaysia), Thailand, Colombia, Chile, St. Lucia, and the Philippines followed with requests for teachers, nurses, medical assistants, community development workers, agriculturists, home economists, surveyors, engineers, lawyers, journalists, mechanics, bricklayers, plumbers, carpenters, and electricians.

The initial Peace Corps programs were established with the help of colleges and universities, international agencies, and private organizations. The first training program was designed and conducted by CARE at Rutgers University for eighty-one volunteers headed for community development work in Colombia. In less than a year, training contracts had been signed with thirty-six colleges and universities. By September, 1962, nearly fifty universities had trained volunteers.

During the first year, five educational institutions signed contracts to administer programs overseas. Notre Dame University, on behalf of the Indiana Conference of Higher Education, conducted the initial agricultural and community development programs in Chile; Colorado State University administered agricultural programs in West Pakistan; and Michigan State University, Harvard University, and the University of California at Los Angeles joined in managing education projects in Nigeria.

In June, 1961, the Peace Corps contracted with two private organizations to administer programs. Heifer Project, a National 4-H Foundation affiliate, supervised an agricultural program on the island of St. Lucia in the Caribbean, and CARE set up and ran the first community development program in Colombia. By the end of the first year of operations, seventeen programs were administered by such private organizations as the Agricultural Technical Assistance Foundation, the Experiment in International Living, International Voluntary Services, the National Farmers Union, the National 4-H Foundation, the Near East Foundation, the YWCA, and the YMCA.

In mid-1962, the Peace Corps announced its first project in cooperation with the United Nations. Twenty volunteers were assigned to serve with the Food and Agricultural Organization (FAO) in Pakistan to help farmers increase crop production. The FAO provided administrative, logistical, and medical support for the volunteers.

Without the help of these organizations, the Peace Corps could never have gotten off to a fast start. However, there were innate difficulties in supervision by outside groups and, as quickly as possible, the Peace Corps developed its own administrative machinery.

## POLICY ON OVERSEAS SERVICE

Basic policy for volunteer service, which has been modified little in the past eight years, was announced at the time the Peace Corps legislation was submitted to Congress.

The Peace Corps would go only to those countries to which it was invited. This policy has been honored, although it is well known that both Sargent Shriver and Jack Vaughn were unquestionably excellent salesmen. Volunteers would work for the host government or for a private agency or organization within the host country and would serve under local supervisors and work with host-country co-workers wherever possible. Volunteers would be active participants in projects, not just advisers. The length of a tour of service would be two years, without draft exemption. A living allowance, based on a cost-of-living index in the host country, would be given to each volunteer to permit a modest living style comparable to that of his co-workers. A readjustment allowance of $75 for each month of satisfactory service would be paid at the completion of service to help a volunteer return to life in the United States.

Volunteers would not have diplomatic privileges or immunities, post exchange or commissary rights, hardship allowances, or vehicles, unless needed for their job. The policy on vehicles has become stringent because most volunteer deaths have been caused by vehicular accidents.

A volunteer would be required to learn the language and to understand the customs of the country to which he is assigned. The importance of this policy has increased with experience, for the Peace Corps has discovered that a volunteer's effectiveness and necessary personal satisfaction are directly related to his ability to communicate with and understand his co-workers. Although fluency in a language or previous language training is helpful, it is not required of an applicant; however, an applicant's ability to learn a language may play a part in determining where he will serve, since some assignments require more than one language. In Niger, for example, the volunteer must speak French and Hausa to communicate effectively; in Ecuador, some jobs require fluency in Spanish and the Indian language Quechua.

A volunteer should be able to discuss the United States intelligently and objectively when questioned and to refrain from political and religious proselytizing. Initial training included numerous lectures on U.S. history, foreign affairs, and culture, but since a high percentage of Peace Corps trainees have attended college, this approach has been changed.

The Peace Corps would be open to all qualified, single Americans eighteen years of age and over and to married couples with no dependents under eighteen, provided each has a needed skill. The record of married couples is excellent. The Peace Corps has found that they adjust better to a new environment and have fewer health problems than do single volunteers, although, because they speak English to each other, they tend to learn the local language more slowly. In 1969, 23 per cent of all volunteers in service were married.)

(A college degree would not be a requirement for service. Nevertheless, college experience or a specific skill improves the chances of a person being accepted.)

( Final selection of each trainee for enrollment as a volunteer would not be made until well into the training program to give both the trainee and the Peace Corps ample time to assess each other. At the same time, high medical, psychological, and character standards were to be met before an applicant would be invited to training.) These policies remain in effect.

The hardships of life in the Peace Corps would be stressed in recruiting materials so that no candidate would misjudge the terms and conditions under which he had volunteered to serve. This policy was overdone in the early years and has been modified.

Volunteers are to live on the same level as their co-workers, which means one thing in a remote village in the Peruvian Andes and something quite different in an urban center like Addis Ababa. Although some volunteers do live in cottages with dirt floors and thatched roofs, the majority have accommodations that include electricity, for at least part of each day, and running water or a nearby well.

(Applicants, trainees, and volunteers could resign from the Peace Corps at any time. The agency wants only those who serve freely. If a volunteer resigns prior to the completion of his two-year assignment, he may have to pay for his transportation home. If circumstances leading to an early return are clearly beyond his control or not of his own making, the Peace Corps pays the cost.)Many staff members believe that the Corps should be responsible for a volunteer until the end of his tour, no matter what the reasons for his return, and, as a result, the policy remains a point of debate. It was recently liberalized by a provision added to the agency's policies and procedures manual that permits the Director to send a volunteer home "for the convenience of the Peace Corps." In such cases, the volunteer's transportation is provided by the agency if he returns home immediately.

## SELECTING VOLUNTEERS

While the basic organization and policy of the Peace Corps was being set up, Shriver and his staff were planning for the first volunteers. There was little need for active recruitment during the first year; the Peace Corps received more than thirteen thousand applications for service in the first six months. Selecting and training volunteers were quite other matters.

On March 22, 1961, Dr. Nicholas Hobbs, chairman of the psychology department at Louisiana State University, was appointed director of Selection. On March 28, he convened a conference of selection experts drawn from the International Cooperation Administration, the U.S. Army, Navy, and Air Force, the National Institutes of Health, the U.S. Information Agency, and several professional and voluntary organizations. In spite of only two days' notice, twenty-one of the twenty-two individuals contacted attended. During this conference, general guidelines for the development of a selection program were established. Other conferences on specific problems followed. At one of these sessions, a group of psychologists worked out the specifications for a Peace Corps entrance examination, the details of which were developed by the Educational Testing Service (ETS) of Princeton, New Jersey. At the same time, the American Institute for Research developed a biographical data form and a personal inventory form to help assess personality traits. The U.S. Civil Service Commission agreed to administer the tests at their centers within the United States and through U.S. embassies overseas.

Before any tests were ready, the Peace Corps was caught by surprise when Ghana submitted its urgent request for teachers for the fall term. The ETS responded to the tight deadline with a test specifically designed to examine potential candidates for the program in Ghana.

( By the end of May, the Peace Corps was ready to administer its first entrance examination. Every person who had applied to the Corps by midnight on Thursday, May 25, was notified by telegram that the exam would be given at a specified testing center on the following Saturday morning. A second test for teachers followed on June 5. The Peace Corps tested 5,210 applicants on those two days. (In 1961, 11,269 tests were given on four separate dates; by the end of June, 1962, an additional 9,163 applicants had been tested.) )

In addition to a questionnaire application and personal references, the Peace Corps requires a full investigation into the background of each candidate invited to training. The Peace Corps asked the Civil Service Commission to conduct these investigations but until they could do so, background checks were handled by the Federal Bureau of Investigation.

## SETTING UP TRAINING

Shriver and his staff were determined that the Corps avoid the errors made by so many groups working overseas. They wanted volunteers to go to their host countries with a knowledge of the culture in which they would live and at least some fluency in the language spoken there. In addition, they believed that volunteers would need to be thoroughly familiar with U.S. history, institutions, and culture and to have strong arguments to counter the accusations of Communists.

With no guidelines for a training program that would provide this background, Lawrence Dennis, head of the Office of Peace Corps Volunteers, arranged a series of institutes to which specialists from government agencies, universities, foundations, business, labor, and professional and academic societies were invited. These men discussed the problems of preparing volunteers for overseas service in general and in specific countries in Asia, Africa, Latin America, and East Asia. At special conferences, they offered advice on teaching foreign languages, area studies, American studies, international affairs, community development, and technical skills, and suggested ways to provide health orientation and physical conditioning. The response to the institutes was excellent. Nearly all the area-studies specialists in the United States attended the general meeting, after which they formed subcommittees and spent an entire night discussing specifics. The next morning, they reconvened to write outlines of suggested study programs.

The story of the Corps's first year was one of crash program piled upon crash program. Fortunately, the colleges and universities responded quickly to the many requests made of them. The response was natural. The Peace Corps needed the resources of the universities, and the schools themselves had much to gain by the expansion of their activities offered by the opportunity for cooperative programs.

## The First Volunteers

The first twelve trainees were selected on June 14, 1961; the first training program began at Rutgers University on June 25; and on August 30, fifty-one volunteers—the first to arrive in a host country—landed in Accra, Ghana, sang the national anthem in the local dialect, Twi, and dispersed to their assignments. The Peace Corps was in business.

From this beginning, the Corps grew rapidly. By the end of 1961, 827 applicants had entered training and slightly more than 600 had gone overseas. By June 30, 1962, there were 1,044 volunteers at work in 17 countries and another 2,939 in training or scheduled for training during the following summer.

These early volunteers were generally well educated (two-thirds held undergraduate degrees and one in ten had an advanced degree) and came from every group represented in the United States and from every part of the nation. They served as teachers in Ghana, Tanganyika, Malaya, Sierra Leone, and St. Lucia. In Colombia, they worked in community development programs. In Tanganyika, they surveyed roads and conducted on-the-job training for their co-workers.

In India, they taught agricultural skills in the Punjab and began the first poultry raising project.) (The latter has led to such an increase in poultry production that Indians today refer rather casually to "the Peace Corps egg.") In addition to their regular assignments, these early volunteers established a Peace Corps tradition by spending extra hours working with children and community groups.

Neither the first volunteers nor the staff in Washington knew what overseas service would bring. The volunteers went armed with tennis rackets to fight boredom and a myriad of shots to protect against disease. But almost on arrival they faced problems.

In many cases, volunteers were unprepared for what awaited them. The life of hardship, which had appeared glamorous in the United States, proved to be tedious and uncomfortable within a few months. Language training was frequently inadequate. On at least one occasion, an entire contingent of volunteers was flown to a country to which they had not been assigned. Some volunteers found themselves on jobs for which they had not been trained, while others arrived to find they had no real job at all. An authority on the growth and care of walnut trees, sent to Brazil, was assigned to a barren section that had no trees of any kind; another volunteer established a successful fishing cooperative in a remote village in northern Peru before a Peace Corps staff member discovered he should have gone to a town in southern Peru. The northern community had been promised a doctor.

Communications broke down, too. A group of volunteers arrived in Nepal to discover that the Nepalese did not know they were coming and the Peace Corps did not know what their assignments were. In the middle of the first year of operations, the Peace Corps received the following letter from a volunteer: "Your letter requesting me, as a Spanish teacher, to complete the Peace Corps questionnaire and examinations for possible assignment in Latin America, reached me here in Nigeria. I am in my fifth month of Peace Corps duty teaching English as a second language."

There were problems at home, as well. Even before legislation had been passed, the press and Congress were scrutinizing Peace Corps operations and watching for signs of trouble. The first incident to receive national coverage involved twenty-one-year-old Charles Kamen, a trainee who had once been ejected from a Rotary Club meeting in Miami for laughing and applauding "at the wrong times" during a showing of *Operation Abolition,* the controversial film made by the House Committee on Un-American Activities about disturbances caused by young people at a Committee hearing in San Francisco. During congressional hearings on the Peace Corps legislation, Shriver was pressured to drop Kamen from the training program at Pennsylvania State University. Shriver refused to do so, explaining that selection was to be based on individual merit alone. On September 26, 1961, just five days after Congress had approved the Peace Corps Act, the agency announced that several trainees at Pennsylvania State University, including Kamen, had been dropped because they did not have skills suitable for the projects for which they had been training. The agency added that they were eligible to be reinvited for service at a later date.

Near the end of the Corp's first year of operations, the press gave wide coverage to the plight of Mrs. Janie Fletcher, a sixty-five-year-old home economist who had been training for service in Brazil. Mrs. Fletcher claimed she had been dropped from the program because she could not follow a rigorous physical education schedule. In a report to Congress, the Peace Corps explained that the decision of the selection board had been unanimous and that by June 30, 1962, 470 trainees had completed the training course, including six in their sixties. The report concluded: "Each of the older volunteers followed a physical exercise schedule consistent with his own capabilities."

The most widely publicized incident—and the most serious

—occurred in October, 1961. Margery Michelmore, a volunteer serving in Nigeria, lost a postcard she had written to a friend back home. In her message, Miss Michelmore described the volunteers' "initial, horrified shock" at the squalor and sanitary conditions in Ibadan. The postcard was found; students at the University College of Ibadan had it duplicated and distributed and called a rally at which a resolution was adopted condemning Miss Michelmore and demanding deportation of all forty Peace Corps members then serving in Nigeria. Nigerian Prime Minister Sir Abubakar Tafawa Balewa publicly demanded that the young volunteer be "unequivocally condemned."

Before the incident escalated further, Miss Michelmore wrote a letter of apology to Nigerian authorities and offered her resignation to the Peace Corps. Although no longer a volunteer, she was asked to remain with the Corps for a brief period to counsel trainees. The agency's first annual report referred to the incident:

> The Peace Corps, till then a generalized concept, became personalized in Miss Michelmore, whose academic qualifications and other qualities for Peace Corps service were obvious. Other Peace Corps Volunteers throughout the world were also alerted to their vulnerability in a way much more effective than a lecture or a written warning.

Within slightly more than a year, the Peace Corps, under Shriver's direction, had grown from an idealistic concept to a functioning agency. Its organization had been established and its basic principles defined; volunteers were at work overseas and plans for an ambitious program were underway. The Corps was ready to build on the groundwork that had been laid during this formative period.

# III

# Headquarters in Washington

In 1965, four years after the creation of the Peace Corps, President Lyndon B. Johnson asked Sargent Shriver to head the newly established Office of Economic Opportunity (OEO) while remaining Director of the Peace Corps. The arrangement lasted only a year, for it was clear that both agencies needed a full-time director. When Shriver was asked to stay with OEO, he agreed to do so, and Jack Hood Vaughn, a foreign service officer, became the second Director of the Corps on March 1, 1966.

Vaughn was not an outsider. He had originally come to the Peace Corps in 1961 after working with the U.S. Information Agency (USIA) and the Agency for International Development. For the Peace Corps, he served as regional director for all programs in Latin America. He left in 1964 when he was appointed U.S. Ambassador to Panama and then returned to Washington to hold the positions, simultaneously, of assistant secretary of State for Inter-American Affairs and U.S. coordinator for the Alliance for Progress.

In his first public address as Peace Corps Director, Jack Vaughn introduced a theme to which he returned frequently:

. . . the cost of peace is no more than the cost of love itself. And here and now, I suppose, is as good a time as any to break down some embarrassments and inhibitions and give this game a name—for of what have we been speaking, toward what have we been groping, if not toward love? I shall not quarrel if it is your style to mask that word with others, like "under-

standing," or "giving," or "generosity," or even that half-way
mystery, "enlightened self-interest."

But if our task is serving the cause of lasting peace, then we
are trying to deliver a coded message without the key—unless
we admit that the key is love, and the message is man's belief
that he can make himself, and every other man, higher than the
animals.

Vaughn explained the attraction of the Corps to the House
Foreign Affairs Committee in September, 1967:

. . . young people are coming to the Peace Corps in 1967 because it is there, a proven idea; an exciting but working reality;
not a novelty, hardly under way, but an organization getting
things done. Moreover, it is an expression of themselves—not
so much a searching as an affirmation. . . . The Volunteers'
identity with the nation [in which they serve] is unmistakable.
They even seem to dismiss in their minds the idea of the Peace
Corps as a government agency. They seem to skip the structure
and identify with the spirit.

But for all the emphasis on love and spirit and references
to the agency as a "functioning noninstitution," the Peace
Corps under Vaughn became a solid professional organization.
The atmosphere at headquarters reflected his leadership. The
pace was more relaxed, the staff more experienced, and the
lines of responsibility more clearly defined than in the earlier
years.

Vaughn initiated a significant change by decentralizing
operations. The associate-director positions established by
Shriver were eliminated, and top overseas staff members
were given the authority to deal with problems on a day-to-
day basis, rather than having to await orders from Washington.
Vaughn also reduced the size of the headquarters staff and
increased the overseas staff to give the volunteers more support. In 1963, there were 716 employees in Washington and
339 overseas. By the end of 1967, when the number of
volunteers overseas had more than tripled, the Washington
staff numbered 676, while the overseas staff had grown to

735. Vaughn made other changes, too. He stressed increased language training for both staff and volunteers and more emphasis on recruiting college graduates with liberal arts degrees. He set up a planning-programing-budgeting system for program review and strongly supported a policy of hiring former volunteers to fill staff positions. And he encouraged the policy of binationalism—the hiring of host-country citizens for positions on overseas and training staffs.

Under Vaughn, major policy decisions were made by the operations committee, which met every Monday at 9 A.M. The committee included the Director, his deputy, the four regional directors, the executive secretary, and the directors of Public Affairs, Administration, and Planning, Program Review, and Research. In addition, a meeting of representatives from all headquarters offices was held every Tuesday and Thursday morning to discuss ideas and current problems. Rarely was there a definite agenda for the meetings, and members of the overseas staff or volunteers visiting headquarters were often invited to speak. Thus junior as well as senior staff members were given the opportunity to contribute information that helped shape policy decisions. Occasionally, and unexpectedly, they helped make policy on the spot.

The agency's approach to security classifications has also fostered a flow of ideas from the headquarters staff. Although the agency is authorized to use Top Secret and other high-level security classifications, staff members have preferred to rely on the classification Limited Official Use, except when leakage might endanger programs still under negotiation, or when an individual might be hurt if the document were widely circulated. Some host-country governments prefer to withhold publicity until all contracts have been signed and volunteer manpower has been assured. This limited use of secrecy has permitted the staff to keep informed about plans and problem areas and has encouraged a feeling of involvement in the devlopment of the Corps.

On March 17, 1969, Joseph H. Blatchford succeeded

Vaughn as Peace Corps Director. A Californian, Blatchford had graduated from the University of California at Los Angeles and had received a law degree from the University of California at Berkeley. At the time of his appointment by President Richard M. Nixon, Blatchford was serving as executive director of Acción International, a privately supported development agency that he had founded in 1960. Acción (Spanish for action) has helped set up community action projects in major urban centers in Brazil, Argentina, Peru, and Venezuela. It is managed and directed almost entirely by the people of the countries in which it operates and is supported mainly by private funds raised in those countries.

When he was sworn into office in April, 1969, Blatchford outlined some of the plans he has for the Peace Corps. He emphasized his intention to further decentralize the agency's operations, to delegate additional authority to overseas staffs, and to restructure Washington headquarters to serve more as a supporting body. He stressed the need to strengthen the methods for recruiting, selecting, and training volunteers and staff and announced that he would seek more blue-collar workers, highly skilled technicians, and mid-career professional men to serve as volunteers. He also proposed the extension of volunteer tours to three years as a substitute for military service, with the final year spent in the United States with an agency such as Volunteers in Service to America (VISTA).

Blatchford's management style differs from his two predecessors' in one important way: he has kept the number of office and division directors who report directly to him to a minimum. Consequently, he has been able to concern himself more with planning and with actively pursuing the goals he has outlined. Under Blatchford's direction, there has already been a reduction of staff in Washington and more autonomy has been given to country directors and their staffs. In July, 1969, he told the House Foreign Affairs Committee:

To improve management, the Peace Corps must be put on a

diet to lose unnecessary services to volunteers, consolidate overlapping functions and eliminate nonessential offices. It must be made lean and trim in order to respond more quickly to requests from abroad and offers to serve. Staff must be better trained. The Peace Corps must establish a better system of evaluating its work, eliminating what does not work and multiplying what does.

In early May, 1969, Blatchford asked Thomas J. Houser to come to Washington to serve as deputy director of the Peace Corps, and the Senate confirmed the appointment on June 12. Houser left a private law practice in Chicago to join the agency. In 1966, he had worked as campaign manager for Charles Percy's successful bid for a U.S. Senate seat, and he had remained with the Senator as special counsel until August, 1967. As deputy director, Houser directs the agency's day-to-day operations.

## "THE FIVE-YEAR FLUSH"

In 1965, prompted by a staff member's suggestion, Shriver asked Congress to add a provision to the Peace Corps Act to prohibit top staff members from serving more than five years with the agency. Congress made the proposed amendment law, specifying that it was not to be retroactive. At Peace Corps headquarters, the private term for this provision is "the five-year flush." Although the Peace Corps has never offered a career to its staff, many believe that the provision endangers the continuity of professional leadership that the agency has begun to develop. In an interview in early 1968, Vaughn expressed his reservations, "I am not enchanted by the figure of five years. I think that six-and-a-half or seven years would be more realistic. A man could work for two years in Washington and then go overseas for two two-year tours, or vice versa, or any of several combinations. This arrangement would give the Corps a great deal more professionalism and continuity."

Although Blatchford agrees with the theory behind the

policy, he would like to see the five-year provision modified. In an interview in July, 1969, he explained why:

> We would be foolish to allow experienced people to escape us. There are only a few old pros around now, those who have been with the agency since it was founded. I'm sure we'll find a way to keep those who want to stay, at least long enough to provide us with some memory. If we don't, as one former staff member put it, we'll continue to reinvent the wheel every year or so. We need new, fresh ideas, of course, but if we don't have some link with the past, we may keep on making the same mistakes.

## THE COSTS OF THE CORPS

In each of the first seven years of operations, the Peace Corps returned unobligated funds to the U.S. Treasury. However, the agency was unable to maintain this record at the end of fiscal 1969, for, after extended debate on all foreign aid programs during the summer of 1968, Congress set the Peace Corps appropriation for fiscal 1969 at $102 million—$10.8 million less than the agency had requested. The appropriation was allocated as follows: training, $23.2 million; Washington administration, $14.2 million; readjustment allowances, $11.7 million; overseas operations, $52.2 million; and miscellaneous, $0.7 million.

In July, 1969, Blatchford asked Congress for $101.1 million for fiscal 1970, pointing out that this was $900,000 less than the appropriation for the previous fiscal year. He added that he hoped to initiate innovations that might increase costs slightly in 1971, and, if so, he would request a higher appropriation in 1970. The House approved the request of $101.1 million, but the Senate cut it to $95.8 million. A compromise authorization bill for $98.5 million was submitted to both houses by a conference committee, and that bill passed the House in October, 1969. Fiscal 1970 is destined to be a frugal year.

In his first presentation to Congress, Shriver estimated that

the annual cost of maintaining a volunteer in service would
be $9,000, adding that he believed this figure would drop as
the agency gained administrative experience. He was right.
The figures for fiscal years 1963–68 demonstrate this trend:

| | |
|---|---|
| 1963 | $9,074 |
| 1964 | $8,214 |
| 1965 | $7,809 |
| 1966 | $7,867 |
| 1967 | $7,458 |
| 1968 | $7,863 |

The rise in the annual average cost per volunteer after the
1967 low was the result of a federal pay raise, the removal
of draft exemption status for Public Health Service physicians
assigned to the Peace Corps as staff doctors, and additional
administrative expenses and mandatory payments to other
agencies.

## HEADQUARTERS ORGANIZATION

Blatchford wasted little time in modifying the organization
of the Corps's Washington headquarters to reduce the weaknesses he saw and to make it conform to his managerial
philosophy. In May, 1969, he asked the management consultant firm of McKinsey & Company to study the Corps's
organization. McKinsey staff members interviewed Blatchford, Houser, and numerous staff members, analyzed the
agency's operations, and submitted a written report with
recommendations to the Director. Blatchford liked the suggestions and has adopted nearly all of them. The new organization chart (Chart II) is almost identical to that proposed
by McKinsey's consultants.

## THE OFFICE OF THE DIRECTOR

The Director of the Peace Corps is appointed by the
President, with the advice and consent of the Senate. The

## CHART II
## The Peace Corps

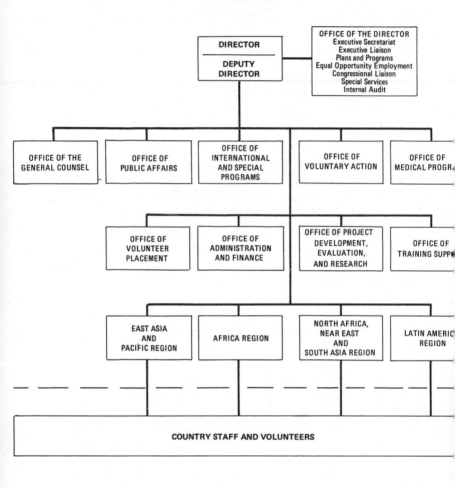

description of his job in the *Peace Corps Manual* is brief and uncomplicated: he is "responsible for the control, supervision, and implementation of all Peace Corps programs." Under Shriver, the Office of the Director was kept small, and this policy has been continued. The deputy director, also a Presidential appointee with Senate confirmation, supervises in the absence of the Director. There are now three special assistants assigned to the Director's Office as well as the Executive Secretariat and the offices of Congressional Liaison, Special Services, and Internal Audit.

The special assistant for plans and programs works with Blatchford on long-range plans for the agency and oversees their development until they are assigned to another office. The special assistant for equal opportunity employment, a carry-over from the tenures of Shriver and Vaughn, is a top staff member who oversees this program in addition to his other duties. The special assistant for executive liaison advises the Director about developments within the executive branch that will affect Peace Corps policy and about the Corps's plans and policies that relate to Presidential programs.

The executive secretary, head of the Executive Secretariat, is responsible for carrying out policy directives, handling communications, coordinating the activities of the Office of the Director, and arranging staff meetings. Congressional Liaison, a part of the Executive Secretariat under Vaughn and now a separate branch of the Director's Office, handles the agency's relations with Congress. (See Chapter XII.)

Special Services establishes policy on emergency home leave, medical-psychiatric evacuations, early terminations of service, overseas transfers, and volunteer deaths. It deals with all personal emergencies—phone calls from anxious parents who have read of a natural catastrophe or an outbreak of violence in the country in which their son or daughter is working, queries from PCV parents who have not had a letter from overseas for some time, or troubles at home in a volunteer's family—and acts as a channel for communication between volunteers and the Peace Corps Director.

## THE REGIONAL OFFICES

Responsibility for conducting the overseas operations of the Peace Corps is divided among four regional offices— Latin America; Africa; North Africa, Near East, and South Asia (NANESA); and East Asia and Pacific (EAP). These offices, working with the Office of Program Development, Evaluation, and Research, are the core of the headquarters organization and the link between the staff in Washington and programs in host countries.

Although each regional office operates independently, there are functions and responsibilities common to all. The staff of each office plans, implements, and supervises all programs within its region; selects, supervises, and supports the staff in each country; and coordinates all activities that directly affect overseas projects, such as establishing new programs, recruiting, selecting, and training volunteers, and providing medical and technical support for volunteers overseas.

Each regional office is headed by a regional director, generally someone with extensive overseas experience with the agency. He reports to the Peace Corps Director and is assisted by a deputy. Under Shriver, the regional directors reported to a central office for program development and operations. Vaughn gave the regional directors more autonomy and had them report directly to him, but the Office of Planning, Program Review, and Research retained the authority to plan and coordinate all programs and had the power of approval over each project proposal submitted by a regional director. However, the decision could be appealed to Vaughn. Under Blatchford, the regional directors and their staffs have been given responsibility for planning, approving, and setting up all programs. Blatchford has retained authority to establish the variety of projects and their priority.

Because of the extensive geographical area and varied cultures within their regions, three regional offices have subdivided responsibilities. The organization of the Africa regional office is the most formal. It contains three divisions—

East and Southern Africa, West Africa (English-speaking), and Francophone Africa (French-speaking)—each of which is headed by a division chief. The NANESA regional office divides responsibility for supervising its operations between North Africa/Near East and South Asia, while the Latin America regional office has staff officers who supervise the programs in Central America and in the Eastern Caribbean. South American operations are conducted by country, as are those in the East Asia and Pacific region.

The key regional staff members are the program and training officers, each of whom oversees operations in one host country. They act as a channel for communications between overseas staff and headquarters staff, help with programing, and work with other offices to set up, administer, and evaluate training programs. Program and training officers report directly to their division chief or to the regional director.

Each regional office also has at least one training coordinator who helps determine the length of training, the site, the staff, and the materials to be used.

## PROGRAM DEVELOPMENT, EVALUATION, AND RESEARCH

The life cycle of a project carried out by the Peace Corps begins with planning and programing, continues with the recruiting, selecting, and training of volunteers, and culminates in an overseas assignment. In the beginning, the agency had no planning or programing; the cycle began with recruiting. Now, the cycle begins overseas and in the Office of Program Development, Evaluation, and Research (PDER), which helps the regional offices with programing and advises the Peace Corps Director on the effectiveness and efficiency of the agency's operations.

The PDER has four major divisions: Project Development, Technical Resources, Research, and Evaluation. Project Development is staffed by specialists in education, agriculture, health, vocational education, and teaching English as a second language who assist country directors with plans for new projects and who provide information and assistance to the Corps's technical specialists overseas. In addition, they work with the Office of Training Support to develop technical curricula for training programs and exchange information on technical matters with such agencies as the U.S. Department of Agriculture and the United Nations.

Additional technical support is provided by the Technical Resources Division, which answers an average of three thousand queries from volunteers and staff each year. Through the division, volunteers can correspond with technical specialists under the auspices of Volunteers for International Technical Assistance (VITA).* Technical Resources also operates a central Peace Corps library, which houses all project, training, evaluation, and research documents.

The Research Division conducts systematic studies of Peace Corps operations that may range from examinations of recruiting techniques to critiques of overseas programs. The studies, conducted by agency staff members, by universities, or by private organizations under contract to the Corps, have dealt with such topics as "Assessment of the Peace Corps Tuberculosis Control Project in Malawi," conducted by the University of North Carolina; "The Peace Corps Educational Television Project in Colombia—Two Years of Research," conducted by the Institute for Communication Research, Stanford University; "Measurement of Peace Corps Program Impact in the Peruvian Andes," conducted by the Department of Anthropology, Cornell University; and "Peace Corps Teacher Training Effectiveness in the Dominican Republic," conducted by the Peace Corps, with the help of Dominican teachers and pupils.

Officers in Evaluation are responsible for providing the

---

* VITA was organized in 1960 by a group of scientists and engineers who wanted to create a structure through which the volunteer efforts of experts could be channeled into a planned program of technical assistance. In October, 1967, VITA merged with Development and Technical Assistance, a similar organization with offices in California. The consolidated operation now functions under VITA's name, with headquarters in Schenectady, New York.

agency with what one former staff member described as "impartial, dispassionate, objective views of what is going on in training and in our host countries." At the request of a country director, program and training officer, or regional director, evaluators visit a host country to determine the effectiveness of individual projects. Local officials and technical experts are often included on evaluation teams. The findings and all resulting recommendations are presented to the country director before the evaluators leave the country and to the regional director when they return to Washington. The information then goes into a short report. Evaluators also examine training programs and prepare studies of agency-wide problems, such as language training, self-assessment during training, technical support for volunteers, and teacher-training programs.

Under Shriver and Vaughn, the agency's staff members were frequently defensive in their dealings with Evaluation. It was then a separate office, reporting to the Director, and was often referred to as the "Office of Espionage." Under Blatchford, however, the gap between the evaluator and the operational staff member has narrowed. As one program and training officer observed:

Evaluations are now aimed at the effectiveness of a project, not at the entire Peace Corps effort in a country, and we're no longer getting reports that include useless comments about how many parties an associate director holds. Many evaluations in the past have been valuable, of course, but they are becoming more effective now that they are being requested by those who figure something is wrong and want an objective assessment.

## VOLUNTEER PLACEMENT

The Office of Volunteer Placement is responsible for recruiting and selecting volunteers. A result of Blatchford's reorganization, it combines the former Office of Selection and the agency's recruiting network that had been supervised by the Office of Public Affairs. Volunteer Placement contains four major divisions: Communication, Processing, Assignment, and Trainee Staging and Assessment.

The Communication Division keeps in touch with potential and actual Peace Corps applicants and coordinates the distribution of recruiting materials to the agency's four regional placement offices. The division also operates a visitor's information center in Washington headquarters and works with other government agencies on the Corps's testing procedures and other services.

Processing handles all applications from the time they arrive at Volunteer Placement until final training assessment is made. Staff members process applications, assign a primary and secondary skill designation to each applicant, draft all letters of invitation, and initiate requests for background investigations of those applicants who accept.

Responsibility for assessing the qualifications of applicants and for matching available volunteers to job descriptions is the primary task of the Assignment Division. Assignment officers are organized by skill area, such as agriculture, education, or health, and by special category, such as older applicants, married applicants, the specially skilled, and handicapped applicants. (When all other requirements and qualifications can be met, the Peace Corps will accept handicapped persons for certain volunteer assignments, usually in education. There have been several blind volunteers who have helped teach the blind overseas, for example.) Trainee Staging and Assessment sets standards and oversees the final assessment of trainees.

The deputy director of Volunteer Placement supervises the Peace Corps's four regional placement offices, whose staff members actively recruit volunteers. Until 1966, the agency did not have professional recruiters. Instead, it relied on agency staff members to make whirlwind tours of campuses once or twice a year. As the war in Vietnam escalated and the problems of poverty and the cities became more urgent at home, recruiting for the Corps became difficult. The "campus blitz," as it was known within the Peace Corps, was not enough, and the agency began to gather a staff of full-time recruiters. At first, only returned Peace Corps volunteers were hired for recruiting assignments, and by March, 1968, nine out of ten recruiters were volunteers who had returned from service in the summer of 1967. Today, most recruiters are still returned volunteers, but they are backed up by specialists who concentrate on attracting agriculturalists, skilled industrial workers, teachers, and nurses to the Corps. Recruiters work out of the four regional placement offices located in Boston, Atlanta, Chicago, and San Francisco. The generalists cover a small area and the specialists travel throughout the entire region. Through this recruiting network, the Peace Corps is able to visit about one thousand colleges and universities each year as well as numerous industries, businesses, and labor unions.

The Office of Volunteer Placement also supervises the School Partnership Program. (See Chapter VI.)

TRAINING SUPPORT

In his reorganization in the fall of 1969, Blatchford set up the Office of Training Support to be responsible for the quality of training programs. Under Shriver, training had been the responsibility of the independent Office of Training. Vaughn dissolved that office and delegated responsibility for training to the four regional offices. Under Blatchford's arrangement, the office oversees training programs but does not have the authority to approve training contracts. That authority remains with the regional offices.

Staff members in Training Support assist the regional offices and country directors with planning, developing, and evaluating training programs. They recommend training institutions and maintain contact with them. The Language Training Division coordinates and evaluates language training programs and recommends or develops language texts, related materials, and language curricula. The Training

Coordination Division oversees the other parts of training.

Training Support also includes the Division of Staff Training. Until 1966, no definite training was provided for staff. Occasionally, staff members going overseas went through training with volunteers headed for the same country; at other times, they were sent to their posts with little advance notice. Old hands still recall the time a candidate was called to Washington to meet Shriver, was interviewed for a full day, and left the next day to supervise the program in India.

When Vaughn returned in 1966, he was presented with the outline of a program for training overseas staff members, drawn up by Daniel A. Sharpe. Vaughn liked the program and made Sharpe director of Staff Training. Sharpe's plan was simple: each new staff member was to be given three weeks of orientation in Washington followed by special training that would include instruction in the local language, culture and area studies, world affairs, and the role of the overseas staff. Whenever possible, the new staff members were to train for a brief period with volunteers and to spend some time in a country other than the one in which they were to work. (This was particularly true for those headed for Latin America.) It was Sharpe's recommendation that wives and children take part in training as well, since they were considered part of the Peace Corps family overseas.

Under Blatchford, staff training will be further refined. The McKinsey Report recommended that training programs be tailored to the requirements of the particular positions so that, for example, a country director's training would be different from that of an associate director, and it appears that this recommendation will be followed.

In addition to providing training for the agency's staff, the division supervises the Peace Corps Fellows Program, initiated by Vaughn for outstanding volunteers. Peace Corps fellows are selected for overseas staff positions at the end of their service and then spend one year working in the agency's administrative and training programs before they go overseas as associate directors.

## Public Affairs

Under Shriver and Vaughn, the Office of Public Affairs was responsible for recruiting volunteers, and publicity and press activities were handled by a separate Office of Public Information. Blatchford has changed that arrangement by moving the recruiting activities to the new Office of Volunteer Placement and combining the former Office of Public Information with the Office of Public Affairs. Public Affairs is now, as its name implies, primarily concerned with the agency's relations with the public.

The Peace Corps was created amidst considerable publicity, and, in the early years, the main job of Public Information was to handle requests from the nation's press. The newness of the agency and Shriver's personal flair for publicity provided a steady flow of copy. The work load and tempo were intense in those years, and the office changed directors frequently. By the time Shriver left the agency, five men had served as director of Public Information.

More recently, the functions of the office have changed. The Peace Corps itself no longer attracts as much attention and there is competition for column inches and air time, with the result that Public Affairs now goes to the media with its own news releases and feature stories. In addition, it produces recruiting brochures for the Office of Volunteer Placement and publishes the *Volunteer,* the agency's monthly magazine. In 1969, the *Volunteer* had a circulation of nearly 100,000. Each issue contains articles written by staff members, volunteers, and returned volunteers on topics that range from the philosophic—"Toward a Social Revolution"—to the pragmatic—"Turning History Majors into Agriculturists."

Public Affairs oversees the Peace Corps Advisory Councils, made up of former volunteers and staff members, community leaders, teachers, and PCV parents, all of whom help to explain the purposes of the Peace Corps and to recruit volunteers. It also maintains the Speakers' Bureau, which schedules talks by returned volunteers and staff members to community and institutional groups upon request.

The Peace Corps Act specifically authorized the creation of a Peace Corps National Advisory Council to "advise and consult with the President with regard to policies and programs designed to further the purposes of this Act." The council is composed of twenty-five citizens appointed by the President. The Peace Corps Act specifies that council members are to be "broadly representative of educational institutions, voluntary agencies, farm organizations, and labor unions, and other public and private organizations as well as individuals interested in the programs and objectives of the Peace Corps." Under Shriver and Vaughn, the council, which normally met twice a year, was kept informed of agency developments by the Executive Secretariat. Blatchford has created, within Public Affairs, the position of executive director of the council and hopes to make the group a more meaningful advisory body. He intends to ask persons to serve on the council who can "relate to the young people in this country and who can help translate the goals of the Peace Corps and what volunteer service means to doubters among our youth."

## MEDICAL PROGRAMS

The Office of Medical Programs is responsible for the medical and psychiatric clearance of all Peace Corps applicants and trainees and for the medical and dental care of volunteers in the field. In addition, the office helps recruit and train doctors and nurses for overseas duty and provides advice on proposed health projects. The Psychiatry Division helps recruit and supervise psychiatric consultants used during volunteer training and makes arrangements for volunteers who terminate their service early for psychiatric reasons. Under a joint agreement, the U.S. Public Health Service, through its Commissioned Officer Corps, details physicians, nurses, and other personnel to the Office of Medical Programs for domestic and overseas assignment.

The agency's medical program has had an excellent record. Only two PCV's serving overseas have died from disease, and the number of volunteers with serious medical problems has been small. Agency doctors have stressed preventive medicine and have initiated several innovative programs. Since animal bites are a frequent problem, volunteers are given pre-exposure rabies vaccine. Although nearly one thousand animal bites have been reported since the Peace Corps began operations overseas—a rate ten times greater than that within the United States—not one volunteer has died from rabies. (The State Department has started a similar rabies-prevention program for its overseas personnel.)

Infectious hepatitis is a very real threat to volunteers because most PCV's are unable to ensure that their food, water, and living conditions are free of harmful bacteria. To protect against hepatitis, the Peace Corps gives all volunteers and overseas staff shots of gamma globulin every four to six months. The effectiveness of the shots had not been thoroughly established when the Corps began to administer them, but a subsequent study showed that the incidence of viral hepatitis was "considerably lower" among those who had received shots than among those who had not.

## ADMINISTRATION AND FINANCE

Administrative support and financial management of the Peace Corps are provided by the Office of Administration and Finance. The office also makes travel arrangements for volunteers and staff members and obtains passports and visas, provides general office services, supervises the printing of agency materials, and handles all foreign and domestic communications, including cable traffic, regular mail, diplomatic pouch mail, and the distribution of agency directives.

The Division of Accounting and Finance is responsible for all Peace Corps financial and budgetary matters, although the separate Budget Division prepares the annual budget. The Division of Contracts negotiates and administers all contracts between the agency and educational, commercial, and non-profit institutions. Contracts cover four main categories: training, overseas support, research, and the development of training materials. More than one hundred and fifty contracts are negotiated each year, and about three hundred contracts are in various stages of completion at any one time. Contracts account for almost one-third of the Peace Corps's total annual budget.

## GENERAL COUNSEL

As chief legal officer of the agency, the general counsel is responsible to the Director for all legal matters that involve the Peace Corps. He and his staff review policy decisions affecting relationships with volunteers, staff, Congress, host governments, and federal agencies. They help draft legislation, participate in congressional presentations, and take part in negotiations for program agreements with host countries.

## INTERNATIONAL AND SPECIAL PROGRAMS

Since its creation, the Peace Corps has been a leader in promoting international volunteerism. When President Kennedy signed the executive order that created the Corps, he expressed the hope that other nations would join in an international voluntary movement to attack the problems of underdevelopment:

> Although this is an American Peace Corps, the problem of world development is not just an American problem. Let us hope that other nations will mobilize the spirit and energies and skill of their people in some form of Peace Corps—making our own effort only one step in a major international effort to increase the welfare of all men and improve understanding among nations.

In October, 1962, the Peace Corps organized a meeting of forty-three nations in Puerto Rico to discuss the problems of training and supplying middle-level manpower to developing countries. The conference was presided over by Vice-President Lyndon B. Johnson. An outgrowth of this conference was the creation of the International Secretariat for Volunteer Service (ISVS), whose purpose is to promote the international exchange of volunteer workers. The ISVS, which works with programs under government and combined government and private sponsorship, acts as a central clearinghouse for information about training and operations and helps coordinate programs to avoid duplication. The Peace Corps Director represents the United States on the executive council of the ISVS.

In December, 1963, at the request of the Peace Corps, Congress added Title III to the Peace Corps Act, which proposed that the Corps

> encourage countries and areas to establish programs under which their citizens and nationals would volunteer to serve in order to help meet the needs of less-developed countries or areas for trained manpower, and to encourage less-developed countries or areas to establish programs under which their citizens and nationals would volunteer to serve in order to meet their needs for trained manpower.

To carry out the purposes of Title III, the Peace Corps created the Office of National Voluntary Service Programs. Under Blatchford it has been renamed the Office of International and Special Programs. This office provides information and guidance to private groups and governments interested in establishing voluntary service programs or in expanding those already in operation. In countries where such programs exist, they are frequently coordinated with the activities of the Peace Corps or with other voluntary service groups. The office works closely with the ISVS.

VOLUNTARY ACTION

Shortly after Blatchford was appointed Peace Corps Director, he announced that he would seek new ways to encourage volunteerism in the United States. To carry out this task, he set up the Office of Voluntary Action to promote volunteer service throughout the nation. Voluntary Action also supervises the Volunteers to America Program (VTA) and the Division of Returned Volunteer Services. (See Chapter XIV.)

The Peace Corps inherited Volunteers to America from the State Department in 1969. The program has been operating on a modest scale, with only slightly more than one hundred volunteers coming to the United States in its two years of operations. Although Congress did not authorize funds for the program in 1970, Blatchford hopes to gain enough support to expand it, with perhaps as many as five thousand volunteers from other nations serving in the United States during the 1970's. In July, 1969, before the House Foreign Affairs Committee, he described the program as an "Exchange Peace Corps" in which the

> Peace Corps would select local leaders and potential leaders to come to the United States for one year. They would be assigned a significant job with an agency which needs their services and will provide their support. They would be trained. They would see firsthand the part-time and full-time voluntary service practiced in this country. Upon return home they would fulfill an obligation to work in national service with the Peace Corps, in an existing voluntary service agency, or in the formation of such an agency.

The reorganization that Blatchford initiated is still taking shape, and there will, no doubt, be changes before the Peace Corps settles into its new structure. But the act of reorganization is significant. It is the first formal change since the Peace Corps began eight years ago, and it demonstrates clearly the pressures that are now shaping the agency's character and the new directions it hopes to follow.

# IV

# The Peace Corps Overseas

Former Director Jack Vaughn, referring to the argument that there are two Peace Corps, one in Washington and one overseas, stated that "in fact, there are nearly sixty Peace Corps—one for each country in which we serve. They are separate and distinct from Washington, and, in many ways, separate from one another." His description is accurate, for the operations in each country are tailored to match the geography, the system of government, and the social and economic needs of the host nation.

The number of staff members in each country is determined by the country's size, the dispersion of volunteers, the number of programs in progress, and the amount of training held within the host nation. Peace Corps operations in Micronesia, India, Colombia, Brazil, and the Philippines require the largest staffs. In February, 1969, there were 47 Peace Corps staff members in Micronesia—16 administrative staff, 4 program technical representatives (PTR's) hired by the agency to provide technical support to volunteers, 4 Peace Corps physicians, 2 medical staff members on assignment from the Public Health Service, and 21 host-country nationals.* There were 46 staff members in India, 36 in Colombia, 31 in Brazil, and 27 in the Philippines. In contrast, the staff in Uruguay numbered 3—a country director, a secretary, and a Public Health Service doctor. In Swaziland, there were two administrative

---

* The agency differentiates between Peace Corps physicians, who are classified as "direct-hire," and Public Health Service personnel on assignment to the Peace Corps.

staff members and a Peace Corps doctor. Operations in Dahomey and Upper Volta required only four staff members each.

There is no typical overseas administrative organization, even though the basic functions of the staff in each country are similar. In smaller countries, business is conducted from a main office located in the capital city. The staff usually includes a country director, a deputy director, several associate directors (called area representatives in some countries, a carry-over from Shriver's era), and a Peace Corps doctor. There is also a secretarial staff, which may include both local citizens and PCV secretaries, full-fledged volunteers serving their two-year tours as secretaries for the Peace Corps. Administrative chores, such as keeping records, meeting payrolls, and administering the budget, are shared by the country director, his deputy, and the secretaries. There may also be a program technical representative who provides volunteers with technical advice.

In larger host countries, administrative responsibility is often divided regionally, with a regional director heading operations in each area and reporting to the country director. Even with such a division, the distances may be so great that the regional or associate director spends from ten to twelve hours just traveling to and from a volunteer's work site. In the larger countries, there are frequently a full-time administrative officer who handles all personnel and budgetary matters and a programing and training officer who coordinates the Corps's plans for programs and training in the host country.

Under Vaughn, regional and associate directors were often generalists who supported all the volunteers within their region regardless of the kind of work the volunteer did. This arrangement put heavy demands on the associate directors, for they had to deal with numerous host-government agencies and had to be willing and able to do the research necessary to answer volunteer questions. Vaughn began a trend toward hiring staff members who were specialists in one area of Peace Corps work and Blatchford has continued the policy. At present, no field staff member is hired who is not a specialist with skills that match the Corps's projects.

## THE COUNTRY DIRECTOR

The chief official in each host country is the country director, who supervises all of the Corps's operations there. Country directors serve under contract for thirty to thirty-six months, as do most other overseas staff members.

The country director's first responsibility is to the volunteers and to those host-country agencies who work with them. His role was summed up by a former country director in a recent interview:

> The country director is father-confessor, guidance counselor, teacher, go-between for the volunteer and host-country agencies, and, along with the rest of the staff, the link between the volunteer and the Peace Corps. If he is a good one, he is also the volunteer's trusted friend. At all costs, he has to avoid spoon-feeding the volunteer while insisting on high performance standards.

Another aspect of the country director's job is the inevitable public relations work he must do. He is expected to represent the Peace Corps at official functions and to be host to important visitors, including congressmen. In addition, he frequently entertains volunteers, local officials, and visitors from Washington at his home.

Within the host country, the country director is responsible to the U.S. Ambassador, and he and his deputy are part of what is known as the country team. This group, composed of high-ranking officials from the embassy, the Agency for International Development, the U.S. Information Service, and other U.S. Government agencies represented at the post, meets frequently to discuss all matters of concern to the embassy. The country director also works with AID mission staff on joint Peace Corps-AID projects and with those host-country officials who are assigned to the Peace Corps or who act as advisers for

Peace Corps projects. The U.S. Ambassador and the country director are ultimately responsible for the approval of all program requests, which are prepared by the country director. Aside from meeting with the country team and keeping all appropriate U.S. officials informed about programs and volunteer activities, the country director's contact with other U.S. Government agencies is slight. In no host country is the Peace Corps headquarters part of the embassy complex, and both staff members and volunteers are discouraged from using embassy facilities. The Peace Corps has treasured its independence overseas and has cultivated separateness.

## THE DEPUTY DIRECTOR

The deputy director supervises the day-to-day operations in the host country. He schedules staff visits to volunteers and assures adequate support for them, answers inquiries and recommendations for programs for host-country agencies, and, if there is no administrative officer, coordinates all administrative matters. When the country director is on leave or visiting volunteers at their work sites, the deputy director assumes the duties of the director. If there is no programing and training officer, he may act as project director for training sessions held in the host country, and, in this role, designs, administers, and coordinates training programs.

## ASSOCIATE DIRECTORS

The associate directors are considered the backbone of the overseas administrative structure. Under Shriver, they were known as area representatives, or area reps, and that designation has remained in some countries. The associate director works more closely with volunteers than any other staff member. His job requires imagination, infinite patience, vitality, physical endurance, and an ability to treat volunteers with firmness and understanding, for the volunteer frequently turns to him with all of his problems, both personal and professional.

The associate director also serves as a liaison officer between the volunteer and host-country officials and may plead a volunteer's case when the latter suggests needed changes in a program. Often he supervises the agency's activities in one region of a host country, with a secretary as his only staff support.

Associate directors are usually former volunteers who served well during their two-year tours and developed special skills in a main area of Peace Corps service. However, agency experience is not mandatory. In spite of a contractual arrangement, there is considerable turnover among associate directors because of the pressures and demands of their jobs. As specialists replace generalists in those positions, Blatchford believes the turnover will decrease.

## SPECIAL OFFICERS

As the Peace Corps began to set up more specialized and extensive programs and moved toward training volunteers in host nations, it became necessary to send special officers to the countries with large Peace Corps contingents. The most recent addition to the overseas staff is the programing and training officer, who works on program plans with the country director and sets up training programs. (In the largest countries, there are both a programing and a training officer.) Large countries may also have regional directors, who carry out essentially the same duties at the local level that the country director performs at the national level, and an administrative officer, who is paymaster, personnel director, budget officer, and sometimes publisher of a local newsletter for volunteers and staff.

## TECHNICAL STAFF

Program technical representatives (PTR's) and contractors' overseas representatives (COR's) are specialists who work with volunteers in specific programs. The COR is recommended and paid for by a private organization under contract with the Peace Corps to administer a program, and he can generally draw on the resources of the sponsoring organization. Program technical representatives are hired directly by the Corps. Almost from the first, there were problems in the relationship between the Peace Corps and the COR's and, in recent years, the agency has relied almost exclusively on its own specialists. In March, 1969, for example, there were seventy-six PTR's in thirty-eight countries and only seven COR's in four countries.

## THE VOLUNTEER SECRETARY

The volunteer secretary program, started under Shriver and maintained by Vaughn, has been a disappointment. It was initiated to offer volunteer service to young women with secretarial training who otherwise might not qualify as volunteers. In recruiting materials, the job sounds glamorous. In reality, however, the PCV secretary is placed in a difficult position. In an interview in the summer of 1968, one volunteer secretary described her situation:

> I found that I was neither fish nor fowl. The other volunteers didn't accept me as a volunteer, and because I had no staff status I was often shunned by the staff. Instead of seeing the host country and meeting its people, I associated mainly with volunteers and staff and host-country officials, who sometimes spoke better English than I. I was cautioned to be discreet about certain matters I had to know about, yet I was constantly pumped for information by volunteers. I felt loyalty to both staff and PCV's, and this put me in a touchy situation.

One reason for the development of the volunteer secretary program was economy. The secretaries receive the same living allowance and the same $75-per-month readjustment allowance as all other volunteers and are not included in the overseas staff employment summaries. One former staff member, who served as a volunteer and as a program and training officer in Washington, believes that the agency "exploits the volunteer secretary. The Corps expects a maximum of work in return for a minimum of exposure to a foreign culture, and it is for this exposure that she volunteered in the first place—certainly not because of the high salary and post-exchange privileges." By law, no more than two hundred volunteer secretaries may be in service world-wide at any one time.

## THE VOLUNTEER LEADER

Anticipating the need for providing volunteer support in remote areas, Congress created the special classification of volunteer leader in the original Peace Corps Act. Initially, volunteer leaders were PCV's with special skills or previous overseas experience. They were enrolled as leaders either at the completion of training or after some service as a volunteer. Appointment as a volunteer leader was not considered a promotion and leaders continued at their regular duties. Although they were not considered staff members, they did enjoy privileges. The volunteer leader was permitted to bring his dependents overseas and was given an allowance to cover their living expenses as well as an extra $25-per-month readjustment allowance.

There were never as many leaders appointed as had been anticipated, primarily because the volunteers resented them and made it very clear they did not want to be supervised by, as they called them, "super-vols." Volunteer leaders often found themselves in the same position as the volunteer secretary—neither staff nor PCV. Vaughn appointed few volunteer leaders and did so only when a job required a trained specialist who could travel frequently, who needed to handle petty cash, or who was required to take on additional administrative responsibilities. The designation volunteer leader is now being revived, but without the quasi-staff connotation it originally had. Blatchford has announced that, until changes in the Peace Corps Act can be made to accommodate mid-career technicians and professional men with families who volunteer for service, he intends to use the volunteer leader provisions in the Peace Corps Act to cover them.

## THE PEACE CORPS DOCTOR

A Peace Corps staff doctor is assigned to every host country in which volunteers serve, and in large countries there may be several doctors, each working from a regional office. In India, for example, there are seven staff doctors; in Micronesia, six. Prior to 1967, Peace Corps doctors were provided by the Public Health Service. In that year, however, Congress amended the Military Selective Service Act to stipulate that Public Health Service officers could no longer satisfy their military obligations through Peace Corps service, and the Corps began to recruit its own physicians.

Although the Peace Corps physician is primarily responsible for the health care of volunteers, he often devotes time to special projects, such as a malaria eradication program or a new curriculum for host-country laboratory technicians. Some doctors also treat local patients while on visits to volunteers or as a part-time member of a local hospital staff. However, the volunteers remain his prime responsibility, and the Peace Corps physician visits them frequently. Invariably, he treats the whole person, for volunteers naturally turn to him when they suffer from homesickness or when their idealism and optimism have been severely tried.

## THE VOLUNTEER

The volunteer is not an employee of the U.S. Government. He has volunteered his services and the U.S. Government has made it possible for him to go abroad and work. He travels on the same kind of passport and visa issued to other private American citizens and is subject to the laws of the country in which he serves. Although the volunteer has fewer privileges than do federal employees serving overseas, he has more freedom. He lives and works closely with his hosts, he can criticize U.S. policies, and he can travel with few restrictions. There have been times when volunteers enjoyed a special status not granted to other Americans. During the rebellion in the Dominican Republic in 1965, for example, volunteers were allowed to cross the lines of both sides by using a simple password: *Cuerpo de Paz.*

Volunteers are responsible to local supervisors. Nurses work under the direction of doctors; teachers follow the directives of their headmasters, and community action workers coordinate their efforts with local officials and government agencies. Because the volunteer is generally independent, well-educated, and working beneath his status, he is an engima to his hosts, who may view him as a nuisance, a threat, or a means for their own aggrandizement. On the other hand, they may see him as he sees himself: an individual who is willing to work hard and sincerely wants to help people. It does not take a volunteer long to realize that he must establish a good working relationship with these officials, for it is abundantly clear that a program without host-country cooperation does not survive.

Rapport with other service organizations and volunteer groups is quite different. PCV's share information and experiences freely with volunteers from other nations and from private organizations and soon discover which nongovernment groups within the host country will cooperate with them. In Latin America, community development volunteers have reported excellent help from local Rotary, Kiwanis, and Lions International clubs, and from both the YMCA and the YWCA.

In many countries, volunteers also deal with radical left-wing organizations. One amusing Peace Corps story illustrates how closely members of the two groups occasionally live and work. In Maracaibo, Venezuela, a volunteer moved from one rented home in a slum area to another just down the street. Local representatives of one of Venezuela's left-wing parties set up headquarters in the house the volunteer had vacated and immediately painted the party's initials on the building. Soon every outside wall contained the letters PCV, which stood for the Communist Party of Venezuela. The volunteer photographed the building and sent a print home with the comment: "Look how much my friends think of me. They advertise that a Peace Corps volunteer once lived here."

The Peace Corps expects volunteers to live in a manner similar to that of their co-workers. Such conditions may range from a comfortable apartment in a city or on a university campus to primitive quarters in a jungle. In most cases, the local government provides housing for the volunteer; if he must rent housing, the Peace Corps reimburses him.

Each volunteer receives a monthly living allowance, which ranges from $36 in Tonga to $160 in Libya. The allowance is paid in local currency and deposited monthly in the volunteer's bank account. In general, the living allowance is comparable to the monthly salary of a host citizen in a similar position and permits the volunteers to live a comfortable, but by no means elegant, existence. The living allowance is used for food, clothing, laundry, entertainment, travel, and similar expenses.

The first volunteers were given tennis rackets, radios, and assorted sports equipment. Since then, however, the Corps has consistently reduced the material goods it supplies and volunteers now receive only a modest means of transport—a bicycle, a horse, or, if necessary, a motorbike—and, if they are in a remote area, a paperback-book locker. Volunteers have always been good at improvising. One volunteer, using local materials, designed a windmill-powered pumping device for irrigating rice paddies that cost only $125 to build. Similar, commercially produced equipment cost $1,500. Another volunteer developed a well-drilling rig using machete blades for about $500. A French drilling company had been charging $3,000 for each well they dug. The rig designed by the volunteer was not only cheaper to use, but its wells produced four times as much water as those dug commercially.

Volunteers earn two days of leave for every month of service and most of them save both time and money for at least one extensive trip throughout the region in which they work. They receive a leave allowance of $9 per day.

Each volunteer is given a thorough physical examination before he enters Peace Corps training and is checked regularly during his tour. Although volunteers suffer from minor problems frequently, few have contracted serious diseases. Peace Corps physicians report that the most frequent illnesses among volunteers are dysentery, gastroenteritis, upper respiratory infections, and skin diseases. The most common ailment is a cold. In a press release that appeared in late 1968, the director of Medical Programs attributed the agency's outstanding health record to "the essential good health of the volunteers, most of them young persons in their early twenties, and what is probably the most extensive preventive care program of any overseas agency."

Most volunteers agree that fluency in the local language makes their work easier and more rewarding. Nurses, agriculturalists, and community development workers often learn a local dialect well, while volunteers working in urban areas or teaching school, with fewer opportunities to learn the language and less need to master it, rarely achieve a high proficiency.

In early recruiting materials and press releases, the agency fed the myth that volunteer service meant rural, simple living and the image has been difficult to overcome. Volunteers with rural assignments accepted simple living and lack of diversion as part of the job. Volunteers in urban centers, however, had to form their own self-image and to justify, at least to themselves, high-level work assignments and comfortable living conditions. To the urban volunteer wanting to be a part of a local culture, facing frustration in his job and questioning his contribution, the rural assignment seems idyllic. The rural volunteer, with some of the same problems, can console himself with being part of a small community in which he is known and, more often than not, included. The problems and contributions of urban-based volunteers are now recognized, and, although the picture of rural service persists, the image problem has become less acute.

At some time during his tour, nearly every volunteer suffers from the phenomenon known as culture shock. Culture shock is exactly what its name suggests—the shock that one experiences from being in a totally new environment. Culture shock may hit a volunteer the first few days overseas, it may not appear for several months, or it may recur frequently as the volunteer's living conditions change. A young volunteer who grew up in Manhattan described her feelings shortly after she began teaching in a Philippine village:

> This is the hardest thing I've ever done. Absolutely nothing is familiar and I often feel totally alone—the physical difficulties actually help, as they take my mind off myself and the feeling of suddenly being cut off from the rest of the world. You cannot imagine the gulf between East and West; and it makes me laugh now to think that I expected to bridge it with a smile and a handshake!

A classic description of culture shock, and one frequently quoted by the Peace Corps, was written by a community development volunteer serving in Peru.

> I live in a picturesque bamboo mat house I built myself. I buy my water from a picturesque boy with a burro loaded down with water cans. I read and write under a kerosene lantern, sleep on a cot, and cook on a camp stove.
>
> Tourists and reporters find this fascinating and "out-door-ish" and envy my experience. They think I'm kidding when I suggest that we trade. How could I pass up living so picturesque! Their mat house would not be so picturesque during a 3 A.M. rainstorm, when water gets in the expensive camera, or during the frequent dust storms that will stop up radios so they can't hear the Voice of America broadcasts. Their water boy won't be picturesque either when they see where he gets his water, or their cot so "outdoorish" when they lie on it doubled up with dysentery.
>
> There comes a day when all this suddenly becomes apparent, all at once. Things are no longer picturesque, they are dirty; no longer quaint but furiously frustrating; and you want like crazy to just get out of there, to go home.

This is called culture shock and you don't find it mentioned on recruiting posters. It happens to one and all, usually about the third or fourth month.

In spite of the difficulties volunteers face, relatively few leave their assignments early. The average annual attrition rate in each of the first eight years of Peace Corps operations was 19 per cent among volunteers who were working overseas, although the rate during training was much higher—close to 70 per cent in some individual training groups. Of those who terminated their overseas service early, 10 per cent left because of failure to adjust to their new environment; 8 per cent returned home because of health problems, family difficulties, or other reasons beyond their control; and 1 per cent returned for more serious psychiatric reasons.

Although much has been written about the volunteer experience, it is best conveyed by volunteers themselves. The following extracts from letters describe common, day-to-day experiences and reveal the volunteers' own reactions to the Peace Corps.

*From a Teacher in the Ivory Coast:*

"The African sun is fierce when you have to pull yourself together after the two-hour noontime break to return to work. All the rest of the world is still sleeping. You can almost hear the buzz of sleep as you walk by the still courtyards and the houses with their shuttered windows looking like closed eyes. The midday meal has left faint odors of wood fires, fish and fried plantain in the air. Chickens and guinea hens have hidden under bushes and the dogs are too drowsy even to scratch their fleas. . . . You pass by the market, where remnants of the morning's activities are strewn about: squashed bananas, spilled tomato sauce, peanut shells. The Foyer Feminin is shaded and cool; the big classroom on the second floor usually catches whatever breeze there is.

"About 2:30 my women begin to drift in, though late-comers will turn up during the ensuing hour. Most look very fresh. Many have babies on their backs or toddlers tagging after them. . . . Some of the students are very young, in their early teens. A few are oldsters, but most are in their 20's. Of course, judging their ages is sheer guesswork on my part and on theirs, too, in most cases.

"The Ivory Coast government set up these Foyers to meet the urgent need for education of women. The men have had a head start in education and have left the women far behind. This has created a real problem: households consisting of a literate father and children and an illiterate mother. Many of the husbands have positions in government, in education, or in business. They are associated with men of similar education. An illiterate wife is incapable of entering into this aspect of her husband's life; thus a chasm exists in the family structure. To bridge this gap, the Foyers Feminins have been created. There are at present 30 Foyers in the cities and towns of Ivory Coast and more are being planned. Enrollments range into the hundreds in the cities and down to a dozen or so in the villages. . . .

"The schoolroom language is, of course, French. My students speak it well, but when they grow excited, they switch to Baoule, the dialect in my village of Yamoussoukro. . . .

"Foyer classrooms are not peaceful and orderly. Babies cry and are nursed, toddlers upset everything possible and wander out of the room so that in the midst of reciting, mothers shout and run off in pursuit. . . .

"What progress have we made in the Foyer?

"First of all, the women, having stepped out of their domestic routines into a disciplined environment in search of something new, have taken a monumental step.

"As for academic progress, the beginners have mastered the vowels and several consonants, the simplest formation of letters, and simple addition. They have read, if mostly by rote, about a half-dozen pages of a primer. . . . In sewing they have made layettes, stitching both by machine and by hand. Also, they have learned to mend and to knit. Knitting in the tropics? Yes, indeed. Ivoriens feel the slightest chill in the air (and we often have it, glory be!) and immediately bundle up their babies in woolen caps and booties until that old sun takes over again.

"The advanced students are about two-thirds of the way through the primer, can read more or less phonetically, can write fairly well, and in arithmetic are on about a level with a second-grader in the States.

"There is the question we all ask ourselves from time to time: what, if anything, can I really accomplish here?

"I tell myself . . . you can at least be a warm, understanding woman among your fellow women, sharing and understanding basic, human things with them. And, since you happen to know how to read and write, you can make every effort to give them these magic keys.

"Nothing spectacular—but there you are."

*From an Architect in Nepal:*

" 'You're an architect—maybe you can tell Mr. John where to place the cornerstone for the new Pokhara College building when the King comes next month.' Volunteer Peter Farquhar had said this to me during our Peace Corps Christmas conferences in Kathmandu. Peter teaches at Prithwi Narayan College, which is presently housed in one bamboo hut at Pokhara; Mr. John is dean of this college.

"Since the two-month vacation period had just begun, my wife, Julie, and I went to Pokhara—she to teach chemistry, and I to see about where to place the cornerstone.

"Pokhara is incredible. It lies in a valley filled with poinsettias and with several lakes that reflect Annapurna Himal and Machhapucchre, 'Fishtail Mountain,' which looms 20,000 feet above and barely 20 miles away. Until recently, this friendly valley could be reached from Kathmandu only by a 10-day trek with porters. Now a 45-minute flight connects Pokhara with Kathmandu.

"Mr. John, the dean, had a Grandma Moses-like water color of the building he hoped to build, but no plans. He knew what it should look like, but wasn't sure what would be in it.

I was sure immediately that his multi-story building would require cement and steel, materials which would have to be flown into "landlocked" Pokhara at great expense.

"Working against the indefinite but imminent visit of the King to lay the cornerstone, I sketched and drew, planning something small and useful, not requiring massive foreign aid but only local fieldstones and slate. I unpacked my X-acto knives and made an irresistible take-apart model, which swayed the college board of governors into beginning work immediately. The board felt that initiated construction would impress the King with the college's willingness to do its part.

"With the students and a borrowed 100-foot tape, we situated the 60-by-90-foot building, creating a 90 degree angle to everybody's joy, by measuring 60 feet along one rope, 80 feet along another from one common point, then using the 100-foot tape as hypotenuse. The jump from class-room learning to real life always takes people a little by surprise.

"The first building adjoins the existing bamboo huts, but will later be part of a family of similar units, to be built as needed and as funds make them possible. . . .

"The King came with a large entourage. A procession of Jeeps drove up through town, through about 500 dhokas (fiesta gates), which the townspeople had erected in his honor. These are made of bamboo or banana palms, with colored paper trimming, photos of the royal couple, and any other colored pictures they could find (one was a magazine picture of a double-decker London bus charging into a department store)—and signs saying swagatam: Welcome.

"The King reviewed his subjects from a rapidly erected stage house, resembling the local peasant huts. Someone had managed to find an easy chair for him. Many people spoke. He spoke. During this long ceremony, Mr. John, the dean, learned that the King no longer lays cornerstones.

"The college secretary did, however, place the models where the King had to see them. While he fingered the models I explained the project in my crude Nepali. He took interest, strode over to the construction site, read the Nepali sign describing the work and the Peace Corps' role in it, smiled, and said he would come to inaugurate the building—much better than laying the cornerstone!"

*From an Urban Community Development Worker in Peru:*

"I live in a giant slum, or *barriada,* on the edge of Chimbote, a city of 120,000 people. The movie "Black Orpheus" showed another *barriada,* more colorful but otherwise similar to mine.

"My neighbors have come down from the mountains, attracted by the money and in hope of a better life. Because of a lack of marketable skills (for generations they have known only farming and grazing), they find it hard to get a job and end up in unbelievable slums, with disease and starvation rampant. Largely illiterate, and sometimes only speaking Spanish as a second language after their Indian tongue, they get almost no public service, and many of their rights aren't protected. The slums around Chimbote stretch for miles and miles, staggering the imagination.

"My job is to get these people, my neighbors, organized, to make them better able to compete in the city for their rights, and to try and get them to raise their standard of living back to the human race.

"I teach in the local school during the days and I teach carpentry to adults at night. Both are important jobs, but I consider them only a front. Teaching kids, while fun for me and hilarious for the rough-housing students, is only an excuse for being in the *barriada.*

"For example, our school has no roof. It would be a ten dollar project and about one day's labor for two or three Peace Corpsmen to build that roof. Yet we don't do it. If we gave my school a roof, it would always be that, a gift, the *gringo's* roof. When it needed fixing, no one would fix it.

"If it takes me a year to talk my neighbors into putting on that roof, it will be worth it. Because it will then be their roof on their school. It would be a small start, but in the right direction. Maybe then we'll take on a little harder project, and step by step build up a powerful organization that is interested in progress and strong enough to do something about it.

"A Volunteer has to be careful, however, and not become too much of a leader. I have said, if I stir up all the action, what will happen when I leave? I hint at things and let my neighbors come up with the ideas and I let them lead the action.

"A really good Peace Corps program receives little credit. Keep that in mind when you read Peace Corps success stories."

# V

# Recruiting and Preparing Volunteers

The initial public response to the Peace Corps spoiled it a little. In the first two years, the publicity given the agency was enormous. Writers and commentators suggested that it personified the spirit of President Kennedy's New Frontier. Inquiries and applications poured into Washington headquarters, generated more by the agency's mystique than by its recruiting efforts. By the end of 1961, the Peace Corps had received more than 13,000 applications and more than 150,000 inquiries about volunteer service. Staff members assigned to recruiting tours found themselves countering the enthusiasm of potential volunteers with a realistic description of overseas work.

## WHO JOINS THE CORPS?

Statistically, the average volunteer in 1969 was 24.6 years old, a college graduate, and a liberal arts major. In the Corps's eight years of operations, approximately 75 per cent of all volunteers and trainees have been twenty-five years of age or younger. Roughly 67 per cent have been male and 33 per cent female. Approximately 96 per cent have had some college education and 80 per cent held at least an undergraduate degree. Of those with a degree, 85 per cent were liberal arts majors.

Volunteers come from every state in the union and every territory administered by the United States. In proportion to population, the West has contributed more volunteers than any other region. Thirteen Western states, with 15 per cent of the total U.S. population, account for 25 per cent of all volunteers. By January, 1969, California had contributed the most volunteers—4,979. New York was second with 3,660. The state of Washington was first in per capita ranking, followed by Vermont, Colorado, and Oregon. (See Chart III.)

From its creation, the Peace Corps has attracted, and sought, liberal arts majors, known within the Peace Corps as A.B. generalists. The attraction is natural. The liberal arts major often does not have career plans and is eager to be part of a movement that he believes worthy of hard work and sacrifice. In turn, the Peace Corps, well aware that these students are available for service, reasons that they can absorb enough knowledge and master sufficient skills in the brief training period to carry them successfully through an overseas assignment.

Although the Peace Corps has actively sought volunteers from minority groups, particularly Negroes, Mexican Americans, and American Indians, the actual number of such volunteers has been small. The agency states, with regret, that Negroes have made up less than 5 per cent of the total number of volunteers.

## APPLICATIONS FOR SERVICE

Although the Peace Corps stresses that volunteer service is a special kind of work and that stiff requirements must be met before an applicant is invited to training, it has been difficult for the agency to establish the difference between being an applicant and becoming a volunteer, or the difference between applying to the Peace Corps and enlisting in a branch of the military services. Application does not automatically lead to volunteer service. It is merely the first step in a process that begins with the submission of an application form and ends at the successful completion of a training program.

Since 1961, over 300,000 Americans of all ages and back-

CHART III

Distribution of Volunteers, by State June, 1968

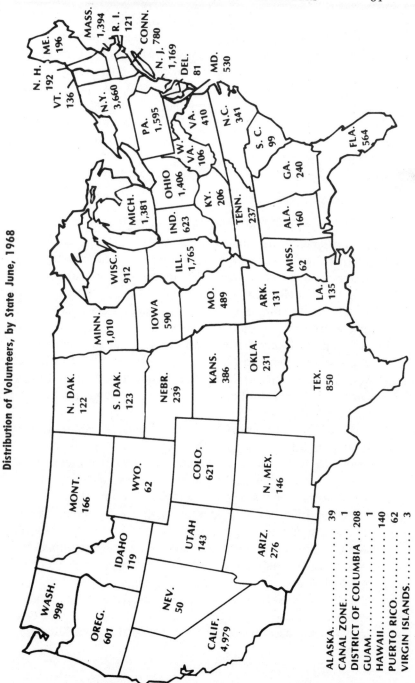

| | |
|---|---|
| ALASKA | 39 |
| CANAL ZONE | 1 |
| DISTRICT OF COLUMBIA | 208 |
| GUAM | 1 |
| HAWAII | 140 |
| PUERTO RICO | 62 |
| VIRGIN ISLANDS | 3 |

ME. 196
N. H. 192
VT. 136
MASS. 1,394
R. I. 121
CONN. 780
N. J. 1,169
DEL. 81
MD. 530
N. Y. 3,660
PA. 1,595
VA. 410
W. VA. 106
N. C. 341
S. C. 99
FLA. 564
OHIO 1,406
KY. 206
TENN. 237
GA. 240
ALA. 160
MISS. 62
LA. 135
MICH. 1,381
IND. 623
ILL. 1,765
WISC. 912
MINN. 1,010
IOWA 590
MO. 489
ARK. 131
N. DAK. 122
S. DAK. 123
NEBR. 239
KANS. 386
OKLA. 231
TEX. 850
MONT. 166
WYO. 62
COLO. 621
N. MEX. 146
IDAHO 119
UTAH 143
ARIZ. 276
WASH. 998
OREG. 601
NEV. 50
CALIF. 4,979

grounds have applied for Peace Corps service. Nearly 240,-000 of those applications have come from college students. Nevertheless, the number of applicants is not a measure of strength, for many who apply do not qualify. Only one in five applicants is invited to training and, of those invited, only 40 to 50 per cent accept. During training, another 25 per cent are lost. Obviously, this severe refining process means that the agency must have an active recruiting program.

RECRUITING VOLUNTEERS

Initially, interest in the Corps was high and Shriver and his staff spent little time on extensive recruiting efforts. In the first few years, the agency employed no full-time recruiters but relied, instead, on agency staff members, who were periodically sent on crash recruiting drives to college and university campuses. Few responded enthusiastically, for such a trip meant that the work in Washington piled up. Little or no thought was given to long-range, planned recruiting, although the National 4-H Foundation, the United Auto Workers, and several other private groups tried to convince the Corps to launch a continuing and professional recruiting program.

By 1965, it was obvious that the agency would have to develop a different approach. Recruiters were being challenged to justify how one could help a government work for peace while that same government was engaged in war, or why Americans should serve in Addis Ababa while Detroit and Newark burned. Yet the Corps continued to send teams of staff members on crash recruiting drives across the country, and it was not until 1966 that the agency hired full-time recruiters and set up the regional operations described in Chapter III.

Today, the agency uses teams of recruiters, nearly all of whom are former volunteers. The mass recruiting that characterized the early years has been replaced by special recruiting efforts aimed at those with needed skills. Staff members in the regional offices determine the number of generalists, city planners, engineers, or public administrators required for a program, and then ask Volunteer Placement if such people will be available. The answer often determines whether or not a program request receives final approval. If it is approved, recruiters then seek persons with appropriate education and background. When volunteers with the necessary skills cannot be found, the Peace Corps simply has to refuse the request or postpone the program until they can be recruited.

But, even with this new approach, recruiting has not become easy. Continuing war in Vietnam and preoccupation with domestic problems have made the Peace Corps less attractive than it was in the early 1960's, and students increasingly have turned to VISTA and local community groups that work within the United States. The number of VISTA applications has risen continually during the past two years while the number of Peace Corps applications has remained the same. In early 1968, at a Peace Corps staff conference, Vaughn summed up the situation. "The honeymoon is over for the Peace Corps. Shifting priorities among our college students will require greater and better recruiting efforts on our part, gentlemen." This shift is one reason why Blatchford has insisted that the Corps switch its advertising appeals to messages that deal specifically with job assignments and skills requested by host countries rather than the low-keyed generalities that have marked Peace Corps advertisements and radio and television commercials up to this time.

## SELECTION POLICY

Selecting volunteers is one of the most critical functions in the agency's operations, for whether the Peace Corps succeeds, fails, or exists at all is almost entirely dependent upon its volunteers.

The broad outline of selection policy was developed by

Dr. Nicholas Hobbs in April, 1961, in a series of conferences with consultants experienced in the selection of overseas personnel. It was decided then that selection would be based on a systematic and extensive study of the individual, using information from several sources and the judgments of professionally trained experts. Selection would begin with the assessment of a thorough questionnaire, designed to reveal as much about the individual candidate as possible. All applicants would be required to take entrance tests, although no applicant would be refused the opportunity to enter training solely on the basis of test scores. Promising applicants would be invited to become trainees but would not be enrolled as volunteers until the successful completion of the training program. In addition, the effectiveness of all selection procedures would be continually evaluated by comparing selection critieria with overseas performance.

As the Peace Corps developed its selection techniques, it became clear that the quality of volunteers was far more important than the number. To train volunteers efficiently and effectively, each host-country program was to be treated separately, with selection and training tailored to fit the particular requirements of the program. It was also established that all applicants would be considered solely on merit, without preference or discrimination because of race, creed, ethnic origin, or political affiliation. Basing initial selection of a candidate on the information in his questionnaire, without requiring a personal interview, appeared to violate a basic hiring technique widely used in government, as well as in private business. Many senior staff members, initially skeptical of this arrangement, agreed to the procedure only after it was decided that final selection would not take place until the completion of training.

THE SELECTION PROCESS

Selection begins with the completion of a volunteer questionnaire. Just by filling out this form, an applicant gives

## Peace Corps Directors

R. Sargent Shriver, Jr., 1961–66, got the Peace Corps off to a fast start and, as a member of the Kennedy Administration, gave the agency its early glamour.

Jack Hood Vaughn, 1966–69, added professionalism to the Peace Corps's operation and expanded its activities to encompass more than 10,000 volunteers at work in over sixty countries.

Joseph H. Blatchford, the present Director, plans to make the Peace Corps more responsive to host-country priorities and to problem areas at home.

Teams of recruiters working out of regional offices across the country visit colleges, professional schools, and businesses to attract volunteers to the Peace Corps. Above, a returned volunteer and a Liberian woman talk with a student at Howard University.

Before going overseas, volunteers attend a training course, during which they study the language and culture of the host country and receive practical job training. Here, trainees heading for Dahomey learn to forge metal and to spray for insect control.

At the Peace Corps's training site on Saint Croix, trainees learn to kill and clean a chicken.

Volunteers completing their training in the Philippines talk with a Peace Corps volunteer already at work there.

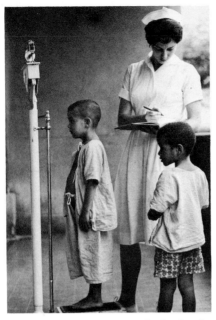

A volunteer nurse in Brazil checks the weight of young patients in a Rio de Janeiro hospital.

A volunteer in Chad helps drill a well.

In Guatemala, a volunteer talks with members of a farmers' cooperative about plans for marketing their crops.

A volunteer uses hand puppets to explain
family-planning to a group of Indian men.

Volunteers work overseas at hundreds of different jobs. They may teach in secondary schools, take part in government vaccination programs, organize cooperatives in urban slums, advise farmers about raising chickens or growing corn, teach at universities or teacher-training colleges, or help plan the development of a nation's cities.

At right, a volunteer working with a local agricultural agency in the Dominican Republic examines a diseased calf. Heifer Project, a 4-H affiliate, distributes cattle to the farmers through the agency, and volunteers teach proper care.

A volunteer in India rides to work.

Before dedication, the last touches are put on a Brazilian primary school built through the School Partnership Program, which the Peace Corps initiated in 1964. Through the program, an American school or organization contributes approximately $1,000 for construction materials and a Peace Corps volunteer works with the local people to build the school.

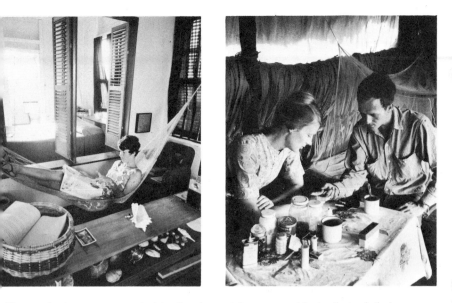

Since volunteers are expected to live in a style comparable to that of their co-workers, living conditions range from the modern and attractive apartment of a university teacher in British Honduras (upper left) to the thatched hut of a volunteer couple working in a new community in the Peten jungle of Guatemala (upper right). More typical, however, is the casual and pleasant housing of three Peace Corps volunteers in Chad (below).

A volunteer teacher gives an English lesson in a girls' school in Ethiopia.

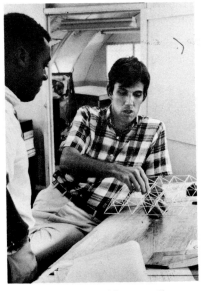

Two volunteer architects talk over plans for a public housing project in Micronesia.

A volunteer in Morocco collects water samples for mosquito research.

evidence of patience and endurance, for the form is twelve pages long, requires answers to more than one hundred separate items, and asks for at least eight references. The applicant then takes the Modern Language Aptitude Test and the Peace Corps Entrance Examination, although the latter is optional in some cases.

When a completed application has been received, staff members assess each applicant for legal and medical eligibility and contact the applicant's job supervisors, personal physician, college dean or high-school principal, and the eight references provided on the questionnaire. A surprisingly high rate of the reference forms—more than 80 per cent—are returned. Generally, they tend to be candid and reliable evaluations. Occasionally, they are amusing, too, as illustrated by the following examples:

"About emotion, he can take it or leave it."

"If dropped into an alien culture, he would be accepted by the members of that culture rather than eaten."

"I have seen her react favorably when her hand was mashed in a car door."

"We feel we have known him for a sufficient length of time to have noticed any seriously weak link in his armor, and we have found one."

"Even police patrolmen that have arrested him in past years stated they liked him."

"I have some reservations about the Peace Corps, none about the candidate."

The candidates are equally frank about themselves. One confessed that "first I thought you had to be an English major to teach English; then I learned different." Another candidate confided that "these are the people whom I feel know me best. If you would like another list of people who do not know me as well, but are in more important positions, please let me know."

The initial assessment of each candidate is based on

information in the volunteer questionnaire, the personal reference forms, academic transcripts, and the test scores. It usually takes three to four weeks to gather this information. When an applicant's file is complete, it is reviewed for evidence of skills, intelligence, ability to profit from a short but intensive training program, ability to adapt to another culture, and adequate motivation for Peace Corps service. If this evidence is present, and there are no legal or medical reasons for rejecting the applicant, his skills and background are matched with program needs. Field investigations, which take from six to twelve weeks, do not begin until an applicant accepts an invitation to training.

In late 1968 and early 1969, field investigations were made by telephone to determine if that method would be a sufficient check and thereby cut down the costs of field investigations. (The Peace Corps reimburses the Civil Service Commission $450 for each investigation.) The results of the experiment were still under study in October, 1969. In the meantime, the Civil Service Commission continues to check each applicant's background.

An applicant need not, and often does not, accept an invitation to training. The major reasons given for not accepting are military obligation, change in date of availability, or dissatisfaction with the program assignment. Since it is impossible to predict the acceptance rate for a given program, the Peace Corps must invite more applicants than are needed, which adds to the complexity of programing.

A CONTROVERSIAL EXAMINATION

In 1963, the Peace Corps flirted with controversy by including in its battery of entrance tests an examination designed to reveal personality and psychological traits. The examination was created for the Corps by a group of Indiana University psychologists. A Civil Service Commission staff member, concerned about the distribution and storage problems the 1-inch thick test was going to cause, scanned a copy of the exam. His concern increased, and he took the exam to Donald R. Harvey, then chief of the Commission's Bureau of Recruiting and Examining. Harvey found parts of the examination repugnant, particularly the sections that probed into sexual attitudes and habits, and was convinced that the test constituted an invasion of privacy. He sent a copy of the exam to Commission Chairman John Macy, with the recommendation that the Commission refuse to administer it. Macy concurred, despite heavy pressure from the Corps.

Nevertheless, the Peace Corps did not discard the controversial examination but, rather, added it to the tests given during training. The agency emphasized then, as it does today, that "all psychological tests are voluntary, and a trainee may reject any test or test item where he feels that his right of privacy is being invaded." The assumption that such tests are justified because volunteers serve in sensitive roles overseas has been sharply rejected by a majority of the staff as well as many psychologists. Most volunteers have found the tests repugnant. Their attitude is well expressed by a PCV who served in Peru. "We all resented the psychologists and their written tests, which were inane and made us feel like guinea pigs."

## SELECTION DURING TRAINING

When training begins, the Peace Corps no longer must rely solely on an applicant's written record, and abilities and personality traits can more easily be evaluated against the requirements of a job. In the early years, most trainees had the feeling that they were under constant scrutiny. Former volunteer Moritz Thomsen described his experience in *The Peace Corps Reader*:

In all three phases of our training, we were studied and appraised like a bunch of fat beeves about to be entered in the State Fair. Our instructors watched us and filed daily reports; the psychologist and the psychiatrist watched us; mysterious little men from Washington in black suits whose names we never learned appeared and watched us. Each weekend, we went on camping trips where we were watched by our camp leaders. The doctor and his nurse watched us; our discussion leaders watched us; our athletic coaches watched us. And even the kitchen help watched us.

Since early 1968, however, the approach has changed. A trainee's strengths and weaknesses are now discussed with him, and staff psychologists explain the results of all testing. The Peace Corps's field assessment officers serve mainly as counselors and the agency tries to maintain a ratio of one officer for every twenty trainees. In addition, early in the training program, trainees learn about living and working conditions in the host country and have the opportunity to meet with host citizens. The training program is explained, and the role of overseas staff described in detail, by members of the staff with whom they will be working, when this can be arranged.

This approach leads to self-assessment by the trainees as they learn what will be expected of them, with the result that many select themselves out of the program. "This is what we want," a staff member explained in an interview in September, 1969:

> In the past too many of our people went all through training and into a job overseas without really knowing what the Peace Corps is all about. The attrition rate in some projects was enormous, and this was not fair either to the volunteer or the host country. Withdrawal should take place as early as possible. The trainee should be urged to assess himself—his motives, his commitment, his skills, his ability to relate with other people. He can only do this if he is made to feel a part of the process, not the victim of it.

About half-way through the training period, each trainee's progress is evaluated by what is known as a mid-selection board. In the past, this was a time of anxiety, for trainees were questioned, their motives were challenged, and they were sometimes badgered in an attempt to test their commitment. Today, the function of the mid-selection board is diagnostic. Board members, generally a field assessment officer, a training officer, the country director or the program and training officer from Washington, and representatives from the training institution, file reports with a field selection officer, who serves as chairman of the board. A trainee's progress is then discussed with him. Near the completion of training, a senior selection officer decides whether or not a trainee will become a volunteer, and his decision is based on the suitability of the trainee for the program and on the trainee's own self-assessment. Since 1968, when the Corps adopted this approach, approximately 65 per cent of all those who dropped out of training did so on their own. In a few training programs, selection has been based entirely on self-assessment.

## Training

The legislation creating the Peace Corps required the President to "make provision for such training as he deems appropriate for each applicant for enrollment as a volunteer and each enrolled volunteer." The Act further provided that the training "shall include instruction in the philosophy, strategy, tactics, and menace of communism," and, in a separate section, decreed that "No person shall be assigned to duty as a Volunteer under this Act in any foreign country or area unless at the time of such assignment he possesses such reasonable proficiency as his assignment requires in speaking the language of the country to which he is assigned."

The Peace Corps has experimented more with training than with any of its other operations. In the early months, the agency considered working with industry, using private organizations with overseas operations, establishing a Peace Corps academy similar to those for the armed forces, or setting up several small training centers throughout the country and overseas. Each of these proposals required more time and money than were available. As a result, the Peace Corps turned to colleges and universities, and the resulting partnership has proved mutually beneficial.

The Peace Corps tailors each training program to meet the needs of an overseas project. The agency's training manual sets the tone for this specialization:

> The design of any training program must begin with the precise definition of the assignment. The nature of the job determines the nature of the training. At the conclusion of his training, the volunteer must be technically, physically, intellectually, socially, and psychologically prepared for the task ahead.

Volunteers in early training programs received a minimum of sixty hours of formal instruction a week, plus outside reading assignments and discussion periods. The program included instruction in language and area studies, American studies, world affairs, technical studies, health and medical training, physical training, and Peace Corps orientation. The trainee spent 40 per cent of this time on language lessons, 20 per cent on technical instruction, and the rest on the remaining subjects, medical and dental examinations, and psychological testing and interviewing. Training lasted from eight to twelve weeks.

Trainees headed for assignments in Latin America usually went to an "outward bound" camp in Puerto Rico for two or three more weeks. There, trainees hiked, climbed mountains, and camped in remote jungle areas with a minimum of food, water, and equipment. The Peace Corps has since eliminated the outward bound experience from training, but many returned volunteers insist that it prepared them for the rigors of volunteer service better than any other segment of the program. Although the outward bound life was more rugged than the conditions in which they lived overseas, they were glad to have been exposed to its challenges.

At the completion of training, those selected as volunteers went through a brief orientation session in the host country designed to give the volunteers first-hand experience with a new culture and to provide additional language and technical training.

In the summer of 1967, the Peace Corps altered its training philosophy. The agency recognized the irrelevance of the lecture hall and began to set up training programs within the host country or in situations more closely approximating working conditions overseas. Training institutions scheduled a portion of almost every program in city ghettos, depressed rural areas, farms, Indian reservations, or in other locations in which volunteers could use their skills and be exposed to attitudes and ways of life unfamiliar to most of them. As a result, volunteers are not only better prepared for their assignments, but they also develop a deeper understanding of the problems of their own society.

Brent K. Ashabranner, former deputy director of the Peace Corps, summed up the evolution of training philosophy in a speech before the American Psychological Association in September, 1967:

In the early days, we set out to separate the men from the boys and came up with what one professor called "a testing rather than a learning situation." Early Peace Corps training was an endurance test. We put the trainee in a classroom [where] for twelve weeks, from six in the morning until ten at night, we stuffed him with facts—some of which, we hoped, were relevant to what he would do overseas.

Next it seemed to us a good idea to . . . throw him into physically demanding situations with which he had to cope. Sometimes we even threw him into a swimming pool with his hands and feet tied, although none of us can quite remember for which country he was being prepared. That was our "Outward Bound" survival era.

Now we know that the trainee cares greatly about surviving with people as well as in places. He wants to know what the Nepali eat and drink, how the nomadic people of Botswana carry water and deliver babies, and how the Micronesians spear their food. We have also found language fluency crucial to volunteer effectiveness. In some of our early programs, trainees sometimes had only a hundred hours of language study. Now we devote from three hundred to four hundred hours to intensive language instruction.

Peace Corps training is no longer formal, classroom instruction. Even language classes are conducted in small groups and in surroundings as different from a lecture hall as can be found. As soon as language proficiency permits, technical instruction and the host country's history, politics, and culture are taught in the language the volunteer will be using on his job.

Peace Corps training today is aimed at preparing a volunteer to do a specific job well. The average training period is thirteen weeks, and much of the earlier subject matter in American studies and world affiairs has been eliminated or reduced. Equal time is devoted to language instruction, including cultural studies, and technical training. Language instructors are often host-country citizens. Cultural and technical studies staff members have first-hand knowledge of the country as well as expert knowledge of their subject. Psychologists are available for counseling, and returned volunteers serve as language instructors, training project directors, or discussion leaders.

Although Peace Corps training has been greatly refined over the past eight years, it remains as physically and intellectually demanding as it was in the beginning. The daily schedule of a group of volunteers preparing to teach physical education in Thailand gives an idea of its intensity:

|       |                      |
|------:|----------------------|
| 6:30  | language instruction |
| 7:30  | breakfast            |
| 8:30  | language instruction |
| 10:30 | technical training   |
| 12:30 | lunch                |
| 1:30  | language instruction |

3:30    area and cultural studies
5:30    physical education
6:00    dinner

In the evening, the schedule varied. On some nights, there were group discussions in which the training staff participated; on other nights, there were lectures or seminars on cultural studies; a few nights were free. Weekends lasted from Saturday noon until Monday morning and were devoted to shopping, touring, swimming, and rest.

## LANGUAGE TRAINING

The Peace Corps has placed special emphasis on language training, for the agency has learned by experience that fluency in the local dialect is crucial for working and living successfully overseas. In its eight years of existence, the Peace Corps has taught more than one-hundred fifty different languages, including French, Spanish, Arabic, Hindi, and Swahili, as well as such exotic languages as Twi, Aymara, and Kru.

In 1967, the Corps began to teach languages by a method called language saturation technique, dubbed LST for short. This technique required that the trainee speak nothing but the language he was learning, regardless of how extensive his vocabulary was. The program was tested in the summer and fall of 1967, and athough it was intense and demanding, trainees responded enthusiastically. At Dartmouth College, where an LST course was being held for volunteers bound for French-speaking West Africa, campus police discovered trainees reporting to the language laboratory as early as four o'clock in the morning. By the spring of 1968, the technique, renamed high intensity language training (HILT), was being used in virtually every training program.

The HILT method has proved effective. Trainees can achieve a language proficiency in twelve weeks equal to that of language majors after four years of college study. A group going to Lesotho was one of the first to use the HILT technique. At the end of their twelve-week training period, their fluency in the native language, Sesotho, was rated on the Foreign Service Institute scale. (The Foreign Service Institute gives fluency ratings in speaking and reading ability from 1 to 5; for speaking proficiency, S-1 indicates the ability to handle elementary conversations and situations; S-2, fluency sufficient for most social and work situations; S-3, the ability to use the language with ease; S-4, considerable fluency; and S-5, bilingualism.) In the Lesotho group, 45 of the volunteers (65 per cent) achieved a rating of S-2, and the rest rated S-1 or S-1+. Once a volunteer is at work overseas, his fluency frequently reaches S-3.

## TRAINING SITES AND INSTITUTIONS

Peace Corps training is conducted by one of five means: in-house centers, colleges and universities, private organizations, split programs, in-country training.

In-house centers are training sites owned or leased by the Peace Corps and staffed by agency employees, including host citizens working full-time for the Corps. The two original centers, Camp Crozier and Camp Radley in Puerto Rico, were established in 1961 and 1962. They were closed in July, 1969, because they were located in remote mountain areas that offered trainees few opportunities to meet and work with local people. Since then, training in Puerto Rico has been conducted at the town of Ponce, where trainees live with Puerto Rican families and meet daily for language and technical training. In 1967, three additional centers were set up at St. Croix and St. Thomas in the Virgin Islands and in Escondido, California. The centers at Ponce and Escondido are used for volunteers heading for Latin America; those in the Virgin Islands, for volunteers going to Africa. In addition, local facilities in each of the six districts of Micronesia have been used to train volunteers who will serve there. About one-third of all Peace Corps volunteers train at these in-house centers or at sites in Micronesia.

Colleges and universities are still the most widely used training sites. In recent years, the Peace Corps has developed close relationships with several campuses and no longer scatters its programs among schools. The most extensive relationship has been with the University of Hawaii at Hilo, where a year-round staff supervises training for the East Asia and Pacific regions. The University of Hawaii has trained more than thirty-five hundred volunteers—more than any other university—and the close relationship has permitted facilities for research and evaluation. This arrangement may forecast future trends.

Private organizations and institutions, the first groups to which the Peace Corps turned, also conduct training programs under contract. Among them, the Peace Corps has relied most heavily on the Experiment in International Living at Putney, Vermont, which, by January, 1969, had trained 2,141 volunteers. Other groups that have conducted training programs are the United Auto Workers, Westinghouse Corporation, Litton Industries, Thiokol Chemical Corporation, the National 4-H Foundation, Educational Services, the Education Development Center, Research Institute for the Study of Man, Caterpillar Tractor Company, Development Resources Corporation, General Dynamics, the Heifer Project, and CARE.

Split programs combine training at Peace Corps in-house centers or at universities and private organizations with a period of training within the host country, known as in-country training. The agency began this program in 1966. The first phase, and the longest and most intensive, is conducted at a training site in the United States or at a center in Puerto Rico, the Virgin Islands, or Micronesia; the second part is held in the host country. This split approach permits the volunteer to adjust gradually to his new environment and seems to be the most successful when the training sites in the host country are such as to encourage volunteers to meet and interact with local people.

Total in-country training is being conducted in an increasing number of host countries. Initially, the agency held training programs in the country in which the volunteers were to work, but these early programs were unsuccessful because both the Peace Corps and the local officials who helped with them lacked experience and were unable to provide the kind of training the volunteers needed. Misunderstandings developed and the approach was dropped. By the end of 1967, however, interest in total in-country training had been revived, and some staff members even proposed that the agency conduct all its training programs overseas. To do so, however, the Peace Corps will have to overcome several difficulties. For one thing, a separate training program must be developed for each project. For another, local officials must be able to select and train their own countrymen to make lectures and discussion sessions interesting and meaningful to volunteers.

There is also a new trend toward continuous training within the host country, a system in which groups of fifteen to twenty volunteers enter training each month. This method combines the obvious advantages of smaller classes with continuity, as well as providing trainees with more opportunities to explore the new culture. Through this approach, volunteer training can be, as one staff member explained, "tailor-made for specific sites where the volunteers will be working."

## INNOVATIONS IN TRAINING

The Peace Corps has tried many experiments in its training programs. Total in-country training was one of the first. Another was the Advance Training Program (ATP) established in 1965 to encourage college undergraduates to apply and to begin training while still in school. Those accepted for the program attended a special 8-week training course in language instruction and area studies in the summer between their junior and senior years. They continued language and area studies through their senior year and attended a final training session in the summer after graduation. Unfortunately, a large proportion of the ATP volunteers never completed training, and the program has since been discontinued.

Joint Peace Corps–university programs, in which volunteers combine Peace Corps work with degree programs, have proved more successful. As early as 1962, Wesleyan University asked the Peace Corps to coordinate its training with their program for a Master of Arts in teaching. Michigan State University initiated a teaching program leading to a master's degree for the volunteers it trained and supported in Nigeria. The University of Missouri established a master's degree in community development for the volunteers it trained for Latin America.

In a recent joint program, the State University of New York at Brockport and the Peace Corps selected fifty math and science undergraduates, who spent two summers and their junior year at Brockport and then went to Latin America as volunteer teachers. Participants in the program received a B.S. degree and were granted provisional teaching certification after the first year of overseas service. When their tour has ended, they may return to Brockport with graduate standing, and, after two semesters of study, will qualify for an M.S. degree and a permanent New York State teaching certificate. Similar degree programs in agriculture have been established at Wilmington College in Ohio and the Davis Campus of the University of California.

Intern programs are another innovation. In the summer of 1967, twenty Harvard and Radcliffe college juniors worked as apprentices to volunteers in Ethiopia, Panama, and Senegal. After completing their senior years, the apprentice volunteers attended a brief training session and returned as volunteers to the country in which they had worked. In another internship program, more than four hundred college juniors spent the summer of 1967 as domestic volunteers with VISTA. After graduation, these interns attended condensed training programs and went overseas.

In another experimental program, the Peace Corps and the Job Corps worked together to select and train a small group of Job Corps graduates for Peace Corps service. In the fall of 1966, twenty Job Corps graduates entered a special 6-week training program, after which seven were invited to enter a Peace Corps training program for industrial arts teachers headed for Malaysia. Five—four Negroes and one Puerto Rican—completed training and went to Malaysia to teach industrial arts in September, 1967. According to a spokesman for the Peace Corps, they became "exceptionally successful volunteers" and related more quickly to their co-workers and adapted sooner and with more ease to their new environment than did many of their fellow volunteers. Since then, Job Corps graduates have served in programs in Jamaica, India, Brazil, Colombia, and Ethiopia.

In 1967, another experiment began when a group of American Indians were selected to take part in a special training session designed to give them the skills and language facility necessary to compete in a regular training program. The idea was first suggested to the Peace Corps by LaDonna Harris, Senator Fred Harris's wife and president of Oklahomans for Indian Opportunity, a private corporation in Norman, Oklahoma. The plan was named Project Peace Pipe. The first summer's training program could not be termed a success, but, as a Peace Corps recruiting brochure explained:

As an experiment, Peace Pipe was designed to raise questions—about the Indian and the Peace Corps. Some of the answers will be long in coming, but it was apparent at the outset that some early assumptions were correct: The Indians did need a special introduction to the world of the Peace Corps, and, as the Indians required an introduction to the Peace Corps, so too did the Peace Corps need an introduction to the ways of the Indian.

In the summer of 1968, thirty-two young Indians were sent to the Peace Corps training center at Camp Crozier in Puerto Rico in a program designated Peace Pipe II. They were given pre-training instruction and then joined a group at Escondido, California, that was being trained for rural community development assignments in Colombia. Of the original number, six completed training and became volunteers.

## THE EVOLUTION OF TRAINING

As the Peace Corps continues to experiment with new ideas and approaches in training, the debate continues over just what a training program should be. A special agency report, "The Making of a Volunteer: A Review of Peace Corps Training—Summer, 1968," observed that within the agency there are as many training philosophies as there are training programs, and that the emphasis of each program is largely determined by its director. It continued:

> The debate is about priorities: Do we want good technicians above all, or do we want good volunteers who are also good technicians? Can Peace Corps-level "technicians" be good unless they also possess the attributes of good volunteers? And conversely, can a volunteer without skills be a good volunteer? The answer we give to these questions determines the direction of the Peace Corps in training as well as overseas. They affect a training program's content, its structure and the methods it uses.

This introspective approach is a long way from that of the early programs when, according to an official who helped direct them, "a small band of hand-picked trainees went to a half-dozen colleges where they embarked upon a vague academic program which had been described over the telephone and in Peace Corps literature in glowing terms." He continued:

> The volunteers' first experiment with what we call culture shock may well have occurred at the training site on opening day. They did pushups in the morning, had three vitamin-packed meals a day, ran through the selection gamut, were pummeled, punctured, and tested. Presto! We had instant volunteers who knew little about their destination, had a lot of guts and remarkable spirit, but not much more know-how than when they started.

The contrast is most dramatic when the description of the early programs is placed next to that of a particularly outstanding training program cited in the agency report:

> Primarily an agriculture program, it assembled a highly skilled technical staff, concerned, competent [returned volunteers] and several host-country professionals, and put them all under an experienced, warm and efficient project director. Trainees started off by planting their fields, thus becoming involved at once in what they would be doing overseas. They learned [agricultural] vocabulary and subject matter in their language classes and eventually did their field work in the host language. Their cross-cultural discussions, led by trained [returned volunteers], focused on their jobs-to-be. Role-playing with the host-country nationals brought out the trainees' American cultural background and again related it to their jobs. The assessment staff saw its job primarily as counselling, not selection, and was interested and involved in all training activities. The trainees weren't lectured to about the Peace Corps; they lived it. The guiding principle of the program was that unless a volunteer had the ability to relate to his co-workers his skills would avail him little.

# VI

# Program Development

On March 1, 1961, when President Kennedy created the Peace Corps by executive order, the agency had no volunteers, little staff, no application form, no tests or testing centers, no selection procedures, no training programs, no evaluation system, and no agreements with nations wanting volunteers. Yet within six months, the agency had sent 120 volunteers to 3 countries and by the end of the year there were 578 volunteers in 8 countries. Six months later, 1,044 volunteers were at work in 17 nations. By June, 1965, there were 8,624 volunteers in 45 countries and in the following year, the number of volunteers passed 10,000. In June, 1969, the Peace Corps had 10,361 volunteers at work in 60 nations. Since the agency's creation, more than 38,000 volunteers have served in a total of 63 countries.

The Peace Corps goes only to those countries to which it is invited, and, conversely, leaves a country when it is no longer wanted. Since the Corps began operations, six nations have requested that volunteers be withdrawn.* The first country to do so was Ceylon. The program there was terminated by a mutual agreement between the governments of the United States and Ceylon after thirty-nine volunteers completed their tours in 1964. In 1967, Ceylon became the first country to reinvite the Peace Corps and volunteers returned there in early 1968. Members of the only group to

---

* In January, 1970, the Malawi Government, following the recommendation of the ruling Malawi Congress Party, formally requested withdrawal of all Peace Corps personnel within six months.

serve in Cyprus were withdrawn in early 1964, when civil strife made their work difficult and hazardous. The Peace Corps program in Indonesia ended in mid-1965—just sixteen months after the first volunteers had arrived there— during a period of deteriorating U.S.-Indonesian relations. In November, 1966, after more than three years in Guinea, the Peace Corps was asked by the Guinean Government to leave the country. Volunteers were reinvited in 1968. (The story of the agency's exit from Guinea is told in Chapter VIII.) The eleven volunteers in Mauritania were withdrawn in June, 1967, after that country broke diplomatic relations with the United States during the Arab-Israeli war. In December, 1967, Peace Corps volunteers were withdrawn from Gabon at that country's request. No reason was given, but there is speculation that former French President Charles de Gaulle influenced the decision. The Peace Corps had been in Gabon since 1963 and had built most of that country's public schools.

Peace Corps operations in three other countries have been reduced or gradually phased out because of internal strife or circumstances stemming from American foreign relations. The program in Pakistan ended when the early groups serving there completed their tours. No additional volunteers were requested by the Pakistan Government, reportedly, because the United States had refused to supply Pakistan with military weapons and supplies. Peace Corps operations in Nigeria were greatly reduced after Biafra declared its independence in 1967 and civil war erupted. In the spring of 1969, Tanzania announced that it was terminating Peace Corps operations there. Faced with mounting criticism over the influence of Peace Corps teachers in Tanzania's elementary and secondary schools, President Julius K. Nyerere made it clear that he believed Africans should be taught by Africans and that Peace Corps teachers were merely an extension of the colonial system. Programs in Tanzania are now being phased out.

BINATIONALISM

As the Peace Corps has become more sophisticated in working with the governments and peoples of other nations, it has learned that including host citizens in planning and operations makes the agency's work more relevant to the host country—and more lasting. In an interview in late 1968, C. Payne Lucas, former regional director for Africa, explained why:

> Since the very beginning we have been saying that there are, or should be, no Peace Corps programs, only host-country programs. We meant well, but in the early years a lot of countries asked for volunteers out of politeness, or out of respect for Jack Kennedy, or because the Peace Corps received so much worldwide publicity that it became fashionable to invite volunteers. Many governments didn't know how they could use PCV's, so they asked for teachers. Actually, many of the second-generation programs were started on the basis of what our early volunteers told us should be going on instead of teaching programs. At any rate, we were still calling most of the shots when Sarge [Shriver] left for [the] OEO.
>
> When Jack Vaughn became Director, we began to mean it when we said, "We want Kenyan programs for Kenyans," and so forth. But we were still only playing around the edges. Finally, some of us began to push for the hiring of nationals to work with us at all staff levels—not just with training. We've made progress. Sierra Leone is a joint partner with the Peace Corps now. We have several of their people on our staff there, and already programing is getting better. No host-country national wants to be responsible for a failure, so a lot more thought is being given to selecting volunteer projects.

In the January, 1969, issue of the *Volunteer,* Brent Ashabranner suggested a model for binational program leadership. He proposed that the director of each program be an official of the host country, assigned and paid by his government, who would have ultimate responsibility for volunteers.

There would be no resident Peace Corps staff in the country, and plans for programs would be worked out in discussions between host officials and a team from Peace Corps Washington. A variation of the scheme might be to have several such directors, one from each ministry receiving volunteers, or to have a resident Peace Corps staff member who would concentrate solely on programing and assume no supervisory responsibility for volunteers. Ashabranner supported his proposal by pointing to the program in Libya:

> One experience that makes me believe that this kind of model is not a fantasy is our experience in Libya. We started a small program there. They requested English teachers; they were adamant that the volunteers not be labelled Peace Corps volunteers. We were not allowed to have a regular office, nor a Peace Corps director per se. We were permitted to send a staff member, but he couldn't travel much, couldn't bring the volunteers together for conferences, etc. The Libyans were perfectly willing to pay the whole freight. We paid for the transportation to and from the country and for training. Everything else was paid by the Libyan government.
>
> The volunteers who went put in two tough years—and during that time the Israeli-UAR war took place with growing intensity of feeling in North Africa about Israel. The volunteers not only survived—they flourished, and they did everything we expect volunteers to do in addition to their teaching jobs. The Libyan government was so pleased they asked for 300 more to replace the original 15. We're sending 125.
>
> Now we can have a Peace Corps director and Peace Corps staff in Libya. We've put one in, but I'm wondering if we should have. Perhaps we should have waited to see if it would work with 125 as it did with 15.

Blatchford gave impetus to this trend in programing on the day he was sworn in as Director of the Corps. He announced then that he hoped to make the agency a more cooperative venture, with host citizens playing a larger role in Peace Corps operations, both abroad and in the United States.

## PRIVATE GROUP PARTICIPATION

In an interview shortly after his appointment was announced, Blatchford said he hoped to lead the agency toward more involvement with private organizations experienced in overseas voluntary operations. If he succeeds, he will have taken the Peace Corps on a full cycle to the original concept of its operations. President Kennedy told Congress and the American public in 1961 that Peace Corps volunteers were to be made available to developing nations:

1. Through private voluntary agencies carrying on international assistance programs
2. Through overseas programs of colleges and universities
3. Through assistance programs of international agencies
4. Through assistance programs of the United States Government
5. Through new programs which the Peace Corps itself directly administers

Shriver underlined the President's directive when he told the Senate Foreign Relations Committee in the summer of 1961 that "we hope to utilize American universities and private voluntary agencies to the maximum." Shriver said he believed that the private sector's involvement would turn out to be a large part of the Peace Corps's total effort and that this cooperation would "thereby avoid the creation of another large government bureau."

Initially, the Peace Corps worked with groups from each of the categories specified by President Kennedy, but there were built-in difficulties in such arrangements. The peak year of private-sector participation in training and program administration was 1963, when sixteen private organizations administered 20 per cent of the volunteers in the field. Since then, the Peace Corps has relied less on the participation of private groups and by January, 1969, there were no programs privately administered, although such groups as the Heifer

Project and the American Association of Health, Physical Education, and Recreation continued to provide technical specialists when such support could not be supplied by the Corps's own technical representatives.

Thomas D. Scott, former director of the agency's Division of Private and International Organizations, discussed the relationships between the Peace Corps and private groups in an article that appeared in the *Annals of the American Academy of Political and Social Science* in May, 1966. In the article, entitled "The Peace Corps and the Private Sector: The Failure of a Partnership," Scott pointed out several reasons why the original plans failed. The Peace Corps, assuming that Congress would insist on preserving the separation of church and state and responding to church groups concerned that some religious organizations would be involved with the agency, announced that "as a matter of administrative policy, the Peace Corps has excluded from contract consideration for the time being, ecclesiastical or church organizations, i.e., those primarily or exclusively under clerical control or authority." In his article, Scott described the implications of this policy:

> With the exclusion of the religious welfare and mission programs from the Peace Corps horizon came a sudden awareness of how few other American voluntary efforts were directed abroad. At that time, it was pointed out that of nearly 20,000 American foundations only 29 were listed as having projects greater than $10,000 overseas. In fact, in the first four years of the Peace Corps, there never was a list of potential and actual private-agency contractors at headquarters that exceeded thirty.

Within Peace Corps headquarters, responsibility for developing overseas programs with private organizations was divided among three divisions—Private Organizations, University Relations, and U.N. and International Agency Programs. Control was further splintered by assigning the administration of university training programs to the Office of

Training and the coordination of university-administered overseas projects to the Division of University Relations. It is not surprising that this internal organization fostered rivalry rather than cooperation and made successful private-sector participation all the more difficult.

In addition, the Peace Corps set stringent requirements that few organizations were able to meet. The agency preferred groups that, in addition to administering programs overseas, were prepared to assist in recruiting and training volunteers and were able to provide technical personnel and logistical support. Only organizations with extensive operations, such as CARE and the Near East Foundation, were prepared and staffed for this kind of cooperative effort.

There were difficulties, too, in the relationships between the Peace Corps and the contractors' overseas representatives who were provided by those private agencies responsible for programs. Before a COR went overseas, he was interviewed by Shriver and as many as ten other staff members, some of whom were the COR's junior in years and experience. Once overseas, he frequently had difficulty working with the Peace Corps staff, who tended to operate in a manner alien to the more experienced, but sometimes less imaginative, COR. In his article, Scott quoted a COR who aptly summed up this situation. "When a [Peace Corps country] representative was in difficulty, it was 'a normal problem of cross-cultural adjustment;' when it happened to a COR, it was 'those damn private organizations!' "

## THE SCHOOL PARTNERSHIP PROGRAM

Through the School Partnership Program, originally called School-to-School when it was initiated in 1964, an American school or associated group can sponsor the construction of a school overseas. The program grew from the efforts of the Rosendale Elementary School Parent-Teacher Association of Schenectady, New York, to find an overseas project on which to spend $750 raised by the PTA. It was suggested to Eugene

Bradley, PTA president, that such a sum would provide building materials for a modest school. Bradley expanded this suggestion into a proposal for a school partnership program and took his plan to the Peace Corps and to other agencies at work in developing nations. He went to Colombia to talk over the idea with volunteers, staff members, the U.S. Ambassador, and local officials in the Ministry of Education, and the encouragement he received helped make his plan a reality. In April, 1964, Shriver announced the formal participation of the Peace Corps in the School-to-School Program. The first project undertaken was a 3-room school in the village of Casa Blanca, Colombia, for which the Rosendale PTA contributed $1,000. Since then, more than one thousand participants in forty-six states have helped finance the construction of more than seven hundred schools in other countries.

To become a partner, an American school must provide between $1,000 and $1,500 to cover the cost of construction materials. A Peace Corps volunteer helps direct the project in the host community and works with the local people in the actual construction of the school. The Peace Corps has definite requirements that must be met before a project begins: The host-country community must have (1) demonstrated an ability to work in a community development project; (2) secured a suitable lot and clear land title; (3) arranged for sound construction plans; (4) provided approximately 35 per cent of the total investment; (5) agreed that none of the partnership funds will go for paid labor; (6) arranged for a teacher; (7) recognized that no further funds will be forthcoming from the sponsoring American group; and (8) given evidence that its political and social climate is stable enough to allow completion of the project.

## SETTING UP A PROGRAM

Despite the availability of organizations and individuals experienced in setting up voluntary service programs overseas, Shriver initially insisted that program development and volunteer assignment were the responsibilities of the Peace Corps, specifically of the former Office of Program Development and Operations. When it was suggested that specialists visit host countries to help develop and organize projects, Shriver often dismissed the proposed trip as a junket. There was little real preparation for volunteer assignments, with the result, in many instances, of outright failure.

By 1963, these early failures had demonstrated the need for realistic programing and had led to the adoption of a system for program development. The basis for a project became a field report known as a 104 form, or project directive, which remains the basic tool in programing. The report is generally written by Peace Corps staff members in the host country and is based on project descriptions provided by a host agency or ministry and by volunteers in similar jobs.

The report focuses on the volunteer and what he will be doing if the described project is approved and assesses the country's need in relation to the goals the Peace Corps has set for itself. Specifically, the 104 form answers the following questions: What is the project and what are its objectives? How many volunteers are required? What kind of training is needed? Where will the volunteers work? Who will they work with and who will their supervisors be? What host-country agency is responsible for the project? What kind of technical support is required and who will provide it? What kind of host-country support will be provided?

If the project is continuing, suggestions for improvement are included. When completed, the 104 form is approved by the U.S. Ambassador in the country and then serves as the basis for a legal contract between the Peace Corps and the host nation. The 104 form is often used to help determine the scope of the training contract with a training institution and to suggest the training format if volunteers are to be trained at one of the Peace Corps's in-house centers.

In 1966, when the Planning-Programing-Budgeting system (PPB) became widespread throughout the federal government, the Peace Corps added a second step to programing.

In addition to the 104 form, the overseas staff prepares a program memorandum in which it analyzes the total program in the host country against the Peace Corps's goals and rates each project according to its relative importance to the country. In the program memorandum, the staff answers such questions as: What are the country's major problems? Which of these might the Peace Corps help solve? What will the volunteer's job be? To what extent will host citizens be involved? The Peace Corps country staff and host-country officials then assign priorities to individual projects and those that are agreed upon are sent to the regional staff in Washington for approval. This process depends as much on the expertise of the host-country officials as it does on that of the Peace Corps staff, and the system works best for countries in which volunteers have been serving for some years and in which local officials have been involved in Peace Corps operations.

There are four criteria for good programing, against which every project request is measured:

1. Volunteers must either be a part of or work closely with an agency within the host country. In addition, there must be a specific, written request for volunteers from the government and an indication that it will support participation by the Peace Corps, perhaps by helping to train volunteers or by sharing a portion of the costs.

2. The volunteer's role must be clearly understood and considered meaningful by the volunteer and his hosts. When evaluating a program request, a regional office examines whether specially qualified volunteers will have jobs that capitalize on their skills; whether the jobs will produce noticeable results and have significant lasting effect; whether the volunteers will displace qualified local people; and whether the volunteers will be in positions that arouse suspicion or distrust.

3. The skills required for a project must match the skills of Peace Corps applicants or individuals Volunteer Place-

ment believes it can recruit, or be general enough to be acquired by volunteers during training.

4. Assignments should offer volunteers considerable opportunity to associate with local people.

After a project request has been approved by the appropriate regional staff and director, the details are sent to the Agency for International Development for comment and to the Secretary of State for approval before the Peace Corps Director gives final approval.

Near the end of Vaughn's term as Director, younger administrators in the four regional offices suggested to Vaughn that he turn responsibility for programing over to the regional directors, as had been done with training. They argued that, if the regional offices know best what their training needs are, then they also are best suited to determine programing requirements. Opponents of the plan replied that a central programing office acts as part of a checks-and-balances system that helps the agency avoid the mistakes of the early years, when enthusiasm for a project often meant disregard for reality. Moreover, they continue, central programing prevents parochialism and promotes objective judgment.

In an interview in May, 1969, a program and training officer agreed on the need for an agency-wide program development office, but added:

> We have never faced up to the fact that overseas staff can put volunteers in any job any time. Local conditions and attitudes can change, and overseas staff members can be swayed by these changes. The program and training officers are in a better position to see the bigger picture, and, certainly, criteria for operations in a host country are better handled from a regional than a central base.

Many staff members believe that program analysis should deal with a basic question that too frequently has been overlooked: Will there be a host-country structure and sufficient resources available to carry on a project without the Peace

Corps? Some countries have not had the structure or funds to back up the agency's effort, and, when Peace Corps volunteers have left, the project has died. The tuberculosis-control program in Bolivia is an example of one instance in which a host country, with pressure from the Peace Corps, developed the means to keep a program going.

Based on the Corps's accepted criteria for programing, the TB control project is a good one. Serums and vaccines have been provided by private drug companies and the World Health Organization and manpower has been supplied by volunteers and Bolivians. The results have been impressive. The first volunteer group, which completed service in the spring of 1969, administered $44,000 worth of drugs and medicines to a total of 160,000 Bolivians. The treatment program has been widely accepted and the incidence of active tuberculosis has been cut back dramatically. In planning for a second group of volunteers to take over the work of the first, however, the Peace Corps insisted that the contract include provisions for additional Bolivian co-workers who would learn to administer the program and would teach others to carry it on. As a result, when the second TB control group completes its service in the late fall of 1970, Bolivian co-workers will be ready to take over the project.

The current program in Nicaragua demonstrates the value of early, careful planning. In 1968, at the instigation of U.S. Ambassador Kennedy Crockett, a team of Peace Corps staff members visited Nicaragua's newly elected President Anastasio Somoza to discuss the possibility of the Corps's going to Nicaragua. The following spring a formal request was received for volunteers to work with farm and community co-operatives, in public health projects, and as baseball coaches. The Peace Corps deputy director from Guatemala, sent to Nicaragua to help plan the program, realized that the proposed projects were not those most needed by the country. Two more experienced staff members were sent from Washington to help with research and planning, and the three men spent from August to December setting up a program. The result: plans for an agricultural credit project, administered through the small loan department of the Nicaraguan Agricultural Bank, limited to farmers with an annual income of less than $3,000. Nicaraguans had done the research behind the study and had proved that the government could carry on the program after the Peace Corps helped get it under way.

## RESEARCH

Within its first year, the Peace Corps established the Division of Research to conduct or supervise studies of Peace Corps operations. It was obvious to those who planned and organized the agency that staff members would need to know about the effectiveness of programs and understand the volunteer experience to insure constructive growth of the agency. The first studies were directed toward improving training and selection; more recent studies have been concerned with overseas operations. The results have been especially useful to staff members concerned with program development, a point emphasized by Vaughn in testimony before the Senate Foreign Relations Committee in April, 1968:

Complete and systematic descriptions of our program activities and quantitative measurement of our program results are extremely useful as tools for improving programs. We are giving more attention to the problem of systematic measurement of program effectiveness, which will allow us to compare one program with another. We have made some progress in coping with the major obstacles to such measurement: the great variety of project goals, the seemingly intangible aims of human development and attitude change, and the political sensitivity involved in Americans doing evaluative studies in another society.

In one of the first research studies, the Department of

Anthropology of Cornell University sought to measure the effectiveness of community action work. Researchers compared the level of community development of thirty Peruvian communities over the two-year period 1962-64 to determine how they had changed when community development techniques were introduced by volunteers. Towns with and without PCV's were rated on a point scale according to the presence of services from government, institutional, or private sources, such as social-service agencies, churches, schools, youth organizations, and clubs. Lima was assigned 100 points and the communities under study ranged downward to a low of 7. The results of the study showed that communities in which volunteers had worked had gained a total of 50 points on the scale; the other communities had gained a total of 6. The researchers also discovered that volunteers had participated in 78 per cent of the activities resulting in point increases and that they were more productive when they worked through local programs and agencies than when they worked independently. In addition, the study showed that the AID Special Projects Program in Peru was twice as effective with volunteer help as without it.

In another study, specialists from the Social Science Research Institute at the University of Hawaii interviewed more than 2,200 Filipinos between 1964 and 1966 to determine the effectiveness of those volunteers serving as co-teachers. The study showed that contact with volunteers had increased the Filipinos awareness and interest in world affairs. In communities where volunteers had not served, 47 per cent of those surveyed had read a newspaper or listened to a radio broadcast sixteen or more days in the preceding month. In communities where volunteers had served, 92 per cent had done so. More important for the Corps, however, the study demonstrated that volunteers were more successful in establishing good relations with their hosts than in carrying out their professional tasks, and the findings pointed out the need for increased training and for a more precise definition of the volunteers' jobs.

## The Program Spectrum

Volunteer assignments cover an amazing range of jobs. A volunteer may teach in a secondary school, run a local health clinic, organize a cooperative in an urban slum, advise farmers about raising chickens or growing corn, teach at a university or a teacher-training college, or help plan the development of a new nation's cities. In general, the work falls into four main categories: education, community development, agriculture, and health. Each of these areas poses different challenges and requires different training and technical support for the volunteers.

## Education

Since the Peace Corps began, nearly half of all volunteers have worked in education or education-related projects. They have worked with ministries to set up new curricula and have taught in primary schools, secondary schools, universities, teacher-training institutes, vocational schools, and special training courses. The Peace Corps prepares most of these volunteers for their jobs, for fewer than one-third of them have taken education courses before they enter training.

Most volunteer teachers face an entrenched system of education patterned after European models in which learning is based on memorization. The texts are often insufficient and irrelevant; the facilities, overcrowded; and the method of discipline, rigid and strict. Countless volunteers have been frustrated by having to teach subject matter inherited from colonial days and largely unrelated to their students' lives. In a report on one African program, Stanley Meisler, a former evaluation officer for the Peace Corps, described education in secondary schools in Africa. His description applies to most of the developing nations.

By the time an African enters an African secondary school, he is a secure and successful rote learner, eager to write down and memorize everything that the teacher puts on the blackboards. This reliance on memorization is reinforced by the fact that the course of his life now depends on passing a single examination. All his reasoning, creativity and initiative in class count for nothing. He has no reason to change from the old, safe way.

Rote learning is reinforced further by outdated textbooks and teachers. Like traditional American educators in the past, the teachers also believe that the essence of education is the communication of a body of information, all based on past experience, to the docile student. If the student can absorb it by memorization, fine. Furthermore, these teachers don't have the patience or concern to attempt changing habits ingrained by eight years of primary school.

The Peace Corps Volunteer, on the other hand, cares enough to try. That may be the greatest resource the Volunteer brings to African education.

In some countries, however, out-dated curricula are being discarded and volunteers are working with ministries and in classrooms to introduce new methods and subject matter. In the Eastern Caribbean, the University of the West Indies has developed new secondary school examinations and is rewriting curricula to conform to the exams. Several volunteer teachers there have stayed on after their tours to help put the new curricula into practice. In Guyana, the Ministry of Education assigned a volunteer to introduce new math in primary schools. He took a teaching job for six months to learn the methods and problems of the teachers, then enlisted the aid of several of them to help him explain new math concepts in seminars and workshops throughout the country. The new math program represents Guyana's first break with rote learning. To introduce the inductive method of teaching science in Nepal, volunteers have produced science-teaching manuals that outline all the steps and materials needed to demonstrate scientific principles through experiments. Volunteers are now helping teachers learn the new procedures.

Teaching English as a foreign language (TEFL) is the largest individual education program. TEFL projects are concentrated in Middle East and East Asian countries, where English is used for trade and government and is almost a necessity for students who wish to do advanced work, especially in science. The TEFL technique, which is taught in training, is audio-lingual, with emphasis on repetition of word patterns and short conversations rather than memorization of vocabulary and grammatical rules.

## COMMUNITY DEVELOPMENT

Even after eight years, there is still confusion within the Peace Corps as to just what community development is. One member of the overseas staff has defined it as "the discovery of elements in a community who are progressive and the support of these elements in any way possible to carry out their ambitions or their objectives." Frank Mankiewicz, former director of Latin American operations for the Corps, described community development as a revolutionary force, the ultimate aim of which is "nothing less than a complete change, reversal—or a revolution if you wish—in the social and economic patterns of the countries to which we are accredited." Others define it simply as helping people help themselves.

Perhaps because community development has never been well defined, the goals of the programs have not been clearly understood. In early projects, emphasis was placed on results. Volunteers initiated projects for which they saw a need and, more often than not, they did most of the work themselves. Not surprisingly, when they left for home their projects were abandoned. Though it seems obvious that a volunteer's efforts have little meaning unless the local people identify their needs and take part, it was several years before the Peace Corps understood this approach and planned programs around it. In *The Peace Corps Reader*, a volunteer described two schools built in his community in Peru. His experience points out the change in thinking that occurred.

In another *barriada* in my town, there are two schools side by side. One is a several thousand dollar complex with classrooms, meeting halls, and a medical clinic.

It was built, brick by brick, by Peace Corps Volunteers, laboring day and night for six months. Architects labored with social workers, pouring cement, laying concrete blocks, putting in lights and plumbing. It is now completed and in partial use. Peruvians call it the *"gringo* school." Not one Peruvian ever lifted a finger to help build that school and it will crumble back to dust before one Peruvian will lift one finger to repair it.

Next door to this complex stands a two-room school, built out of grass mats, without windows or lights and with a dirt floor. It was built because the *barriada* grew and because classroom space was needed. The teacher, a Peace Corps Volunteer, talked the parents of the students into building those two rooms. The school was put up in one day. Volunteers only gave limited aid in construction. I consider the grass-school a success, and ten times more valuable to the community than the big complex it sits next to. Now the grass school is being replaced by another massive school, [but] even with the grass school gone, I still think it will remain a symbol to the *barriada* people of what they can do—working together.

Community development volunteers are now advised to begin slowly. They look for the real needs of the community —those which both they and their hosts recognize—and talk with neighborhood leaders to find those who will assume responsibility. The first community effort may be a campaign to clean up the streets. The next, a boys' baseball team. Then a meeting may materialize during which more pressing community problems are discussed. Eventually, government agencies are contacted and more ambitious projects undertaken. Water and sewer lines might be installed, an access road built, a consumer cooperative started, a credit union established, or an athletic field or playground built. According to one volunteer, "It all starts—and sometimes develops fast—once a community identity is established."

Because of the early emphasis on results and the confusion

over goals, the Peace Corps made mistakes in community development work. Volunteers, poorly trained and without a clear understanding of their roles, were sent to jobs that proved frustrating and futile. In Ecuador, volunteers were assigned to local agencies to assist with city planning, waterworks management, and highway design. When local elections brought a change in administration, co-workers and supervisors were replaced by supporters of the victors and the volunteers found themselves in meaningless assignments. In Chile, volunteers working with local social assistance programs were given neither specific tasks nor resources to work with. They spent two years trying, in vain, to develop a program.

Volunteers were also sent into urban slums to help local residents organize basic services for themselves. These assignments were perhaps the most difficult of all, and the number of urban-based volunteers who returned early was more than twice as high as for those in rural assignments. Vaughn admitted in an interview in 1968 that

> if we could do things differently, we would have sent fewer volunteers to the urban areas of Latin America, and that was my responsibility. I believe we expected too much of them in community development in the cities. We sent them to the large urban centers and said "go to work" without being specific. Many of them were handicapped by not having a real command of the language. We have tried to change this in training.

In Vaughn's last two years as Director, the agency reduced the number of volunteers sent to urban areas.

Today, about 25 per cent of all volunteers work in community development. The Peace Corps has learned that success in such jobs requires a special kind of volunteer, skillful in communication and human relations. Most community action volunteers spend some time in training working and living with the poor in places such as Spanish-speaking Harlem so that they understand the cultural, economic, and political issues they will face. They also learn to set up a government structure, to establish a system of communications, and to gather meaningful data from a community. For practical experience, they may work with a local group to solve a community problem, such as purifying a water supply or obtaining credit or technical assistance for an agricultural project. Volunteers are also given leadership training, and a few are assigned to programs in Latin America that are specifically designed to provide such training for local community leaders.

## PUBLIC HEALTH

The agency's health programs are aimed at changing people's habits, teaching better health care, and controlling diseases. In May, 1969, there were nearly 1,000 PCV health workers, a total that included such specialists as environmental health and home economics experts, laboratory and medical technicians, nurses, occupational and physical therapists, and X-ray technicians, as well as generalists trained to attack a specific problem. In Brazil, volunteers are helping to control schistosomiasis. In Thailand and the Philippines, they have helped establish successful malaria eradication programs. In Bolivia, Malawi, Korea, and Malaysia, they have launched tuberculosis control programs, and in India, Turkey, and Tunisia, they are encouraging family planning. The emphasis is on preventive rather than curative medicine, with family planning, child care, personal hygiene, and sanitation among the most common programs.

The problems of the volunteer health workers range from fears, superstitions, and cultural taboos to political squabbles over how a local government intends to use its money and the difficulties of fighting communicable diseases that do not stop at national boundaries. In some instances, these problems have led to so small a return on the Peace Corps's efforts that the agency has chosen to concentrate on other types of programs.

## AGRICULTURE

In the first year of operation, 14 per cent of all volunteers worked in agriculture. The program was cut in half the following year, but has been increasing steadily since. In 1968, about 10 per cent of all volunteers had agricultural assignments, and the Peace Corps estimates that, by 1970, that number will have risen to more than 25 per cent, with the percentage in some countries much higher. Most of these volunteers are generalists who learn a skill such as rice cultivation or poultry-raising in training.

Agricultural volunteers work at exceptionally varied jobs. They help farmers upgrade produce, establish grade standards, improve packaging methods, and enlarge markets. They train agricultural extension workers and teach in high schools and training centers. They set up systems for gathering and maintaining data on pricing and production for farm products and help establish cooperatives for purchasing, credit, marketing, processing, and transportation. They help build and operate irrigation systems, set up shops for the maintenance and repair of farm equipment, and teach adult classes in farm mechanics. They care for livestock, treat animal diseases, and help in livestock slaughter and processing programs.

The volunteers' biggest problem is resistance to change. Farmers, unable to visualize the results of a new method, are reluctant to try it. This situation is particularly unsettling for professional agriculturalists. One volunteer who graduated from an agricultural college and served in Venezuela explained his situation:

I had no training in tropical or sub-tropical agriculture before I came into the Peace Corps, and I saw my first banana growing at the same time the generalist volunteers did. I found that I could learn more quickly about tropical crops than the others because of my training, but I was also frustrated by the primitive methods the farmers were using. I never did quite adjust to thinking in terms of simple, basic farming. On the other hand, the generalists were learning all the time and many of them found it fascinating. They didn't stop to think to themselves "Lord, these people are backward" and then worry about it like I did.

There are programs that do not fall into these four categories, such as architecture, city planning, law, accounting, and public administration, and there will no doubt be others as the Peace Corps moves toward more specialized technical assistance. But the Peace Corps's activities can best be understood by looking closely at a few programs rather than trying to survey all of them. Each region has presented different problems and each has been the scene of different experimental ventures. The programs and countries discussed in the following chapters were selected because they are representative of the agency's operations in many nations, because they pose particular problems, or because they are unusually interesting.

# VII

# Latin America: Emphasis on Community Action

The Peace Corps's operations in Latin America are, and always have been, larger and more extensive than in the other regions. In the first annual report to Congress, the agency reported that as of June 30, 1962, there were 345 volunteers serving in Bolivia (35), Brazil (43), Chile (63), Colombia (103), El Salvador (25), Jamaica (38), St. Lucia (15), and Venezuela (23). At that time, another 485 trainees were preparing to go to Honduras, Bolivia, British Honduras, Dominican Republic, Venezuela, Ecuador, and Peru. From that beginning, the number of volunteers working in the Latin America region expanded rapidly to a peak of 4,034 at the end of fiscal 1967. By May, 1969, the total had dropped to 3,191 volunteers at work in twenty countries. Of these, nearly 1,300 worked in community development projects in rural areas or urban slums, 748 were in education programs, 499 in agricultural work, and 111 in public health projects. The rest were in such special programs as forestry, mining, rural electrification, fisheries, and municipal management. Latin America is the only region in which the Peace Corps has put its greatest emphasis on community development, and it is here that most of the theories about community action work have been developed and tested.

The philosophy of community development set forth by the Latin America regional office is a mixture of idealism and

TABLE I

The Peace Corps in Latin America
An Eight-Year Summary of Volunteers in Host Countries
at End of Fiscal Year

| | 1962 | 1963 | 1964 | 1965 | 1966 | 1967 | 1968 | 1969 |
|---|---|---|---|---|---|---|---|---|
| Brazil | 43 | 168 | 210 | 548 | 639 | 601 | 580 | 456 |
| Chile | 63 | 99 | 106 | 294 | 397 | 392 | 254 | 197 |
| Colombia | 103 | 229 | 561 | 544 | 506 | 522 | 576 | 467 |
| El Salvador | 25 | 21 | 49 | 55 | 51 | 105 | 119 | 87 |
| Jamaica | 38 | 32 | 62 | 77 | 70 | 101 | 117 | 112 |
| Eastern Caribbean Islands | 15 | 14 | 17 | 5 | 45 | 89 | 124 | 131 |
| Venezuela | 23 | 83 | 117 | 265 | 292 | 352 | 262 | 206 |
| Bolivia | 35 | 112 | 126 | 220 | 266 | 303 | 219 | 230 |
| British Honduras | | 33 | 18 | 49 | 33 | 42 | 45 | 35 |
| Costa Rica | | 26 | 65 | 61 | 107 | 154 | 98 | 83 |
| Dominican Republic | | 144 | 171 | 85 | 101 | 140 | 161 | 121 |
| Ecuador | | 156 | 236 | 309 | 211 | 255 | 247 | 200 |
| Guatemala | | 27 | 105 | 83 | 69 | 140 | 151 | 85 |
| Honduras | | 27 | 46 | 103 | 107 | 174 | 167 | 152 |
| Panama | | 28 | 76 | 133 | 196 | 171 | 174 | 112 |
| Peru | | 285 | 293 | 379 | 301 | 349 | 283 | 137 |
| Uruguay | | | 18 | 4 | 48 | 65 | 31 | 14 |
| Guyana | | | | | | 44 | 51 | 43 |
| Paraguay | | | | | | 35 | 56 | 65 |
| Nicaragua | | | | | | | | 30 |
| Totals | 345 | 1,484 | 2,276 | 3,214 | 3,439 | 4,034 | 3,715 | 2,963 |

realism. The agency's directors frankly say that community development is an approach that must be shaped by practical experience. One Latin America regional officer believes that volunteers are doing far more than building roads, bridges, or schools, or establishing cooperatives and credit unions. He explained that, if the volunteers

> leave leaders and community organizational structures behind, we will have accomplished our purpose. We are trying to reach a population of 100 million people. When a significant number of them are fully awakened to their social and political responsibilities and potential, they will become a force for reform, and the Peace Corps no longer will be needed. It will have done its job.

# LATIN AMERICA

Shading indicates countries in which Peace Corps volunteers are at work.

This philosophy reflects the ideas of Frank Mankiewicz, at one time the agency's leading spokesman on the theory and practice of community development. Mankiewicz was one of the first to advocate active participation in community affairs by volunteers. In his article "A Revolutionary Force," which appeared in *The Peace Corps Reader,* he stressed that "the political and social development of a country can only come through the infusion of a kind of revolutionary spirit such as the Peace Corps represents and which more and more Latin American governments now welcome." Not everyone on the Peace Corps staff is willing to go this far, but whether they view community development work as sparking reform or just helping people help themselves, the test of theory comes when a volunteer arrives in a country and goes to work.

## THE FISHERIES PROGRAM

In cooperation with the U.N. Food and Agricultural Organization (FAO), the Peace Corps has launched a pioneer regional project, the multinational Central American fisheries program. Six Central American countries are involved—Guatemala, El Salvador, Honduras, Nicaragua, Costa Rica, and Panama—all of which have long coastlines on the Pacific or Caribbean, a need for protein foods, and a small or nonexistent commercial fishing industry. The program began in 1967, when the FAO launched a six-year fisheries research and development program in Central America and the Peace Corps sent volunteers to take part. Working with the national fisheries offices of each country, the PCV's help with administration and planning, assist in the development of fisheries projects, conduct resource surveys, and teach marketing to local fishermen. Two groups of volunteers have been trained for the program, and in July, 1969, there were 5 volunteers serving in Guatemala, 6 in El Salvador, 10 in Honduras, 8 in Nicaragua, 7 in Costa Rica, and 9 in Panama.

To staff the program, the Peace Corps has relied on generalists as well as specialists in food processing, marine biology, nutrition, economics, and education. The agency tried to recruit fishermen, but they argued that such a venture would only aid their own competitors, and few volunteered. The fisheries volunteers trained as a group in Puerto Rico and Florida before going to their respective countries for additional instruction. The primary contractor for the training program was the Atlantic and Gulf Fisheries Supply Corporation.

COLOMBIA

The first community development workers sent overseas by the Peace Corps went to Colombia in 1961. By the end of the first year, they were immersed in self-help programs at fifty-five locations. With village leaders, they planned and helped construct schools, aqueducts, health centers, athletic fields, bridges, and roads. They started libraries and taught courses in community action, agriculture, and family hygiene. They helped build parks and telephone systems, started cooperatives, and helped dig wells. They worked in a home building project, helped with 4-H programs, and were engaged in reforestation, electrification, and farm pond construction. In one instance, they even fought a plague of red ants and saved the lives of two Colombians with first aid. From this auspicious beginning, the program in Colombia has grown to include agricultural extension work, rural nursing, nutrition and health programs, teacher training, secondary education, small business administration, and educational television.

Today, Peace Corps operations in Colombia are the largest in Latin America, and, with the Philippines, India, and Malaysia, the largest in the Peace Corps world. In May, 1969, there were 533 volunteers working in Colombia and an additional 30 in training. The latter are scheduled to play an important role in a national agricultural extension program the Colombian Government has begun.

Since 1964, volunteers have helped establish the largest educational television system (ETV) in any of the world's developing nations. A side effect has been significant modernization of the Colombian school system because of ETV's impact on school and classroom organization. With volunteer help and materials from AID, the ETV network increased its audience from 200 schools and 38,000 pupils in 1964 to 1,250 schools and 350,000 pupils in 1966. Today, the students audience is estimated at more than 500,000.

The first volunteers assigned to the ETV program worked in the studios and trained Colombian co-workers to staff the system. When this phase of the program was completed at the end of 1967, volunteers concentrated on working directly with teachers to demonstrate the effective use of ETV. In 1967, a research team from Stanford University's Institute for Communication Research studied the ETV program in Colombia. Their report, entitled "The Peace Corps Educational Television Project in Colombia—Two Years of Research," summed up the program's impact:

> ETV requires adherence to a schedule, the following of a curriculum, the advance planning of lessons—in short, a reorganization in the interests of education. Moreover, it has involved thousands of individual teachers actively in education who before had been little concerned with anything but maintaining discipline and supervising memorization by pupils.

Within just five years, the ETV program has developed into an independent host-country institution. The final ETV volunteer group will complete their tour at the end of 1969, and no new groups have been assigned to the program. There may be some extensions of service among volunteers now in Colombia, but for all practical purposes, the Peace Corps seems to have worked itself out of a job. The experience in Colombia has helped pave the way for similar ETV programs now under way in Jamaica, Malaysia, Peru, and Ethiopia.

DOMINICAN REPUBLIC

The Peace Corps went to the Dominican Republic in August, 1962. Since then, volunteers and staff have survived the overthrow of President Juan Bosch in September, 1963, a rebellion in the spring of 1965, and an invasion by U.S. Marines to quell the uprising. In many ways, the country is an enigma for the Peace Corps. Rafael Leonidas Trujillo Molina made it his personal domain from 1930 until he was assassinated in May, 1961. Since that time, it has taken on many aspects of a U.S. trust territory, but with a national constitution in full force. AID has assigned the country a priority second only to South Vietnam. American influence can be seen everywhere from the Hotel Ambajador on the outskirts of Santo Domingo to department stores and record shops with their shelves and tables full of American products. The *peso* is artificially kept at a one-to-one ratio with the U.S. dollar and prices for most goods in the cities are outlandishly inflated. The volunteers, wealthy on their $125-per-month living allowance when compared with the Dominicans with whom they live and work, feel the inflationary pinch. Those assigned to urban centers, Santo Domingo in particular, can barely make the allowance stretch from one month to the next. Rural volunteers are able to save modest amounts if they budget carefully.

The major complaint of Dominican volunteers is not the cost of living, however. It is the overwhelming American influence. The volunteers claim that too often programs have not been Dominican programs; they have been AID programs, or State Department programs, or Peace Corps programs. A volunteer who served there described the situation:

Volunteers in the Dominican Republic find themselves fending off the excesses of American influences while they try to wipe out the indifference, the fears, the distrust of others, and the lack of personal drive that complete dictatorship fosters. These people still remember Trujillo best—those in the rural areas— and they don't understand either democracy or the need for individual initiative. On the one hand, we face the challenge of indifference; on the other, we run into situations like the one I found not too long after I arrived. I was assigned to a program in rural community development, and eventually I needed some technical support. I went to the Dominican ministry I had been told was in charge of the program and told them my problems. I was told to go see Mr. —————— of AID "who knows all about it." It didn't take me long to discover that AID really runs things in the Dominican Republic.

In this tiny nation, the Peace Corps has emptied its entire bag of projects. Urban community development, rural community development, agricultural extension, home economics, public health, tuberculosis control, mental health, teaching and teacher training, teaching the blind, forestry, physical education, sports and recreation, and fisheries—all have been tried at one time or another. In May, 1969, there were 133 volunteers in the country, including 78 in rural and urban community development work, 49 in teacher training, and 6 in university education.

Community development in the rural areas has worked well in the Dominican Republic, and it is perhaps significant that a number of volunteers have asked to extend their tours to complete projects they helped begin. In contrast, urban community development has waxed and waned, as it has elsewhere in the Latin America region. It was given a strong boost, however, through the efforts of eight volunteers who arrived in 1966 to work in a variety of urban jobs—university teaching, tuberculosis control, recreation and Boy Scout programs. Through the difficulties they encountered, they began to develop an approach for urban community action projects in which they viewed youth work as a way to establish themselves in a community. Once accepted, they could then begin to initiate more ambitious projects. A staff member with similar ideas about community development work called them together for a conference, out of which grew an urban community development program that gave each of the eight volunteers a fresh start. They began to meet regularly to compare notes and to give each other what one member called "our own technical support." Eventually they agreed on a philosophy that emphasized the promotion of leadership and group participation in the *barrio* and gave less weight to the search for special projects to start.* One of the volunteers elaborated on the approach: "The volunteer should concentrate on developing leaders within the *barrios* rather than being the leaders themselves. Sure, we can teach by example, but as long as we organize projects instead of leaders, we will simply be filling a leadership gap which the Dominicans should be filling." This approach to community development now underlies all the agency's community action programs.

## BRAZIL

The first agreement for volunteers between the Peace Corps and Brazil was signed in 1961, and the first volunteers —43 of them—arrived in late March, 1962. Most of these went to urban or rural community development assignments. Since then, more than 3,000 volunteers have served in Brazil. In May, 1969, there were 460 volunteers at work in rural and urban community development projects, agricultural cooperatives, health projects, a rural electrification program, and a schistosomiasis control program. In 1969, operations in Brazil required more than 30 full-time staff members, including 5 administrators, 6 physicians, 2 program technical representatives, and 12 associate directors.

Brazil has posed an unusual number of problems for the Peace Corps. Size, diversity, and poverty are but three. Volunteers have always gone to its poorer sections and many have worked in urban slums. Some volunteers have lived in such remote cities as Rio Branco, Cáceres, and Boa Vista, which is 2,000 miles from Rio de Janeiro and can be reached only by riverboat or air. The greatest hazard, though, has been a feeling of ineffectiveness. In some instances,

* *Barrio* translates literally as "district." Although its meaning varies slightly from country to country, it generally connotes an urban slum.

officials in Brazilian community action agencies have found the problems of the slums so impossible that they have hesitated to give jobs to young, unskilled volunteers. Other officials have made clear their feeling that technical assistance and financial aid are far more important than anything a volunteer can do. To compound the situation, Brazil has no central agency responsible for community action programs.

The lack of a coordinated effort has also plagued rural community development volunteers, who have had to rely on local resources, AID money when available, and ingenuity. In the rural areas, volunteers have set up 4-H clubs, initiated craft projects, developed fishing and agricultural cooperatives, helped construct schools, roads, and bridges, worked on irrigation and sanitation projects, promoted nutrition and proper child care, and taught primary grades.

One of the most interesting activities is the school lunch program. In 1963, 1,118 schools were serving meals to roughly 97,700 children. Volunteers and Brazilian co-workers went to work to enlarge the program, and by the end of 1966, 5,185 schools were serving meals to 379,826 children. Brazilian agencies and Food for Peace helped with the project, which was so well received that in 1967 a group of volunteers was trained specifically to carry it on. Volunteers have also worked on irrigation, land resettlement, road and bridge construction, and surveying projects associated with a program similar to the Tennessee Valley Authority that will affect 5 million people in Brazil's 2,000-mile long São Francisco Valley.

In general, volunteers serving in Brazil's rural areas have had little trouble in establishing good relations with local people, but many have left with the feeling that there would be no follow-up by government agencies and things would return to what they were before the volunteers came. The problem is not uncommon.

## VENEZUELA

The Peace Corps has been serving in Venezuela since 1962, when twenty-three volunteers arrived there to work in urban community development projects and teach physical education. The early volunteers were clustered in the country's urban centers, which turned out to be a mistake, for the volunteers were not prepared to cope with the problems of the *barrio*. The exodus from the cities began in 1966, when the agency placed volunteers in agrarian reform and rural cooperatives programs. Although the successful nationwide physical education program remained, the Peace Corps suggested that the Venezuelan Government begin training its own people to carry it on. In May, 1969, 254 volunteers were serving in Venezuela—76 in rural cooperative projects, 73 in physical education and youth training programs, 45 in community development projects, 20 in agrarian reform programs, 2 working as secretaries, and 38 in a municipal management program.

The Peace Corps began the municipal management program in 1966. Thirty-two volunteers with degrees in law, architecture, planning, engineering, and political science were assigned to work with city councils throughout the country to help elected municipal officials improve services to their constituents. The program's director is a Venezuelan attorney, the first host-country national to serve in such a position for the Peace Corps. Technical support for the program is provided by Venezuela's National Foundation for Community Development and Municipal Improvement. The program emphasis has been on city management, urban planning, and public administration.

All the members of the first municipal management group lived in *barrios*. Some served on the staffs of city councils, while others worked directly in the communities to help establish credit unions and to plan community projects that would improve living conditions until public services could be provided by the government. Valencia, for example, now has a garbage collection service in its *barrios* as the result of a volunteer's efforts. A second group of municipal management volunteers arrived in Venezuela in early 1969.

## PERU

The Peace Corps went to Peru in 1962 with 160 volunteers who worked in rural and urban community action programs, taught school, and helped establish cooperatives. Since then, groups have worked in forestry, industrial training, teacher training, handicraft, agricultural extension, and small business management projects. In May, 1969, there were 169 volunteers at work in the country.

The small business management program, one of the Peace Corps's most unusual, began in 1967 with thirty-one volunteers and has been so successful that the Peruvian Government has asked for more. Volunteers in the program assist small businessmen or managers of cooperatives while training Peruvian co-workers. They help prepare loan applications, negotiate loans, and supervise the use of funds; they prepare market and production studies, help solve marketing problems, develop inventory and financial controls, and help plan for expansion. Some volunteers provide assistance to such support agencies as regional banks, development corporations, productivity centers, cooperative associations, universites, and produce, marketing, and consumer cooperatives.

## WHAT NEXT?

It is risky to predict what the volunteers serving in Latin America will be like, but they may well follow the tradition of speaking out that has characterized their predecessors. For some unknown reason, Latin America volunteers have been more outspoken than those in any other region. They have seldom hesitated to "tell it like it is" publicly and have written devastating articles about lack of host-country cooperation, incompetent Peace Corps staff members or volunteers, the disappearance of Peace Corps idealism, the increasing bureaucracy both in Washington and overseas, and their attitude toward U.S. involvement in Vietnam. They have also produced inspiring statements about volunteerism and many written defenses of the Peace Corps.

Whatever tone Peace Corps volunteers may take toward their work, it is likely that the Peace Corps's efforts in Latin America will continue to be rooted in community development, education, and agricultural technical assistance. But within the sphere of community development, staff members predict a change in tactics: they hope to have more host citizens directly involved in the projects. It is safe also to predict that technical assistance programs will continue to be emphasized, with projects like municipal management in Venezuela, educational television in Colombia, small business management in Peru, the Central American fisheries program, forestry and municipal planning in Chile, and rural electrification in Brazil and Ecuador duplicated throughout the region.

# VIII

## Africa: From Education
## to Rural Transformation

The early programs in Africa were concentrated in education and the statistics released by the Peace Corps tell the story: In 1963, Peace Corps volunteers constituted more than one-third of the degree-holding instructors in Ghana's secondary schools and more than one-third of all teachers in both Ethiopia and Nyasaland (now Malawi); by 1965, more than half of the degree-holding secondary-school teachers in six African nations were volunteers and more than two-thirds of the volunteers serving in Africa were teachers. Emphasis on education continues, although the program has been expanded from chiefly secondary education to include university, primary, and vocational education, as well as teacher training. Of the 2,672 volunteers at work in 23 African countries in May, 1969, 1,788—two-thirds—were teaching or helping to train African teachers. The other volunteers worked in a variety of jobs—221 in argicultural assistance, 361 in urban and rural community development, 142 in public health programs, 74 in social work, 33 in public administration, 18 as small business advisers, and 12 as home economics extension workers.

The volunteer teacher faces a system of education based on memorization with a curriculum often irrelevant to the needs of the country. According to one volunteer, "the African educational system as we found it was based on the wholesale preparation of students for middle-class, white

TABLE II

The Peace Corps in Africa
An Eight-Year Summary of Volunteers in Host Countries
at End of Fiscal Year

| | 1962 | 1963 | 1964 | 1965 | 1966 | 1967 | 1968 | 1969 |
|---|---|---|---|---|---|---|---|---|
| Ghana | 51 | 129 | 136 | 110 | 111 | 208 | 242 | 181 |
| Nigeria | 109 | 258 | 508 | 634 | 719 | 719 | 248 | 93 |
| Sierra Leone | 37 | 120 | 159 | 150 | 233 | 236 | 273 | 258 |
| Tanzania } Tanganyika } | 35 | 26 | 125 | 326 | 366 | 290 | 143 | 8 |
| Cameroon | | 39 | 88 | 103 | 118 | 77 | 61 | 50 |
| Ethiopia | | 278 | 402 | 565 | 566 | 432 | 389 | 395 |
| Gabon | | 41 | 70 | 35 | 49 | 71 | – | – |
| Ivory Coast | | 49 | 51 | 56 | 83 | 71 | 80 | 102 |
| Liberia | | 132 | 272 | 335 | 399 | 317 | 299 | 327 |
| Niger | | 16 | 12 | 43 | 48 | 129 | 156 | 45 |
| Malawi } Nyasaland } | | 42 | 97 | 230 | 231 | 153 | 123 | 140 |
| Senegal | | 34 | 62 | 51 | 55 | 75 | 119 | 98 |
| Somali Rep. | | 35 | – | 58 | 80 | 96 | 73 | 51 |
| Togo | | 44 | 59 | 56 | 49 | 109 | 102 | 85 |
| Guinea | | | 52 | 95 | 81 | – | – | 28 |
| Kenya | | | | 129 | 197 | 229 | 253 | 277 |
| Uganda | | | | 35 | 56 | 118 | 123 | 97 |
| Botswana | | | | | | 56 | 50 | 68 |
| Chad | | | | | | 30 | 38 | 46 |
| Mauritania | | | | | | 11 | – | – |
| Gambia | | | | | | | 16 | 14 |
| Upper Volta | | | | | | | 44 | 52 |
| Lesotho | | | | | | | 66 | 57 |
| Dahomey | | | | | | | 26 | 37 |
| Swaziland | | | | | | | | 44 |
| Totals | 232 | 1,243 | 2,093 | 3,010 | 3,421 | 3,427 | 2,924 | 2,553 |

collar jobs, while the great need is for progressive farming
and vocational training." C. Payne Lucas, former African
regional director goes further:

We feel that the teaching methods used in the schools of Africa,
be they buried in the bush or located in the most modern cities,
need to be more demanding of the African student. Methods
must be employed to capture his imagination with examples
about which he has emotions and insights. He must be challenged to argue, to demonstrate, to experiment, to discuss, to

# AFRICA

Shading indicates countries in which Peace Corps volunteers are at work.

question, and, finally, to accept and to learn. We have referred to it as the African's journey from rote to reason [and] this has been our overriding contribution to Africa.

Recently, the Peace Corps has begun what it calls a rural transformation program. In part, the new direction stems from the reports of early volunteer teachers who saw the need for agricultural assistance and rural development and feared an overemphasis on education. According to one volunteer, "the secondary schools are creating a dangerous class of people. The students are not willing to accept the manual labor available and cannot find the jobs they feel they deserve." It is also the result of an increased interest among African leaders in developing their countries' rural areas. The program includes agricultural extension work, the construction of feeder roads and schools, public health and home economics projects, well-drilling, irrigation, reclamation of wetlands for farming, land resettlement, and general rural community development.

BINATIONALISM

While the effort to include host-country nationals in programing, training, and project supervision is not exclusively that of the Africa region, binationalism has been more dramatic and more widespread in Africa than in any other region. In Sierre Leone, host instructors now plan and direct all training for volunteers who will serve in their country, and two officials from Sierre Leone have helped recruit volunteers in the United States. The director of the teacher-training program in Liberia is a Liberian. Three Ethiopians are serving as Peace Corps associate directors in that country. The Peace Corps physician in the Ivory Coast is an Ivorian. The associate director in charge of the social workers in Senegal is a Senegalese, and Africans from several nations serve on the staff of the Peace Corps training centers at St. Croix and St. Thomas in the Virgin Islands.

## TRAINING FOR SERVICE IN AFRICA

The Africa region has been a leader in the movement toward in-country training. In the past year alone, more than half of all volunteers headed for Africa received most of their training in the host country. For training carried out in the United States, the Africa regional office uses its training centers in the Virgin Islands. Volunteers scheduled to serve in French-speaking Africa train at St. Croix, while those going to English-speaking countries train at St. Thomas. All volunteers who will be teaching English as a foreign language, regardless of the African host country, spend a portion of their training in a program directed by the University of California at Los Angeles. In 1969, they practiced their skills at La Pocatiere, Quebec.

## BLACK AMERICANS FOR AFRICA

To encourage black Americans to volunteer for Peace Corps service in Africa, the agency has developed training programs in cooperation with Atlanta University in Atlanta, Georgia, and Shaw University in Raleigh, North Carolina. The Atlanta University program, set up with the help of the American Forum for African Study, a nonprofit educational corporation, permits students to serve as Peace Corps volunteers in Ghana while working toward advanced degrees in Black studies, African studies, or education. The first group of volunteers were to begin their graduate work and Peace Corps training at Atlanta University in January, 1970. A second group will begin training the following September. The volunteers will be given additional instruction at the University of Ghana and will be able to take course work there during vacation periods. The program agreement specifies that the degree work is not to interfere with Peace Corps duties. The program is not limited to black students.

The Shaw University program, which began in the fall of 1969, sends volunteers to work in the Harambee Schools

Program in Kenya.* The volunteers receive graduate credit and are eligible for job placement service when their tours have ended. The program was developed with the help of Volunteer Training Specialists, a Washington-based firm.

## PULLING BACK IN TANZANIA AND NIGERIA

The Peace Corps is being phased out of Tanzania, which at one time was host to more than four hundred volunteers, most of whom were teachers. President Julius Nyerere at first welcomed such an impetus to his nation's educational system, but in recent years he has become critical of the Peace Corps. He recently stated than Tanzania needed more technical assistance and technical training and claimed that "the Peace Corps has changed its character—some of its idealism has gone out, and now? Now it is a problem." In May, 1969, there were only eight volunteers, all soil scientists, still at work in Tanzania, and the agency does not expect additional volunteers to be requested before they finish their tours at the end of the year.

Nigeria is another country in which Peace Corps operations have been greatly reduced. In May, 1967, there were about 800 volunteers there. By April of the following year, that number had dwindled to 291 as a result of the civil war that followed the secession of Biafra. By October, 1968, there were only 189 volunteers left and two proposed programs had been cancelled. In May, 1969, only 104 volunteers remained—21 in elementary education, 11 in secondary education, 70 in teacher training, and 2 in rural community development work. Recently, however, the Nigerian Government requested 65 volunteers to work in agricultural and community development programs and expressed the hope that the Peace Corps would play a major role in the postwar reconstruction.

* Harambee, a Swahili word, means "Let us all pull together."

Exit from Guinea

The Peace Corps was asked to leave Guinea in 1966 for the most bizarre of reasons. On October 28 of that year, a Pan American jetliner, on a regular flight from New York, made a scheduled stop in Dakar, Senegal, to pick up Guinea's 19-man delegation on its way to Addis Ababa, Ethiopia, to attend a pre-summit conference of the Organization of African Unity (OAU). During a scheduled stopover in Accra, Ghana, the entire Guinea delegation was taken from the jetliner at gun point by the soldiers and police of Lt. Gen. Joseph Ankrah, head of Ghana's ruling military government. The delegation was informed that it was being held hostage in the hope of bringing freedom for one hundred Ghanaians who, according to General Ankrah, were being detained in Guinea against their will. Guinea and Ghana had been feuding since February, 1966, when Ghana's former President Kwame Nkrumah had taken refuge in Guinea after being ousted by a military coup. Guinea President Sékou Touré had proclaimed Nkrumah co-president of Guinea.

From the capital of Guinea, Radio Conakry accused the United States of complicity in the delegation's detention and launched virulent attacks against both the United States and Ghana. When Peace Corps Country Director Henry R. Norman and his staff heard of the incident, they decided that volunteers in the Conakry area should report for work as usual the following day. If they acted otherwise, it was believed, the basic Peace Corps principle of noninvolvement in host-country politics would be exposed as hypocrisy. Although a few volunteers managed to get in several hours of work, all were soon placed under house arrest. The tense atmosphere at Peace Corps headquarters was relieved only when a volunteer stationed up-country near Telimele called headquarters to complain that an order for vitamins for his chickens had not arrived. He was planning to deliver an order of eggs in Conakry and said he would pick up the vitamins then. Shouting into the phone, Norman told the volunteer, "Sit on your eggs in Telimele until they hatch, and stay the hell out of Conakry." The surprised volunteer knew nothing of the anti-American attacks.

Although the entire Guinean delegation was released and sent home after a special OAU mission reported that none of the Ghanaians it had interviewed in Guinea wanted to return to Accra, the anti-American attacks continued. At a rally honoring the returned delegation, Touré expelled the Peace Corps, thanking them for their help but making it clear that they were no longer welcome.

As the Peace Corps prepared to depart, Vaughn sent a message of support to Norman. He said, in part, "I wanted to convey to you and your great volunteers and staff my personal pride and that of the Peace Corps in the way you have conducted yourselves in a long series of difficult situations. If you must leave, it must be with dignity and friendliness. . . . Exit smiling."

But the Peace Corps did not exit smiling. Tears overcame the entire contingent, and many predicted that the Peace Corps would return. They were right. Guinea reinvited the Peace Corps in 1968, and twenty-eight volunteers arrived in Conakry in June, 1969, to work for the Ministry of Transportation. Waiting to greet them was Peace Corps Country Director Henry R. Norman, who had agreed to return long enough to help reestablish the Peace Corps in Guinea. The new volunteers will take over where the previous group stopped in training Guineans to maintain and repair motor vehicles. An interesting footnote to the story is that the Minister of Transportation for whom the volunteers will work is Karim Bangoura, the former Guinean Ambassador to the United States, who had worked quietly behind the scenes to have the Peace Corps reinvited to his country.

## ETHIOPIA

Ethiopia has been host to some of the largest and most varied Peace Corps programs. In May, 1969, there were 442 volunteers at work there—165 teaching in schools and universities, 89 working in educational television, 63 teaching English as a foreign language, and 125 working in rural and urban community development programs, including 60 assigned to water resources and agricultural development projects. In addition, the Peace Corps presence in Ethiopia may have influenced the creation in 1964 of the Ethiopian University Service, a domestic volunteer program in which university students spend one year in the service of their country.

Education has been the main Peace Corps activity in Ethiopia, although there is now a trend toward rural community development and agriculture. Ethiopia has the distinction of having sponsored one of the agency's most highly publicized failures, a road-building project. More than sixty volunteers worked on the program over three years, but the government was ill prepared to use them and little was accomplished.

Peace Corps teachers in Ethiopia have taught at every level from primary grades through Haile Selassie I University and by 1967 the agency could quote an impressive statistic: every Ethiopian student then in secondary school had been taught by at least one volunteer teacher. In the past two years, however, the emphasis has been on in-service courses for teachers and away from classroom teaching. Until 1968, most PCV teachers in Ethiopia worked in Addis Ababa or other urban centers, although the Peace Corps staff had attempted to get permission from the Ministry of Education to go into the country's rural areas. In 1969, the Ministry agreed to a 50 per cent reduction of volunteer teachers in Addis Ababa, and PCV teachers were assigned to remote areas for the first time. By June, 1969, there were no volunteer English teachers at Haile Selassie I University, and by June, 1970, there will be no volunteers at the university in any capacity. This change is partially the result of the country staff's effort to disperse volunteers and partially the result of anti-Peace Corps feelings that have developed among university students.

During 1969, the Peace Corps had sixteen staff members in Ethiopia including seven associate directors assigned to the provincial capitals. Ethiopia is one of three African countries in which the Peace Corps has regionalized its operations.

## KENYA

In May, 1969, 283 volunteers were serving in Kenya—200 as secondary school teachers, 44 in agricultural projects, 30 with Kenya's Land Resettlement Scheme, and 9 as teachers in a nurses' training program. Peace Corps operations required nine staff members—a country director, his deputy, three associate directors, two program technical representatives, and two physicians.

The most famous program in Kenya is land resettlement. With independence, the new Kenya Government made land redistribution a first priority and over 1 million acres were bought and divided into small holdings. The cost has not been small; land resettlement accounts for half of the Kenyan Government's annual expenditures for agricultural programs. The land resettlement program reversed the usual trend in agriculture by moving from large-scale to small-scale farming in a short period of time. The result was an initial decline in production, and it became apparent that efficient, modern farm management practices were needed.

Two years after the land resettlement scheme was initiated, the Kenya Government asked the Peace Corps for volunteers to work with local landowners. By the end of 1966, Peace Corps volunteers made up one-third of the field staff of Kenya's Department of Settlement. Working as department officers, they directed individual resettlement schemes, served as agricultural extension advisers, cooperative specialists, water development technicians, and livestock consultants, helped reorganize milk production and marketing, taught farm equipment maintenance, negotiated contracts with food processing plants, and generally helped the new landowners adopt efficient farm management practices. A recent Kenyan Department of Settlement annual report observed:

> Volunteers have shown a marked ability to come to grips with the many problems they are faced with. In particular, much good foundation work has been done in the preparation of the cooperative society estimates and as a result of this work a technique for general application has been established. Their patient coaching of cooperative communities has been of particular value.

The number of volunteers working on resettlement will undoubtedly decrease as Kenyans learn to take over farm management, for there is pressure in Kenya, as in other African countries, for full Africanization of national development.

## DAHOMEY

The Peace Corps was invited to Dahomey in 1967, and the first volunteers arrived there the following year. By May, 1969, there were 26 volunteers working in agricultural programs and rural community development and another 13 in training. In that same month, the government of Dahomey requested 25 more volunteers to assist in agricultural development and health programs. Volunteer jobs in Dahomey have included such diverse and specialized agricultural assignments as grain storage, school gardens, animal husbandry, tropical agronomy, cooperative organization, and farm mechanics. Female volunteers have worked in public health and child care programs.

The pilot villages program has been the most publicized. In 1964, the Dahomean Government set up three villages in which young farmers interested in learning improved agricultural skills could work cooperatively. The pioneers, as the members were known, were initially recruited and trained by the Dahomean Army, and the program was initiated under the auspices of an Israeli technical aid program. AID subsequently granted the equivalent of $600,000 for the establishment of the first three villages in the form of houses, community buildings, equipment, tools, agricultural commodities, and the services of a technical adviser under contract to the Near East Foundation. In early 1967, the villages were shifted from army control to the Rural Development Service, a division of the Ministry of Rural Development and Cooperation, and in 1969 two additional villages were set up. Sixteen Peace Corps volunteers began working in the program in 1968. In teams of two, they have taught animal husbandry (primarily the raising of rabbits and other small animals), animal traction, crop rotation and cultivation, cooperative management, and farm mechanics as well as personal hygiene, child care, and sanitation.

## MALAWI

It was in Malawi that the Peace Corps first proved that generalists could be trained to carry out a health program aimed at the control of a specific disease. In November, 1964, forty-three volunteers, working in teams with Malawian assistants, began a program of curative and preventive tuberculosis therapy in which they treated patients at home rather than in hospitals. It was hoped that the program, in addition to controlling TB, would provide training for the Malawians to carry on the program, provide a base for the expansion of the country's health services, and show other nations that such a program is feasible. During their first year in the field, the volunteers took a census of 30,000 people and tested 85 per cent of them for tuberculosis. This background work made possible the first national projection of the incidence of TB cases in Malawi—between 45,000 and 50,000. (At that time, there were only 800 hospital beds available for TB treatment.) A University of North Carolina research team under contract to study the effectiveness of the program reported that the volunteers' rate of diagnostic accuracy was 68 per cent. A rate of 75 per cent is good for most public health purposes and the team predicted that, with increasing experience, the volunteers would reach this level of accuracy. They did.

## CHAD

The largest and most populous nation in former French Equatorial Africa, Chad is one of the least developed African countries south of the Sahara. The Lake Chad region, traditional junction of trade routes from the Mediterranean and the Nile Valley to Africa's equatorial rain forests and the Niger Basin, is the site of a water resources development program, one of the agency's most interesting projects. The program is supervised by Chad's Ministry of Water and Forests and includes both well-drilling and irrigation. In the well-drilling portion, the volunteers, each of whom works with a group of villages, teach drilling methods and help dig shallow wells six to fifteen meters deep. A Peace Corps-AID program for deep wells has also been started. In the irrigation portion, volunteers design and construct irrigation systems fed by wells, rivers, or Lake Chad and test for water purity.

## THE FUTURE IN AFRICA

The Peace Corps will expand its program in Africa in 1970 when volunteers go for the first time to Mali and the island nation of Mauritius.

Throughout the region, education will continue to be the agency's major activity in the immediate future, with the emphasis on teacher training and vocational education. In addition, the rural transformation program will be enlarged and the volunteers recruited for it will have increasingly specialized skills. This trend has already been established and nearly every host country now has volunteers at work in rural community development, rural health, or agricultural projects. The Peace Corps also hopes to send volunteers to help with equipment maintenance and repair and may play a role in the development of large regional programs in irrigation and electric power.

# IX

# North Africa, the Near East, and South Asia: Agricultural Assistance

Most diverse of the Peace Corps regions, North Africa, Near East, and South Asia (NANESA) begins at the Atantic Ocean and runs through the heartland of the world's earliest civilizations to India. It includes Morocco, Tunisia, Libya, Turkey, Iran, Afghanistan, Nepal, India, and Ceylon. In May, 1969, the NANESA region had the smallest number of Peace Corps volunteers—1,930. Education was the largest program, with 979 volunteers in teaching assignments, including 671 who taught English as a second language. There were 617 volunteers in agricultural work, the largest regional agricultural program, and 160 volunteers in public health assignments.

 Unstructured community action programs have not worked well in NANESA, and few volunteers are given such jobs. Robert Steiner, former regional director, explained why during an interview in 1968:

> We say we come as doers, not advisers. So far as I am concerned, community development implies just the reverse. Leadership training, organizing groups—all of this means "We are Americans and therefore know more than you, so let me show you how you should be running your lives." We tried that approach, and we weren't slapped down. We were simply ignored. Then we began to give our volunteers a handle as a means of entrance to a community, a specific kind of training

TABLE III

The Peace Corps in North Africa, the Near East, and South Asia:
An Eight-Year Summary of Volunteers in Host Countries
at End of Fiscal Year

| | 1962 | 1963 | 1964 | 1965 | 1966 | 1967 | 1968 | 1969 |
|---|---|---|---|---|---|---|---|---|
| India | 26 | 115 | 153 | 401 | 754 | 1,133 | 750 | 536 |
| Pakistan East ⎱ | 29 | | | | | | | |
| West ⎰ | 28 | 172 | 191 | 141 | 35 | – | – | – |
| Morocco | | 56 | 102 | 133 | 117 | 83 | 94 | 118 |
| Tunisia | | 94 | 48 | 135 | 192 | 252 | 230 | 192 |
| Afghanistan | | 35 | 62 | 136 | 181 | 207 | 171 | 164 |
| Ceylon | | 36 | – | – | – | – | 42 | 30 |
| Cyprus | | 23 | – | – | – | – | – | – |
| Iran | | 41 | 36 | 149 | 272 | 267 | 167 | 191 |
| Nepal | | 65 | 96 | 120 | 150 | 221 | 179 | 185 |
| Turkey | | 39 | 114 | 338 | 481 | 225 | 158 | 161 |
| Libya | | | | | | 18 | 13 | 161 |
| Totals | 83 | 676 | 802 | 1,553 | 2,182 | 2,406 | 1,804 | 1,738 |

for a specific job. The volunteers were then accepted in their villages because they were contributing something. Once this happened, in subtle ways, we began to work toward community action—a suggestion here, a comment there. Finally, people began to come to volunteers for advice. They began to ask questions. At that point, community development began.

It has been in NANESA, perhaps more than in the other regions, that Peace Corps leadership has insisted on responding to the priorities set by the host governments and that volunteers have worked consistently within the limitations of the host country. The Peace Corps supplies little equipment and there are few joint programs with other U.S. Government agencies to provide institutional support or resources for volunteers. More than anywhere else in the Peace Corps world, volunteers in NANESA are assessed as individuals and finally accepted or rejected as individuals.

Volunteers in NANESA are confronted with difficult languages, centuries-old traditions, strict codes of conduct, a low status imposed on women, and a myriad of other cultural

NORTH AFRICA, THE NEAR EAST, AND SOUTH ASIA

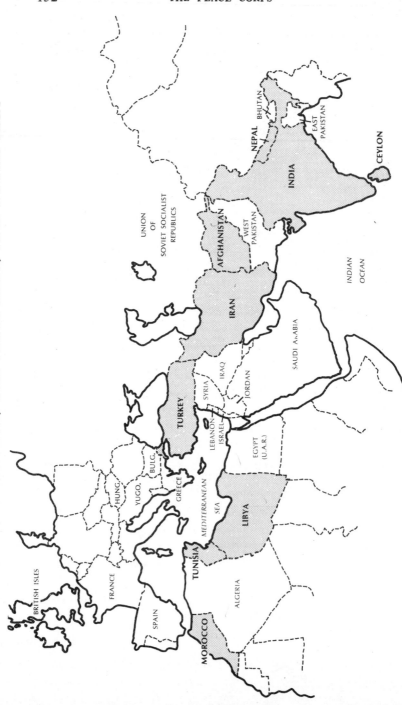

Shading indicates countries in which Peace Corps volunteers are at work

differences. Although the same conditions exist in nearly every country where volunteers work, they seem to be more abundant in the countries of NANESA and it is generally conceded that NANESA is the toughest region in which to serve. Former volunteer Jerry Leach described some of his experiences in an article entitled "Culture As An Invisible Prison," which appeared in *The Peace Corps Reader:*

> In Turkey . . . a full bus pushes people into atomsplitting embrace, and no one really seems to mind. In addition, some social situations require bodily contact between members of the same sex as a sign of friendship. This entails being held by the elbow, interlocking arms while walking, kissing on both cheeks, walking shoulder-to-shoulder, being kissed on the hand, talking at unnaturally close range . . . or occasionally holding little fingers. Our reflex is to pull away in shock from such advances. The Turk sees such withdrawal as cold or superior.

The position of women in NANESA countries accounts in large measure for the reason why male volunteers serving there have outnumbered females four to one. (In the other regions, the ratio has been two to one.) Assignments for young, unmarried women in NANESA are, with few exceptions, restricted to teaching, nursing, and other public health duties, and very few have been placed in community development jobs. A volunteer who served in the region explained why:

> Assignments for women must be well planned. They are accepted now in India as nurses, nutritionists, specialists in family planning, and other health and family care projects, but very few farmers I met would accept a girl as a community development worker or an agriculturalist. Young single girls doing such work would have no credibility.

## TRAINING FOR NANESA

NANESA officials have moved consistently toward in-country training and the use of host citizens as instructors, especially in language training. Such NANESA languages as Marathi, Punjabi, Farsi, Turkish, and Arabic are among the most difficult to learn—according to the Peace Corps, only Amharic, Korean, and Thai are more difficult—and NANESA administrators admit that language training has been one of the biggest problems. As a result, they have relied more on split programs, with the first portion of training held at a university and the rest in the host country, than have the other regions. They do not use any of the Peace Corps's permanent training centers. The region's three main U.S. training institutions are the Center for Research and Education, Estes Park, Colorado; the Experiment in International Living, Putney, Vermont; and the Development and Resources Corporation, Hemet, California. In recent years, NANESA groups have also trained at the University of Kentucky, the University of Oklahoma, and the University of New Mexico. The first program of continuous in-country training in NANESA began in Afghanistan in the fall of 1969.

## INDIA

India's Prime Minister Indira Gandhi accompanied a group of Peace Corps volunteers on a chartered flight from New York to New Delhi after her official visit to the United States in October, 1968. During the trip, she told the volunteers.

It is difficult for any society to change, but especially so when the society has been so tradition-bound. To transform it into modern society when we are of such vast size and such different levels of development is an extremely difficult job and one of real magnitude. We are going along, sometimes not as fast or as efficiently as we would wish, but we have to deal with human nature and we have to progress with the people's consent. I think that India is on her way in spite of the problems. . . . I think that we will face them and when we have people from outside who give us understanding and friendship, it makes it that much easier. . . . So I wish you all good luck and good wishes for your work.

Mrs. Gandhi was addressing the seventy-second group of Peace Corps volunteers to go to India. The first group— twenty-six volunteers who worked in the Punjab—arrived in December, 1961, and the program increased steadily to a nearly unmanageable 1,133 volunteers by 1967. That figure is considerably lower now. In May, 1969, there were 568 volunteers working in all but four of the seventeen Indian states. More than half of them—330—worked in agricultural projects; 65 taught English or conducted science teaching workshops for local teachers; and the others worked in public health, nutrition, rural community action, family planning, and small industry projects. To support the program, there were 46 staff members, including 23 administrators, 6 program technical representatives, 3 Peace Corps physicians, 4 Public Health Service personnel, and 10 Indians. The central office in New Delhi coordinates the entire program and the regional offices in New Delhi, Bombay, Calcutta, and Bhopal oversee projects in surrounding states.

With food production India's number one priority, the Peace Corps has sent volunteers to work in agricultural projects that range from irrigation to farm mechanization. In the state of Maharashtra, most of the volunteers work in animal husbandry where they serve as assistant managers of cooperative poultry farms, teach broiler and layer production in poultry extension projects, assist with poultry marketing, and teach cattle raising. A program for swine production and marketing is planned. In Mysore State, volunteers work as extension agents for the state Department of Agriculture in land development, irrigation and drainage, mechanized farming, and crop cultivation projects. In Orissa State, they assist local agricultural extension agents demonstrate the use of mechanical farm equipment. In the Punjab, they work in the government-sponsored Intensive Agricultural District

Program, which began in 1961 with financial help from the Ford Foundation to promote the use of high-yield seed and efficient farming methods. In the north and northwest sections of India, volunteers have had such success with poultry raising projects that the price of eggs is now low enough for all but the completely poverty-stricken to buy them. For the first time, there are nearly enough chickens and eggs to meet the demand.

Family planning has a priority second only to food production. India's current population is officially estimated at 534 million people and is increasing at the rate of more than 1 million persons each month. Since 1966, volunteers, primarily married couples, have been working with local groups to explain the purpose, benefits, and methods of family planning, and volunteer nurses have been training Indian medical personnel in the use of the interuterine device. To get their message across, the volunteers use group discussions, films, dramatics, posters, puppets, and any other audio-visual aids they can invent. Other volunteers have been working in child care and home economics programs and teaching personal hygiene, sanitation, and nutrition to Indian mothers, who are less skeptical of birth control when they realize they can improve their child's chances of reaching adulthood.

## TURKEY

The Peace Corps arrived in Turkey in 1962 with thirty-nine volunteers scheduled to teach in secondary schools and work on community development projects. The program there built rapidly, reaching a peak in 1965 with 590 volunteers—the third largest Peace Corps program at that time. Peace Corps and Turkish officials now admit that the program developed too rapidly and without proper planning. It was cut back and by May, 1969, the number of volunteers had dropped to 232—217 in education projects, including 119 teaching English as a foreign language, and 15 in child care work in orphanages. Future programs in Turkey seem to be headed toward technical assistance. Originally, liaison work with the Peace Corps was handled by the Cultural Affairs Department of the Turkish Foreign Ministry. Liaison is now the responsibility of the Technical Assistance Department.

The switch in emphasis was triggered in 1967 when the Peace Corps began to help promote Turkey's tourist industry. Five volunteers were assigned to regional offices of the Ministry of Tourism to organize adult English courses, to advise local investors on the kind of accommodations tourists require, and to help the Turks improve existing hotel and restaurant facilities. Three of the five had had previous hotel management experience. The idea caught on and Turkey requested more volunteers to expand the program. In late 1968, another group went to work in local government tourism offices in southern and western Turkey. Their job is to stimulate community interest in creating and upgrading tourist attractions, and to do so they help with maps, translate signs and menus, teach courses in English and hotel-restaurant management, promote clean-up campaigns, and act as advisers to hotel and restaurant owners.

The tourism program was given special impetus by Bruce Kokernot, a volunteer English teacher. In the winter of 1968, Kokernot spent hours of his own time erecting signs to direct straggling skiers on Mount Uludag, the site of a government-run ski resort. Officials of Turkey's forestry service were impressed and asked Kokernot to organize ski patrols on the mountain. The Peace Corps approved. Kokernot's efforts had special meaning; in February, 1967, a volunteer married couple had frozen to death on the same mountain after losing their way while skiing in a thick fog.

What has not worked in Turkey is community development, primarily because, according to a former staff member, "the volunteers had no identifiable goals and no real skills and the Turkish villagers never did know what the volunteers were up to." One volunteer recounted a typical failure. He had spent a year trying to convince the villagers to build a shelter at the bus stop on the main road. Finally, in frustration, he built the structure himself, but did not add the roof, believing that the local residents would complete the shelter. The roof was never built. Instead, the villagers used the shelter to wait for the bus, with water pouring through the support beams during rainy weather.

## TUNISIA

Tunisia is one country that abounds with material proof of the Peace Corps's presence—the dozens of new buildings in white concrete or rough native stone designed by volunteer architects. Tunisia has few architects of its own, and the PCV architects have played an important role in the country's development. Assigned to the Ministry of Public Works, they have designed everything from mosques to new communities, using, as much as possible, local materials and traditional elements of Tunisian art. Several have also designed playground equipment for a nationwide preschool program that is partly staffed by PCV teachers, and others have established schools to teach drafting to high school students. One volunteer is now on the faculty of Tunisia's first school of architecture, which opened in 1968.

## AFGHANISTAN

The first volunteers went to Afghanistan in 1962 to teach in secondary schools and the Corps's main effort there continues to be education. In May, 1969, there were 170 volunteers serving in Afghanistan and an additional 50 in training. Of those at work, 136 were teachers or teacher-trainers, 16 were assigned to community development and agricultural projects, and 18 female volunteers traveled throughout the country administering smallpox vaccinations.

The smallpox vaccination program is one of the Peace Corps's most unusual. The program was conceived when the

Afghan Government, planning a country-wide smallpox vaccination program, discovered that it could not use male Afghans to do all the inoculations because taboos prevented village women from permitting male doctors to vaccinate them. Similar prohibitions involving the proper role of women discouraged Afghan women from accepting the task, and so the government turned to the Peace Corps for help.

Based in provincial centers and traveling in pairs with government vaccination teams, the volunteers spend 80 per cent of their time going from village to village or seeking out the encampments of the nomadic Kochi tribe. One NANESA official commented:

These gals lead probably the toughest existence in the Peace Corps. They travel by donkey, horse, camel, and foot into villages where foreigners have never visited before. They also perform public health and child care chores, and their great difficulty is that they are never in one location long enough to make more than superficial friendships. Their arrival really provides excitement. The Afghan women are curious about the girls' clothes and are amazed that they don't have lice. They fuss over their make-up and are appalled by their brashness. It becomes an education for both sides.

Selection for the program is also tough because the assignment requires a high level of physical stamina and emotional maturity. A typical day begins at six o'clock in the morning with a breakfast of tea and nan, an Afghan bread similar to Mexican tortillas. Then, while the male vaccinators go to a place where the men are gathered, the volunteers set up their operations in the women's quarters. In addition to administering vaccine, they dispense advice about nutrition and child care. If there is no village resident who can read and write, one volunteer records information while the other vaccinates, for the government requires that the name of each person vaccinated be recorded. At the end of the day, equipment and supplies are packed and the trek to the next village begins. After two or three weeks in the field, the vaccination team returns to its base of operations for fresh supplies and a brief rest.

## THE PEACE CORPS IN NANESA

Plans for the NANESA region include changes in Peace Corps operations as much as they do new programs. The regional staff in Washington hopes to improve language instruction, to provide more thorough training for overseas staff members, and to include more host citizens in training and overseas programs. Before he left the agency in 1969, the region's director Robert Steiner talked about the Peace Corps's effectiveness and admitted that

> it is tough to come up with any tangible proof of Peace Corps impact in NANESA—except in Nepal and Afghanistan, which are small enough so that change is very visible. We have to feel rather than measure impact. The fact that our host countries continue to ask for volunteers is about the only measure of success. We can point to the buildings and new planned communities in Tunisia and to the fact that until we went to Afghanistan women there did not have the right to vote. And we certainly can claim success in helping to increase food production in India. By and large, however, it is mainly a matter of attitude change in NANESA. It is a tough region for the volunteer. He can't hide his inadequacies behind a loan or a bulldozer. An American who can survive two years in NANESA can survive anywhere.

# X

# East Asia and the Pacific: Experiments in Technical Assistance

The Peace Corps program in the East Asia and Pacific region (EAP) began slowly. In the first year, 384 volunteers served in three Asian countries—Malaya, the Philippines, and Thailand. By 1963, there were 976 volunteers in the three original host countries plus Indonesia, Sabah, and Sarawak. With the Peace Corps's withdrawal from Indonesia, however, the number of volunteers dropped to 847 by the summer of 1965. At that time, Latin America had 3,214 volunteers; Africa, 3,010; and NANESA, 1,533. The disparity between EAP and the other regions was frustrating and disappointing to the EAP regional staff.* Within two years, though, the number of volunteers in EAP had grown to 2,045—an increase of 1,198 with only two new host countries added: South Korea and Micronesia. Volunteers in Micronesia accounted for better than two-thirds of the total increase, a fact that alarmed some congressmen and stimulated considerable debate on Capitol Hill.

Today, the EAP region includes Malaysia, the Philippines, Thailand, South Korea, Micronesia, Western Samoa, Tonga, and the Fiji Islands. Of the 2,553 volunteers there in May, 1969, 76 per cent—1,938—were teaching at all levels from

* At that time, the Peace Corps, like the Department of State, called the region the Far East. The Peace Corps changed the designation in 1965 after a member of the Philippine Senate commented, "I notice that my country is referred to by the U.S. State Department as part of the Far East. I ask, 'Far East of what?'"

161

primary grades to universities. An additional 450 volunteers worked in health programs, including a tuberculosis eradica-

TABLE IV

The Peace Corps in East Asia and the Pacific:
An Eight-Year Summary of Volunteers in Host Countries
at End of Fiscal Year

| | 1962 | 1963 | 1964 | 1965 | 1966 | 1967 | 1968 | 1969 |
|---|---|---|---|---|---|---|---|---|
| Malaysia | | | | 378 | 561 | 583 | 495 | 495 |
| Malaya | 67 | 169 | 206 | – | – | – | – | – |
| Sabah/Sarawak | | 91 | 124 | – | – | – | – | – |
| Philippines | 272 | 472 | 286 | 227 | 571 | 601 | 720 | 662 |
| Thailand | 45 | 227 | 245 | 242 | 356 | 321 | 228 | 283 |
| Indonesia | | 17 | 31 | – | – | – | – | – |
| Korea | | | | | | 92 | 310 | 265 |
| Micronesia | | | | | | 448 | 625 | 478 |
| Western Samoa | | | | | | | 129 | 115 |
| Tonga | | | | | | | 114 | 88 |
| Fiji | | | | | | | 51 | 139 |
| Totals | 384 | 976 | 892 | 847 | 1,488 | 2,045 | 2,672 | 2,525 |

tion project in Malaysia and malaria control projects in the Philippines and Thailand. There were 74 volunteers in agricultural and rural community development jobs, including a group of volunteers working in a Head Start program with the Office of Economic Opportunity in Micronesia and a group of volunteers working in urban and regional economic and development planning in the Philippines. While at one time East Asia and Pacific was the smallest of the Peace Corps regions in both numbers of volunteers and host countries, it now has more volunteers than NANESA, and in recent years its programs have been among the most innovative. The emphasis has been on education and public health, but the latter is giving way to agricultural and community development work and to projects in the areas of public administration, law, and developmental planning. With city and regional planning already under way in the Philippines, the region's staff members are looking forward to similar programs in Malaysia and Thailand.

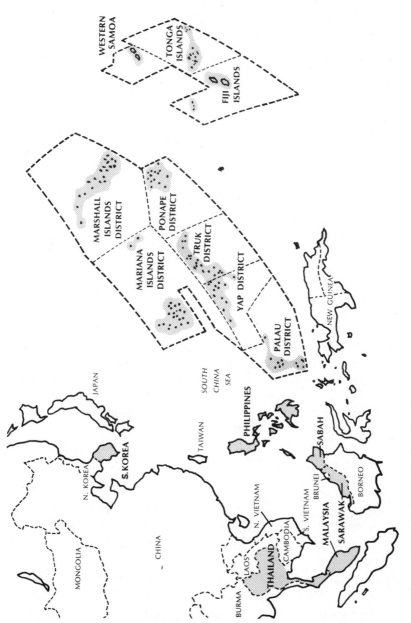

Shading indicates countries in which Peace Corps volunteers are at work.

## TRAINING FOR ASIA

Over the years, EAP administrators have led the movement in the Peace Corps to adapt liberal arts college graduates to public health projects and to decentralize volunteer training. With the support of new leadership in the other regional offices, the EAP staff took advantage of the change of Peace Corps directors in 1966 to press for responsibility for their own training, arguing that they were more aware of the needs for their region than a training office headquartered in Washington. When the Office of Training was dissolved and each region given responsibility for administering its own training programs, EAP turned almost exclusively to the University of Hawaii, where the staff worked with university officials to establish a permanent center at Hilo. Today, about six hundred volunteers headed for Southeast Asia and the South Pacific train there each year. Ross Pritchard, former EAP regional director, discussed the advantages of this arrangement in an interview in 1968:

> We knew that the environmental and human resources of the University of Hawaii would lead to a better and continuing partnership. Proper cycling of our training programs at a permanent center also allowed us to hire a full-time, year-round staff. This soon led to excellent relationships between operations in the field and our operations officers in Washington, and we found we didn't have any need for training officers in Washington.

With the addition of Micronesia and Polynesia to the East Asia and Pacific region in 1967, EAP administrators began to look for training sites in the Micronesian islands. Training facilities were first set up on the island of Truk for volunteers who were to work in Truk District. Today, all training for Micronesia is conducted within the country, and Micronesians help with the programs. Volunteers who will work with high-yield rice varieties train at the International Rice Research Institute outside Manila and some volunteers in crop production, community development, or public works projects train in Taiwan.

## A Change in Emphasis

Many of the health programs initiated in the EAP region are now being phased out and replaced with projects that more closely follow the priorities for development set by the host country. In an interview in Washington, a Peace Corps staff member discussed the reasons behind the change:

> While our health programs were generally in an auxiliary position to our educational programs, they followed a valid philosophical concept for a developing nation. We found, however, that resources just were not available to do the massive job that was needed. Counterparts could not be found to work with volunteers, and when they could be found, they couldn't be assigned in many instances because their salaries placed too heavy a load on public budgets.

Those health programs in which host governments are highly interested, tuberculosis control in South Korea, family planning and tuberculosis control in Malaysia, and malaria control in the Philippines, will probably continue but they will be, according to an EAP staff member, "small, high impact programs." The malaria control program in Thailand is ready to be taken over by Thais and will not be renewed.

New programs in the EAP region include public administration and development and economic planning. An EAP staff member provided an illustration of the new approach:

> Western Malaysia [had] settled on an agricultural program for an area on the [Malay] peninsula that was economically depressed but was ideal for land reclamation and rich in soil. The government was ready to move in and start a massive educational program in crop production, mechanization, and marketing. Then a lone volunteer with a degree in agricultural

economics visited the area and asked, "How are you going to get the crops to market?" It was a good question. There were no roads or any other suitable means of transporting goods. Building a system of feeder roads and several main highways has become top priority for the area. This project, we hope, forecasts the new emphasis—economic and development planning.

## THE SHADOW OF VIETNAM

National hatreds and the war in Vietnam have retarded the growth of programs in Southeast Asia. Many countries in the area are wary of a U.S. presence in their country—in any shape or form—and have made no response to overtures by Peace Corps officials. But the level at which the war is most acutely felt is that of the individual volunteer. Many must reconcile within themselves working for the same government that is fighting a war in Vietnam and some are publicly confronted with the issue by friends as well as opponents. In Thailand in particular, volunteers have had to work to maintain an identity apart from the U.S. military presence. In general, they have avoided contact with military personnel, who, as a result, consider them "strange, stuck-up, and stand-offish." A former volunteer explained the situation:

We were not necessarily anti-GI. A lot can be hidden behind a facade of bravado. Some of [the soldiers] were infuriated, though, when our PCV girls refused to date them. I got tired of explaining why the girls couldn't date them—that in Thailand, girls who date soldiers are considered to be prostitutes. Finally I gave up trying to explain and avoided them when I could. Frankly, we didn't get to see them too much, unless we went into the towns near where they were stationed. Most of the ones I met couldn't understand how I could live with the Thais and why I wanted to work with them. I suppose it could be considered amusing that some of our hosts were suspicious of us because they thought we might be spies, while the GI's considered us different, kooks, and Commie-lovers.

The Peace Corps itself came closest to the conflict in Vietnam in 1966 when, for almost six months, a group of staff members in Washington debated whether or not volunteers should go to South Vietnam if an invitation were extended. The staff was divided on the issue, and Vaughn waited until he had heard both sides of the debate before announcing that the Corps would not go to Vietnam.

Three factors had a major bearing on the decision. Staff members were concerned about placing volunteers in physically dangerous situations. They also felt that no amount of restraint could prevent volunteers from having ultimately to collaborate with military intelligence personnel and the Central Intelligence Agency. In carrying out their assignments, volunteers would come in contact with the Viet Cong and those sympathetic to the National Liberation Front and would undoubtedly become privy to information that would be of use to intelligence agents. One Peace Corps official outlined the danger in such a situation:

> Consider, for example, the mixed feelings a volunteer would have when he learned of an ambush that had been planned by the Viet Cong. Sure, he would agonize over it, because it is likely he would have friends on both sides of the political fence. But he just couldn't stand by and let the ambush happen. He'd finally make for the nearest military outpost and tell the story before he would let Americans die. Putting a volunteer in this kind of a situation would be asking too much of him.

The overriding factor, however, was expressed succinctly by that same official: "Why in hell should the Peace Corps be in Vietnam while our policy is one of seeking a military solution to the Vietnamese problem? To go there until the fighting stops would be the height of hyprocrisy."

But even many of those who argued against going into Vietnam wanted the Peace Corps to be prepared to accept an invitation if it came, and today, many staff members hope to send volunteers there as soon as a peaceful settlement is reached. "I believe," said one, "that to be effective [such a program] would have to be a massive effort involving thousands of volunteers. Certainly it should be a multinational undertaking."

## THE PHILIPPINES

The government of the Philippines was one of the first to request Peace Corps volunteers and within a year, 272 PCV's had been sent there. At one time, there were more than 800 volunteers in the Philippines, and more than 2,000 have worked in the country since 1961. Of the 712 volunteers there in May, 1969, 676 were teaching or training local teachers, 17 helped with a malaria eradication project, and 19 worked in the Bicol regional planning project.

In terms of numbers of volunteers, the Philippine program is the agency's largest, and the volunteers are scattered from the northern island province of Batan to southern Sulu. There are 12 regional offices and 27 staff members.

By far the largest number of volunteers in the Philippines have worked in education programs. In the early years, they were assigned only as teacher aids because school officials feared that Filipino teachers would balk at having foreigners in the classrooms and little would be accomplished in an atmosphere of jealousy and resentment. The volunteers soon found that they had been given nonjobs, and frustration was widespread. Today, the volunteers have risen to co-teacher status and are now helping to train local teachers. Under the current program, a volunteer teaches in a Filipino school for a semester or two and then works with a Filipino co-worker in a team-teaching arrangement. The emphasis in primary and secondary schools is on math, science, and teaching English as a second language. Volunteers with master's degrees in science, math, and English have recently begun to train college and university teachers.

Early in 1969, volunteers began to staff Philippine agencies responsible for development planning. They work primarily in the Bicol region, a group of north-central provinces with similar languages. The volunteers help coordinate provincial and city plans and translate them into regional schemes. They plan road systems, harbors, and water supplies, survey manpower resources, and work with industry. The Bicol program has produced one interesting spin-off: three volunteers and their Filipino co-workers have organized the nucleus of a similar program in the Western Visayas, another island group in the Philippines.

The newest program in the Philippines will make use of the miracle rice strains developed at the International Rice Research Institute. A group of volunteers scheduled to arrive in late 1969 will work with local farmers to demonstrate the use of the new rice strains, to teach irrigation and fertilization methods, and to encourage the farmers to use their land year round by growing vegetables off season.

## MALAYSIA

Peace Corps programing in Malaysia has been the most diversified in the EAP region. In early 1969, there were 506 volunteers serving there—367 as teachers, 42 in a rural health program, 22 in rural community development, 25 as industrial arts teachers, 24 in a tuberculosis eradication program, and 26 in a combined agricultural and fisheries project. The country has provided the Peace Corps with some of its most remote assignments, including posts among the descendants of the headhunting tribesmen of northern Borneo. In 1967, Malaysia paid the Peace Corps a fine compliment when it launched a domestic volunteer service program patterned after the Corps. Most of the local volunteers are college undergraduates.

New directions in programing have been initiated in Malaysia with two specialized programs. Volunteers with degrees in economics have gone to Sabah and Sarawak to work as economic planners for the central government and to help set up regional agricultural development schemes. One of their main contributions has been to coordinate the collection of agricultural data. Twenty-five volunteers began training in the fall of 1969 to work in the Accountant General's Office in the Ministry of Treasury to help modernize Malaysia's budget system to permit performance budgeting and advance planning. The U.S. Bureau of the Budget and the General Accounting Office are helping with training.

## THAILAND

In May, 1969, there were 223 volunteers serving in Thailand—71 working in rural health programs, 60 teaching English, 34 teaching in primary and secondary schools, 26 working in rural community action projects, 16 teaching physical education, and 16 engaged in malaria control.

In 1968, the rural community action volunteers began modest irrigation projects in northeast Thailand near the Mekong River and started a rural public works program to develop potable water supplies, including a network of small reservoirs, in the same area. Accompanying the English-teaching programs is an extensive teacher-training project in colleges and central schools where English is used. Thirty volunteers have recently begun to work in the upper Mekong area in swine and poultry husbandry and in land cultivation. Two civil engineers will soon be engaged in rural construction in the northeast, and the Thai Government has expressed interest in obtaining volunteers with degrees in agriculture to help with the development of the Mekong Basin. In the fall of 1969, twenty volunteers began training to work in a leprosy control program in the northeast, and plans are under way for volunteers to work with the Ministry for Community Development in a rice production project.

## THE PEACE CORPS IN PARADISE

In early 1966, the Peace Corps became the pawn in a game of international chess, and, for the first time, played only a minor role in the decision to send volunteers overseas. In May, 1966, the Johnson Administration announced through Arthur J. Goldberg, then U.S. Ambassador to the United Nations, that several hundred Peace Corps volunteers would be sent to Micronesia, a U.N. trust territory administered by the U.S. Department of the Interior. In his announcement, Goldberg acknowledged that there had been "some criticism" of U.S. administration there and said that the commitment of Peace Corps volunteers to Micronesia showed U.S. "determination to discharge our full responsibility as trustees."

Just after Goldberg made his statement, the Peace Corps began an intensive 1-month recruiting campaign on campuses to interest potential volunteers in serving in Micronesia. Despite the fact that only a few weeks remained in the spring semester, a record three thousand applications poured in, and by the next spring, there were 448 volunteers at work in the South Pacific. The attraction may have been provided by a now-famous recruiting brochure that announced on its cover: "The Peace Corps Goes to Paradise." The cover photograph showed a stretch of beach, a dug-out canoe sitting offshore, and a string of tiny islands on the horizon. In the foreground, two bare-footed South Sea Islanders climbed a coconut palm. Inside, the brochure explained that the paradise was not without disease, illiteracy, or poverty, despite its allure.

More than 3 million square miles of the Pacific Ocean are peppered by the 2,141 Micronesian islands, 97 of which are inhabited by 100,000 persons. The population is increasing at the rate of 3.6 per cent a year and will double by 1985. There is a severe teacher shortage and half of the territory's classrooms fail to meet basic standards of construction, ventilation, and protection from the weather. The island economy is almost entirely dependent on the production of copra, and processing methods and crop destruction by disease and rats prevent bumper crops. There is also a need for agricultural diversification and for more small businesses, not only to provide services for the Micronesians but also to take advantage of increased tourism.

To help fill these needs, the Peace Corps has provided teachers, agriculturalists, fishery experts, community development workers, small business advisers, and volunteers with specialized backgrounds in law, engineering, architecture, nursing, and communications. When volunteers arrived in Micronesia, they conducted the islands' first census to provide a base for medical assistance and future programing, and launched an extensive public health program.

Nevertheless, Congress was displeased with the program in Micronesia and pressed the Corps to explain by whose authority volunteers had been sent there. The answer was not simple, for the host government in this case was, and still is, the U.S. Department of the Interior. In May, 1967, the Senate Foreign Relations Committee told the Peace Corps that it should not undertake such major programs without congressional approval. In its report to the Senate approving the agency's authorization for fiscal 1968, the committee noted that the number of volunteers then in the trust territory represented a ratio of 1 volunteer for every 195 Micronesians. It further calculated that, based on the Peace Corps's projections, the ratio would drop to 1 to 130 by the end of 1968. The report added:

> While the aims and purposes of this pilot program are certainly admirable, the committee questions whether they are consistent with the mandate Congress gave the Peace Corps. If programs of the same magnitude were to be undertaken in Latin America, for example, the achievement of a ratio of 1 Peace Corps Volunteer for every 130 inhabitants would require a Volunteer corps of nearly 2 million persons. Certainly this is not what Congress had in mind when it authorized the Peace Corps. The committee believes that no further programs of this intensity should be undertaken by the Peace Corps without further authorization by Congress.
>
> It may even be questioned whether the Peace Corps ought to be in Micronesia at all. It is a U.S. trust territory, and if the

United States has fulfilled its trust to the inhabitants badly, then those responsible for this condition ought to be also responsible for its remedy.

The Peace Corps's role in Micronesia, according to many staff members, is to serve as a catalyst for cohesion. That role is being fulfilled in part by the teaching of English, which will give the Micronesians a common language.

The Peace Corps's first year in Micronesia was not distinguished by cohesion, however, and its programs became enmeshed in family squabbles with the Department of Interior. Jealousies cropped up between Interior and Peace Corps administrators and disputes arose over policy matters. By 1968, both sides were telling Congress that fences had been mended, quarrels had been patched up, disruptive personnel had been replaced, and the two agencies were working in concert.

By mid-1969, the Micronesian program included a total of 496 volunteers—118 working in health, economic development, and public works projects, 306 teaching English as a foreign language, and the rest working in a Head Start program with VISTA volunteers or serving as specialists in public administration, legal counseling, architecture, and other technical assistance programs. Public health projects have been nearly phased out and there are no plans to expand them.

WHERE TO NEXT?

Until peace in Vietnam comes, it is unlikely that Peace Corps volunteers will be invited to any additional countries in Southeast Asia, although the agency would welcome invitations to Indonesia, Laos, and Cambodia, and hopes to go to Vietnam itself when the war ends. Education is likely to remain the agency's main effort in the region, but there will be increased emphasis on agricultural projects, especially agricultural education and the organization of cooperatives,

rural community development, and economic and development planning. The Mekong Basin development program
will offer an opportunity for the Peace Corps to send teams
of volunteers to work in a series of related projects, and the
agency hopes it will have the chance to make its plans real.
For the moment, however, expansion is improbable. Vietnam holds the key.

# XI

# Interagency Relationships

Within the federal bureaucracy, the Peace Corps is semi-autonomous. It sets its policies and determines its programs with a minimum of coordination with other federal agencies, and since there are few areas in which the Peace Corps's work overlaps with that of other departments, it has been able to go its own way with little interagency conflict. As would be expected, its closest working relationships are with those agencies operating overseas. However, other federal departments work with the Peace Corps on joint projects to recruit and train volunteers and, in one case, to administer a program overseas. The Civil Service Commission, completely apart from programing or policy development, provides several services to the agency.

## The Civil Service Commission

The Peace Corps does not publicize its activities with the Civil Service Commission and few prospective volunteers are aware that the Commission administers the Peace Corps Entrance Examination and the Modern Languages Aptitude Test. In recruitment brochures and radio announcements urging young Americans to join the Corps, readers and listeners are told that they may take the tests at "more than five hundred testing centers throughout the nation," but no mention is made that these locations are, in fact, a part of the Civil Service Commission's network of testing centers, or that the Commission administers the tests. This omission apparently is a carry-over from the early days of the agency, when Shriver was trying to establish an identity for the Peace Corps outside the usual image of a federal bureaucracy. In fact, Shriver had hoped to avoid using the Commission altogether. When the Peace Corps was being organized, he searched for a private organization to administer the tests but found none that could guarantee integrated testing centers in the South. Reluctantly, he turned to the Civil Service Commission, the only federal agency with access to fully integrated testing facilities at the time.

Although the Commission had administered testing programs for other federal agencies, it accepted the Peace Corps request with reluctance. One Commission staff member recalled that "unbelievable publicity had been given to the scheme, which most of us thought unworkable, and Shriver had invited nearly our entire population to apply. We weren't sure what kind of a response to plan for." According to a former staff member, the Commission agreed to cooperate because "John Macy, who was then chairman of the Commission, was interested in fulfilling what he felt was the Commission's role as the personnel arm of the federal government. We were also fully aware that the President's brother-in-law was running the Corps."

The Commission laid careful plans for conducting the first examinations. In anticipation of demonstrations and an influx of what were then known as beatniks, the agency alerted all its employees and asked that regional directors and other high-level staff members oversee the testing. Police departments were asked to stand by in the event of trouble. To the Commission's surprise, the testing went smoothly, without protests, picketing, or disturbances of any kind. The expected beatniks did not appear and the only outsiders present were press photographers and television cameramen who were given permission to photograph applicants arriving at testing centers and to take pictures from the back of the examination rooms.

The Commission has since served as the testing agency for the Peace Corps under a memorandum of understanding signed in 1961. The first examinations were scored by the Educational Testing Service, but the Commission took over this responsibility in 1962. The Peace Corps reimburses the Commission for such costs as storage and maintenance of the exams and distribution, collection, and scoring of tests. The Commission does not interpret examination results but transmits test scores directly to the Peace Corps's Office of Volunteer Placement.

In addition to providing testing services, the Civil Service Commission conducts investigations of all those invited to Peace Corps training and those hired for staff positions. This service, too, is provided under a memorandum of understanding and the Peace Corps reimburses the Commission $450 for each field investigation. In 1968, the cost of investigations reached $4 million. An investigation of a prospective volunteer is the same in-depth check conducted for any person being considered for a sensitive job in the federal service, although Commission investigators also look for evidence of maturity, motivation, and the ability to succeed on a job in a foreign environment. The investigators make no judgments on the information gathered, but simply forward their findings to the Peace Corps, where the data becomes part of an applicant's record.

The area of greatest controversy between the Peace Corps and the Commission has been staff employment. At the time the Peace Corps was being shaped, Shriver suggested that the legislation contain a provision granting the agency a number of supergrade positions that need not be filled from the Commission's supergrade pool. The Senate did not object strenuously to this request, but the issue became a *cause célèbre* for a number of House members and the topic of a good portion of the House debate. In the end, Shriver had his way and House and Senate conferees agreed to allow the Peace Corps twenty-five supergrade positions without regard to civil service registers.

In 1962, the Peace Corps sent a request to the Commission that the agency be permitted to hire persons for Grade 13 through Grade 15 positions, those just beneath the supergrade level, under Schedule B. (Schedule B positions do not require competitive examinations or assignment to a civil service register.) The request caused debate within the Commission. Ultimately, although it did not approve placing the positions under Schedule B, it did authorize the Peace Corps to recruit for temporary noncompetitive appointments to middle-management positions. This authority was extended annually until 1965, when Peace Corps staff members were given Foreign Service Reserve officer status similar to the employment and rating system that exists for USIA and AID staff appointments. At that time, the Peace Corps's professional staff was removed from Civil Service Commission jurisdiction, an arrangement that worked out to the satisfaction of both the Peace Corps and the Commission.

## THE DEPARTMENT OF STATE

The Peace Corps works more closely with the Department of State than with any other federal agency. The Peace Corps Act provides that the Secretary of State oversee the operations of the Peace Corps and that the Peace Corps coordinate its activities with State. Sub-sections (c) and (d) of Section 4 of the Act contain the main clauses outlining this relationship:

(c) (1) Nothing contained in this Act shall be construed to infringe upon the powers or functions of the Secretary of State.
(2) The President shall prescribe appropriate procedures to assure coordination of Peace Corps activities with other activities of the United States Government in each country, under the leadership of the Chief of the United States diplomatic mission.
(3) Under the direction of the President, the Secretary of State shall be responsible for the continuous supervision and

general direction of the programs authorized by this Act, to the end that such programs are effectively integrated both at home and abroad and the foreign policy of the United States is best served thereby.

(d) Except with the approval of the Secretary of State, the Peace Corps shall not be assigned to perform services which could more usefully be performed by other available agencies of the United States Government in the country concerned.

The wording of the Act leaves wide latitude for interpretation and a Secretary of State who so desired could probably exercise tight control over Peace Corps activities. Although this has not been the case, the fact remains that the relationship between the Department of State and the Peace Corps could alter drastically with major changes in the administration of either agency.

The initial relationship between the State Department and the Peace Corps was established by Dean Rusk. As one of the Presidential advisers who helped shape the Peace Corps, Rusk was instrumental in determining the role the agency should play in the nation's foreign affairs. During a conference of returned volunteers held in Washington in the spring of 1965, he told his audience:

One important element in our relations with the rest of the world is the reflection of the interest in and the attitudes of the American people towards the ordinary people in other countries. We deliberately did not catch you up in the day-by-day and week-by-week problems of foreign policy. The relations between the American people and peoples of other countries are not channeled just through the problems which governments have with each other. But I hope very much that we can enlist a considerable number of you in our own work in the future.

Rusk understood the importance of independent operations for the Peace Corps and insisted that it be allowed to keep its distance from the State Department. He stated his reason succinctly: "To make the Peace Corps an instrument of foreign policy would be to rob it of its contribution to foreign policy."

Rusk's cordial view of the Corps did not filter down evenly within the State Department, nor was his cordiality fully returned by Peace Corps staff and volunteers. When the Peace Corps was created, members of the Foreign Service expressed serious reservations about the agency and its possibilities for success. They predicted that sending virtually untrained young Americans overseas to work alongside host-country citizens could only make a shambles of the nation's foreign relations. They were sure that Peace Corpsmen would embarrass the United States through blundering amateurism.

The Peace Corps, in turn, has guarded its independence with the ardor of a jealous lover. According to one Peace Corps staff member,

> There are some hair-raising tales that could be told about the power struggle between the Peace Corps and some State Department people. . . . someday they may reach the light. Suffice it to say that we had to be on our guard. Some of the career officers over there would have loved to call the shots for us. I will say that whenever this was tried, Rusk called them off. We agree that our contribution to American foreign policy is one of people-to-people relationships, not government-to-government diplomacy. To continue to make this contribution, we have to be independent.

The Peace Corps has developed a reputation for arrogance that is not always undeserved. Volunteers and staff have a tendency to believe that their contributions are more meaningful to the host country because they work directly with the local people. A former volunteer who served in Peru thought that volunteers condemned the efforts of Foreign Service officers too quickly:

> I felt that many of us were unfair in our rejection of what they

were trying to accomplish. Most Peace Corpsmen quickly acquire the snobbishness of the downtrodden, sometimes forgetting that pride and dignity also go along with poverty. I can remember that it happened to me. I came down out of the mountains one time after eight months of isolation. It was evident that I had been working with sheep herders. The first American I saw was a young Foreign Service officer who would have looked more at home on the streets of Wilton, Connecticut, and I snubbed him. Suddenly, my martyr complex came to the surface and I felt superior and resentful at the same time. It was nothing more than bad manners on my part. I'm sure all he saw when he looked at me was a dirty, smelly American kid who was badly in need of a shower and a shave. I wanted him to look upon me as a hero. Now, I figure his was a tougher job than mine. No matter how long he served in Peru, he remained a stranger. I was not a stranger in my community.

The directives of Section 4 of the Peace Corps Act are carried out in a formal way in Washington. Top-level officials of the Department of State, the Agency for International Development, and the U.S. Information Agency are kept informed of all negotiations and plans for programs. AID officials are asked for comments on proposed programs and the Secretary of State approves all program requests. Occasionally Peace Corps program and training officers attend briefing sessions at the State Department. Annual reviews of the entire assistance program in a host country are attended by program and training officers as well as the appropriate Peace Corps regional director. Otherwise, Peace Corps staff officers seldom have more than informal contact with their counterparts at State.

The State Department handles all Peace Corps cable traffic to and from host countries, although it is transmitted without State Department clearance. All other official overseas Peace Corps correspondence is handled by diplomatic pouch, also the responsibility of State.

Most of the contact between the Peace Corps and other U.S. agencies with overseas operations takes place overseas.

The Peace Corps country director reports to the chief of the U.S. diplomatic mission and is a member of the country team, which coordinates the total U.S. foreign policy and foreign aid programs in the host country. The U.S. Ambassador or chief of mission must approve all program requests made by the Peace Corps before they are sent to Washington for further action. Peace Corps associate directors may have occasional contact with AID counterparts when material support for volunteers is required or when a joint Peace Corps-AID project is in progress. Volunteers themselves rarely find a need for direct relationships with AID or embassy staff. In times of crisis, however, embassy and AID personnel rally to offer whatever assistance is required. When the Peace Corps was asked to leave Guinea, for example, AID staff members helped round up volunteers from outlying areas and arranged for transportation out of the country, while the embassy staff worked through an entire weekend to close out the volunteers' financial records and cut through the red tape involved in termination of service.

The working relationships between Peace Corps staff members and other U.S. personnel overseas continues to be cordial but distant. A State Department desk officer with experience in two South Asian countries where the Peace Corps serves related that "country teams generally work well together, but close contact remains at the top. Otherwise, the Peace Corps goes its own way and handles its own affairs."

## THE AGENCY FOR INTERNATIONAL DEVELOPMENT

Early relationships between the Peace Corps and the Agency for International Development were dismal. The men who created and ran the Peace Corps viewed its role as far different from that of AID and encouraged distance between the two agencies to maintain an independent position for the Corps. They criticized many AID programs as misdirected and made clear their belief that foreign aid money should be used for self-help projects. In turn, AID and other Foreign Service personnel tended to view the Peace Corps as immature and unrealistic. But in spite of opposing views and occasional hostility between the two agencies, they did undertake some cooperative projects that worked out well. The educational television program in Colombia is one example.

When Vaughn returned to the Peace Corps in March, 1966, he issued a directive urging Peace Corps overseas staff members not only to cooperate with AID but to look for projects that would benefit from joint programing. Vaughn was aware of the shabby relationships that existed between the two agencies from his tenure as the Peace Corp's regional director for Latin America. Since the directive, coordination has improved. However, it is generally AID that seeks Peace Corps help, and frequently cooperation depends more on personalities than on established policy. When a joint program is set up, AID usually supplies material, financial, and technical support for the volunteers and the Peace Corps maintains control of the project.

One example of a successful joint project is the malaria eradication program in Thailand. AID officials there had tried to initiate such a program on their own but had been unsuccessful because the Thai workers did not understand the importance of the program and would work only when closely supervised. Since AID did not have enough personnel to work closely with the Thais, it turned to the Peace Corps for help. Volunteers already working in community development programs began to set up mosquito control units with guidance from AID specialists and to explain the work they were doing to the local people. Within a short time, Thais began to volunteer to help. With the program tentatively under way, the Peace Corps sent another volunteer group to Thailand specifically trained for malaria control. With AID still supplying technical advice and materials for the project, the Thais now will carry on the program themselves.

In spite of the close working relationship that has developed in some countries between the Peace Corps and AID, the approach to foreign assistance by the two agencies remains distant, and many overseas staff members and volunteers have been cautious in recommending interagency cooperation. However, Blatchford has indicated that he would like to see more volunteers with technical skills recruited for overseas service and more technical assistance programs initiated. He has stated publicly that he will seek more interagency cooperation and has created the position of special assistant for executive liaison to encourage joint efforts. If he is successful in carrying out his plans, the agency's relationships with AID will no doubt become closer.

## THE U.S. INFORMATION AGENCY

The Peace Corps has remarkably little contact with U.S. Information Agency staff, either overseas or in Washington. The USIA is informed of Peace Corps activities and consulted about the agency's public information role in the host country, but it issues no official announcements for the Corps. In the host country, news about Peace Corps programs comes from local agencies with whom the Peace Corps works, and the country director or his deputy deal with reporters interested in other matters. Separateness is deliberately maintained to assure credibility.

## INTELLIGENCE AGENCIES

Although leftist groups throughout the world have accused the Peace Corps of being a cover-up for espionage, there is no evidence of any use of the Peace Corps by the Central Intelligence Agency (CIA) or any other intelligence group. The Peace Corps is extremely sensitive about this issue and has taken precautions to protect itself from such charges. At the insistence of Shriver, President Kennedy issued a strongly worded order that there was to be no interference with the Peace Corps or any attempt to infiltrate its ranks by the CIA or any other U.S. intelligence agency. In addition, intelligence agents were not, through any guise or pretense, to attempt to gather information from staff or volunteers. At the same time, agreements were signed by Shriver and Secretary of State Rusk that continue to prevent volunteers from employment by an intelligence group of the federal government, including the CIA, for five years from the time of their separation from the Peace Corps. If former volunteers or staff members choose a career with an intelligence agency, the agreement provides that they cannot be sent to any country in which they served. Furthermore, no one who has ever worked for an intelligence agency, even in military service, can become a Peace Corps volunteer or staff member, nor can anyone who is or has been married to a person with such a background.

## THE DEPARTMENT OF THE INTERIOR

When the Peace Corps went to Micronesia in 1966, relations with the Department of the Interior nearly regressed into a brawl. Interior had been governing the islands under a U.N. trusteeship since the end of World War II, and the circumstances leading to Peace Corps involvement—accusations by the United Nations that the United States had done a poor job of helping the Micronesians—caused immediate friction. That atmosphere has changed considerably over the last three years, and the agencies now work together in relative calm.

In Micronesia, the Department of the Interior performs a role similar to that assumed in other programs by the host government. Program requests may come from an office in the Interior Department, the Micronesian Congress, a Micronesian district legislature, or an independent local organization. Requests must be approved by the Interior Department official in charge of each district, then reviewed by Micronesian officials, and given final approval by the High Commissioner of the trusteeship, another Interior official. In addition, Interior Department staff members supervise training programs, all of which are held at training sites within

Micronesia. The Peace Corps provides its own training staff.

This arrangement has led to little more than a talking relationship between the Peace Corps and the Interior Department in Washington, but in Micronesia, the program has become a truly cooperative venture between Peace Corpsmen, Interior staff, and Micronesians.

## THE DEPARTMENT OF COMMERCE

Early in 1967, the Peace Corps received a request from the U.S. Department of Commerce to help establish a chain of weather observation stations in the outer Micronesian islands. The Department's Environmental Science Services Administration, which contains the U.S. Weather Bureau, shipped observation stations and equipment in kit form to the islands and the Peace Corps worked with the Micronesian Government to assemble the stations on strategic islands on Micronesia's perimeter. Volunteers with little or no prior knowledge about weather reporting assembled and operated the stations by following printed instructions. The PCV's filed regular weather reports while training Micronesians to man the stations. The first eight stations were set up in 1967; seven more were built and put into operation in 1968. By May, 1969, all fifteen stations were manned by Micronesians and the Peace Corps was no longer involved in the project.

## THE OFFICE OF ECONOMIC OPPORTUNITY

Relationships between the Peace Corps and the Office of Economic Opportunity have always been cordial, in part because of Shriver's influence and in part because so many former Peace Corps staff members and volunteers have gone to work for OEO after Peace Corps service. Within the United States, the Peace Corps and OEO have worked together on joint training programs and have initiated several experimental ventures such as that involving the Job Corps graduates. In Micronesia, volunteers have been assigned to OEO's community action agencies to serve as construction supervisors or program administrators. In all cases, OEO provides the salary for a co-worker, who is trained by the volunteer.

## THE PUBLIC HEALTH SERVICE

The Public Health Service aids the Peace Corps in recruiting medical personnel and continues to assign physicians to the Corps for overseas service. Until Congress amended the selective service laws so that military obligations could not be met through Peace Corps service, the Public Health Service provided the Peace Corps with its entire medical support overseas.

## OTHER AGENCIES

For many years the Department of Agriculture has sent experts abroad as advisers to foreign governments on such subjects as crop production, extension services, and soils research. The Peace Corps uses these experts in a number of its agricultural training programs and occasionally relies on them for technical advice and support within the host country.

The Bureau of Indian Affairs helped the Peace Corps launch Project Peace Pipe, a program to recruit American Indians for service in Latin America. The Bureau provided $20,000 for the salaries of two full-time recruiters for the project.

The Peace Corps joined in a cooperative venture with the Bureau of the Budget and the General Accounting Office in the fall of 1969 when the three agencies began working together on a training program for accountants headed for Malaysia.

# XII

# The Peace Corps and Congress

---

During his opening remarks in support of the Peace Corps legislation in 1961, Sargent Shriver told the House Foreign Affairs Committee:

> All of us connected with the Peace Corps are well aware of the fact that the Peace Corps is in a very real sense a child of this House. The appropriation cf $10,000 authorized last year by the House of Representatives for a study of a Peace Corps-type program marked the beginning of serious efforts to bring the Peace Corps to reality. The Peace Corps belongs to many people who long have believed that the United States must constantly seek various avenues of approach to the world's staggering problems. During the exploratory stages of the program we have tried to keep clearly in focus the will of Congress—as well as the aspirations of many thousands of Americans who want to play a personal role in their Nation's response to the world's needs.

Shriver could just as correctly have acknowledged that the Peace Corps is a child of Congress, since impetus and support for the agency came from both the Senate and the House. Congressmen Henry Reuss and Thomas Morgan, Senators Richard Neuberger and Hubert Humphrey had all proposed schemes similar to the Peace Corps and were instrumental in rousing interest in the program.

There was little doubt about backing for the Peace Corps in the Senate. Even as doughty a conservative as Senator Barry Goldwater of Arizona expressed enthusiasm for the idea and admiration for young Americans who applied for service. Fellow conservative Senator Bourke Hickenlooper was initially skeptical of the scheme and of the amounts of money Congress appropriated to the Peace Corps, but as time passed he became more a friend than a critic of the agency. The response in the House was similar, although there was more outspoken opposition when the Peace Corps legislation was debated.

Over the years, congressional support has not changed appreciably and the Corps continues to enjoy bipartisan backing in both houses. However, approval has not been given without extensive debate and admonitions that there be closer congressional supervision of Peace Corps operations. Nor does the continuing support mean that the Peace Corps's friends on Capitol Hill have not taken issue with the agency's administration. It has been amply demonstrated in committee hearings and on the floor of both chambers that the idealism motivating the Peace Corps is one thing; programing and volunteer behavior are quite different matters.

## An Annual Visit

The Peace Corps goes before Congress each year to request monies to finance its operations. The request for annual funds is accompanied by a congressional presentation, which contains statistical summaries of the agency's activities and a detailed account of its accomplishments, programs, and current budget. Requests for modifications, changes, additions, or deletions in the existing Peace Corps Act may also be recommended.

The agency's existence is renewed annually by an amendment to the authorization clause of the Peace Corps Act, which is modified to designate a new fiscal year and to indicate the amount the agency is authorized to receive from Congress during that period. The authorization merely sets a maximum amount that may be appropriated, but without this authorization, the Peace Corps would die.

During hearings on the legislation, Peace Corps administrators appear before the Subcommittee on Foreign Operations of the House Appropriations Committee, and it is here that battles have been fought. There are two reasons for contention. Although proposed changes to the Peace Corps Act and the authorization for funds are considered as separate bills, the actual appropriation request for the agency is part of the total foreign aid package submitted by the Agency for International Development. In the past years, AID and the programs it administers have fallen into disfavor within Congress, and Peace Corps appropriation requests have been put at a disadvantage. In addition, the long-time chairman of the subcommittee, Representative Otto Passman of Louisiana, is an avowed critic of the Corps.

As a result of President Johnson's ordered reduction in federal spending, the hearings in 1968 raised special problems for the Peace Corps, as they did for all agencies requesting funds for foreign aid programs. Through 1967, the Peace Corps had been granted every request it had submitted to Congress. Although appropriations did not always reach the maximum authorized, they were sufficient for expansion of operations. Furthermore, the agency had returned unobligated funds to the U.S. Treasury every year through fiscal 1968 and on several occasions had readjusted its request for authorization of funds downward after initial submission of its budget request. This reputation for economy had won the agency widespread favor in both houses.

BATTLES IN CONGRESS

Both Sargent Shriver and Jack Vaughn found formidable opponents in Congress. For Shriver, it was Congressman Harold R. Gross of Iowa, a member of the House Foreign Affairs Committee. During Shriver's first appearance before the Committee, Gross severely reprimanded him for inviting House members to breakfasts at which he discussed the Peace Corps and answered questions about its operations and administrative practices. Gross suggested that Shriver had violated the antipropaganda and lobbying law and said that he was sending a report on the breakfasts to the Justice Department. "Under the circumstances," he added, "I have no hope that anything will be done about the matter," a reference to the fact that Robert F. Kennedy was then Attorney General.

Even after Shriver left the agency, Gross continued to be a critic of the Peace Corps. In June, 1968, during House debate on the Peace Corps authorization bill, Gross moved to amend the proposal to authorize $97 million for fiscal 1969. The agency had requested $112.8 million. Gross argued that the President had ordered a 10 per cent reduction in government spending and a 10 per cent reduction in personnel by December 31, 1968, and that $97 million reflected a 10 per cent reduction from the $107 million that had been appropriated for Peace Corps operations for fiscal 1968. He also moved to recommit the bill to committee, an action tantamount to killing it. Gross's motion lost by only seven votes—the closest vote on any Peace Corps measure since the agency was founded. A roll call vote was taken on the bill as reported from committee, which authorized $112.8 million for fiscal 1969. It passed by a significant margin— 292 to 61, with 80 abstentions.

Jack Vaughn's most outspoken opponent on the Hill was Congressman Otto Passman. The battle between the two men broke into headlines in July, 1968, when partial testimony of a closed hearing by the Subcommittee on Foreign Operations of the House Appropriations Committee was made public.

On a tour of Southeast Asia earlier in the year, Passman had met a group of Peace Corps volunteers in Bangkok who had expressed objections to the Vietnam war and to the military build-up in Thailand. A Peace Corps staff member present at the meeting reported that both Passman and the volunteers made their points with reason and little show of emotion, although the Congressman was obviously disturbed by what he heard.

The testimony, made public in July, 1968, revealed that Passman was thoroughly angry with the volunteers and with a policy that permitted them to speak so freely. Passman insisted that Vaughn require volunteers to support U.S. policy, especially on Vietnam and told him, "Your concept of our foreign policy is such that I do not think you should be in the position you hold." Vaughn then stressed his belief that volunteers should not be tied too closely to government policy while serving overseas. The conclusion of the testimony that was released follows:

Mr. Passman: If I had a chartered plane, I would have brought back some of those Volunteers from Bangkok when I was out there recently. I was shocked to hear them expressing themselves vocally in opposition to our Viet Nam policy. . . . The Peace Corps Volunteers do not have to comply with the same rules and regulations that our Foreign Service officers do, do they?

Mr. Vaughn: No.

Mr. Passman: Certainly not. I wish I could have the privilege of having this committee travel with me to see how vocal these Volunteers are. At the same time this conversation was going on, there may have been at least 50 young Americans killed in Viet Nam, while these Volunteers are expressing themselves vocally to me in opposition to our policy in Viet Nam. . . .

No American, to my way of thinking, should be permitted to go abroad until he takes that same oath of allegiance to this great country that the people down at the State Department take.

Mr. Vaughn: Let's talk about Dean Rusk, Secretary of State.

Mr. Passman: What about Dean Rusk? Let us see what Mr. Gaud [Director of AID] said. He said that all of his people going abroad have to support our foreign policy or they do not go abroad.

Mr. Vaughn: Dean Rusk has said repeatedly that Peace Corps Volunteers are not a part of U.S. foreign policy, not to be considered as such, and if they were. . . .

The released testimony ended on that fragmentary note.

Vaughn was not the only person to defend Peace Corps policy to Congressman Passman. A month later a volunteer who had served in Thailand wrote a letter to the Congressman in which she suggested that foreign nationals would be wary of an American who agreed with all his government's policies. She added that volunteers attempt to convey to host-country citizens the ideals and personal freedom that are identified with the United States, including freedom of speech and the right to dissent. She wrote, "You may argue it is good to be able to speak freely within the country, but it is dangerous outside the country because foreign nationals could easily misunderstand. I believe you underestimate the intelligence and sensitivity of non-Americans."

## PART OF THE FOREIGN POLICY ESTABLISHMENT?

The Peace Corps has always resisted being identified too closely with the U.S. foreign policy establishment, but it is a federal agency funded by Congress and its independence from national policy positions must be balanced against the reality of its existence. In general, the Peace Corps has operated at the limits of its freedom. Both friends and critics in Congress have pointed out the difficulties inherent in the agency's position.

In the presentation before the Senate Foreign Relations Committee in April, 1968, Senator J. William Fulbright discussed the incompatibility between the goals of the Peace Corps and the nation's Vietnam policy. During the hearings, he asked Vaughn, "Don't you think there is any inconsistency between what the Peace Corps is doing in India and what the United States is doing in Vietnam?" Vaughn said that he did not believe so, adding that, "We go abroad to serve people in the host country, not to serve the U.S. foreign policy. The Peace Corps is not an arm of our foreign policy." Fulbright responded that he thought it must be "very difficult for our young people to go abroad under the present circumstances" and that he personally would be "embarrassed" to serve as a

Peace Corps volunteer while the United States continued its present policy in Vietnam.

Fulbright also pointed out that the total budget requested by the agency for the 1969 fiscal year was only "enough to run the war in Vietnam for about two days. We are spending about $80 billion a year on military affairs [and the Peace Corps request] is only $112.8 million . . . that's a great commentary on our priorities."

Other members of Congress have attacked the Peace Corps for not aligning itself more closely to U.S. foreign policy. At the time the agency was created, Congressman August E. Johansen voiced concern over the Peace Corps's ambivalent concept of its foreign policy role. More recently, during debate on the Peace Corps authorization bill in the House in June, 1968, Congressman Robert Taft, Jr., of Ohio, raised questions about the agency. Taft said:

> Mr. Chairman, I rise in support of [the] bill and advocate strongly the continuation of this effort that the United States has been making. I think it is a very fine effort.
>
> In supporting the bill, however, I think it would be remiss not to comment at least briefly upon the hearings that took place before [the House Foreign Affairs] committee at which Mr. Vaughn appeared. As a result of his appearance, supplementary views, somewhat critical of some aspects of the Corps, occurred. They occurred, I believe, because . . . the principal argument . . . made for the continuation of the Peace Corps was that it is of great benefit to America [by] the building up of experience and character of the Volunteers.
>
> Well, this may be. But it seems to me in the long run the true justification of the Peace Corps . . . must be related primarily to U.S. foreign policy. To lose sight of that fact, it seems to me, would be a great mistake. I think perhaps the administrator . . . lost sight of it in his testimony as he appeared before our committee, for . . . there was no discussion of the real need or progress of the individual country-to-country programs.

Congressman Taft concluded by suggesting that members of

the House Foreign Affairs Committee visit volunteers in the field because "I do not think there is enough information on the part of the members . . . or this Congress about the impact within the countries themselves to make constructive suggestions as to how it might be improved and better related to the overall foreign policy of the United States."

The supplementary views to which Taft alluded were authored by Congressman E. Ross Adair, of Indiana, for himself and several other members of the House Foreign Affairs Committee who felt that Peace Corps operations required closer congressional supervision, that administration of these operations could be improved, and that the number of Peace Corps employees receiving annual salaries in excess of $12,-000 had increased disproportionately to the number of volunteers.

## DAY-TO-DAY RELATIONS WITH CONGRESS

The Peace Corps maintains day-to-day contact with individual members of Congress through the Office of Congressional Liaison, a part of the Director's office. Congressional Liaison coordinates the preparation of material for congressional presentations, keeps the Director informed of all activity on Capitol Hill that involves the Peace Corps, and maintains records of materials relating to congressional hearings and actions that concern the agency. The office also handles routine inquiries from Capitol Hill, which are generally from constituents awaiting assignment or from anxious PCV parents.

Not all inquiries are routine, however. The freedom of speech issue that arose over the dismissal of a volunteer in Chile and the flap that followed publication of a photograph of a bearded trainee enroute to Micronesia drew letters from congressmen who wanted a full explanation of the incidents. Staff members drafted a reply for each inquiry. (See Chapter XIII.)

Congressional Liaison also provides individual senators

and representatives with information on Peace Corps activities related to their districts. The information may range from notification of contracts let to individuals, firms, or universities and the names of schools participating in the School Partnership Program to description of unusual contributions by individual volunteers. Some congressmen maintain their own files on volunteers from their districts. The late Senator Robert F. Kennedy, for example, wrote a congratulatory letter to each volunteer from the State of New York at the time he was selected and sent another letter at the completion of service. Congressional Liaison provided the information that made this kind of personal attention possible.

## A FRIEND DEPARTS

The Peace Corps lost one of its best friends on Capitol Hill when Congresswoman Frances P. Bolton of Ohio retired in 1968. Mrs. Bolton had made headlines by calling the Peace Corps a "terrifying idea" when it was first publicly proposed by John Kennedy. Over the years, however, she became an ardent supporter. She used to delight Shriver's staff by chiding and badgering the Director during his appearances before the House Foreign Affairs Committee. She would take Shriver to task for his attention to detail, then suddenly object that she did not have time to absorb all the information in his voluminous presentation. Because of her deep interest in Africa, she was known affectionately by her colleagues as the African Queen. She made frequent trips to Africa, during which she became friends with a number of volunteers with whom she exchanged letters, and she was probably more familiar with the agency's operations there than any other member of Congress. With her departure, the Peace Corps lost a staunch ally and a good friend.

# XIII

## Life in a Goldfish Bowl and Other Problems

Sargent Shriver used to caution volunteers and staff preparing for overseas duty that they would be living in a goldfish bowl. He warned them that all Peace Corps personnel would be under constant, and sometimes critical, scrutiny by the press, host-country officials, and the people of the communities in which they were to live and work. Shriver was right; the scrutiny has been constant. Volunteers and staff members are stared at, laughed at, touched, and jostled. Their living quarters are often invaded by curious neighbors and their behavior is a source of gossip and entertainment. A volunteer from the NANESA region expressed a familiar complaint. "Sometimes I wish to hell everybody would go away. The whole damn town camps on my doorstep and I have to climb over them to get in or out." A volunteer serving in Venezuela described his situation:

> I can't be alone in my own barrio for a moment. The children expect me to be all-knowing. The women confide things with me that would make a psychiatrist blush. The men expect me to prove my manhood—their word is *machismo*—in more ways than arm wrestling and the consumption of liberal amounts of beer and rum. I sometimes want to close the doors and shutters to my cottage and pull the whole damn thing in after me.

This constant public exposure is exhausting but unavoidable,

197

and volunteers and staff soon learn that privacy is a precious commodity.

Whether a volunteer's reception in the host country is characterized by friendly curiosity, indifference, or open hostility, he has to face the fact that it takes time to gain the confidence and cooperation of his hosts. One of the early volunteers assigned to Sarawak took the advice of a former British Colonial Service officer. "Don't expect results too fast, and take six months to settle in, if necessary." On the job, the volunteer traveled discreetly among the Iban tribesmen. He was painted with tatoo motifs, dressed in native garb on ceremonial occasions, and adopted as a son by one of the tribal chieftains. As a result, he was able to launch a successful 4-H club program through which, as the Ibans put it, "we're getting progress."

Occasionally, the Peace Corps is accorded an identity quite apart from the official U.S. presence. During the fighting in the Dominican Republic, Peace Corps volunteers were the only Americans permitted to pass safely through the lines of the opposing forces. One volunteer came across a Dominican in Santo Domingo who had just finished painting "Yankee Go Home" on a wall. "Well," said the volunteer, "I guess that means me. I'll get packed." "Oh, no!" said the Dominican, "I meant the Yankees, not the Peace Corps."

## IN THE SPOTLIGHT AT HOME

Close scrutiny of the Peace Corps is not limited to volunteers and staff overseas. Since its founding, the agency itself has received widespread attention at home, which Shriver and his staff deliberately encouraged to raise interest in the Corps. One of the first Americans to volunteer, with tongue in cheek, was Art Buchwald, then a columnist for the *New York Herald Tribune*. Immediately after President Kennedy created the agency by executive order, Buchwald wrote:

One of the most urgent areas requiring technical skills and help is the French Riviera. There are people on the Riviera walking around half-naked, lacking shelter, and many still don't own their own boats. . . . As a volunteer of the Peace Corps we would be willing to drop everything this summer and go down to the Riviera to help them. We would live the way they do, eat the food they do, share their hopes and show them that an American is not too proud to become one of them, no matter what hardships he has to face.

Other publications also made light of the idea in a gentle way. The *New Yorker* published a cartoon depicting a switch-board operator answering the phone at agency headquarters with, "Peace Corps, hi!" *Playboy* pictured a youthful Corps-man in a jungle setting, flanked by two alluring, scantily clad local girls, being lectured by a female volunteer with the words, "Well! Wait 'til President Kennedy hears about *this!*"

There were more substantive comments, too, and, in effect, debate on the program was held publicly months before Congress acted on the Peace Corps bill. The late George Sokolsky, a columnist with conservative leanings, dismissed the Peace Corps as a "Children's Crusade." Others were full of advice about how volunteers should behave, what countries the Peace Corps should go to, and what kinds of assignments volunteers should be given. There were statements from congressmen, ministers, educators, and national leaders. A newsletter for public relations consultants even suggested that, since the Peace Corps would be "a public relations activity," each "battalion" of volunteers should include "a PR representative."

The Russians were not silent, either. Two weeks after the executive order creating the Peace Corps was signed, Moscow Radio made the first direct Soviet attack on the agency. Predicting that the Peace Corps was "doomed to failure," the broadcast, an English-language commentary, said the Corps was designed to "use youth as a pawn in the hands of the political strategists in Washington, to pursue goals that are anything but selfless." The commentary added that there was "every justification" for suspecting there was a "crafty plot" behind the plan. Admitting that the idea of sending young volunteers to countries in need of skilled workers was "meritorious," the broadcast said a second glance showed that the Peace Corps was "very far from being the altruistic organization whose main task . . . was to provide selfless aid for nations in need." It concluded with the charge that "U.S. monopolies" were trying to take over newly independent nations from colonizers.

## THE CREATION OF A MYTH

In the summer of 1962, Shriver achieved a major public relations coup when he arranged to take a large number of newsmen to Puerto Rico to spend a week going through the volunteers' daily schedule at a training camp. From this experience came the first stories about the rigors of Peace Corps training, and the Peace Corps image began to take shape. The result was the creation of a mythical volunteer, aptly described in the agency's third annual report:

> The realities of Peace Corps life . . . have little in common with the stereotype which persists in the minds of the American public. Otherwise known as "the Peace Corps image," the stereotype is a sweaty but wholesome American youth, motivated by visions of self-sacrifice and adventure, who is living in a mud hut in a jungle, somewhere across the seas. This image is the *real* volunteer's nemesis; it is almost his greatest burden.

Though the press has exhibited less interest in the Peace Corps in recent years, this false image of the volunteer and his life overseas persists. The agency's sixth annual report again treated the problem:

> In a very real sense, there are still two Peace Corps: one, the reality of life overseas and the considerable change that is wrought in those who experience it; and two, the romantic, self-congratulating image the public has carefully created over

the past six years. There is no similarity between the two and very little communication. The more anxiety the public feels about Vietnam or the Middle East, the more impenetrable the fantasy Peace Corps becomes.

## FLAPS AND NEAR FLAPS

In spite of constant public scrutiny and the unfamiliar and sometimes difficult circumstances in which volunteers live and work, the Peace Corps has had a remarkable record for good conduct overseas. More than 38,000 volunteers have served in 63 nations since 1961, yet few Peace Corpsmen have been guilty of embarrassing their nation or their countrymen or involving themselves in an event of international proportions. This record is due in part to the good sense of the volunteers and in part to the alert actions of overseas staff, who from time to time extricate a volunteer from trouble or, if the offense is more serious, arrange to send the volunteer home while attempting to smooth out the situation with host officials.

Sometimes what does not happen tests the staff's equanimity. One such nonincident occurred shortly after Margery Michelmore's notorious postcard was found in Nigeria. After talking with volunteers on his overseas trips, Shriver generally wrote brief notes to each volunteer's parents that went something like this:

Dear Mr. and Mrs. ————,
I had an enjoyable visit with your daughter, ————, today, and she is in good health and busy working in her new assignment for the Peace Corps. You would have been proud to see how well she is working with her host country friends. I am certain you will hear from her shortly and that her commitment and enthusiasm will come through to you in what she writes.

Sincerely,
SARGENT SHRIVER

Shriver took care of this task while flying from country to country, and normally he used postcards, which were returned to the United States in diplomatic pouch and mailed from Washington. Following a particularly long and gruelling two days in an African country, Shriver was pressed for time and asked the Peace Corps representative (now known as a country director) to have a staff member type out the message. He agreed. Shriver signed the blank cards and they were placed in the glove compartment of the jeep in which Shriver was taken to meet his flight. After Shriver's departure, the Peace Corps representative and his staff returned to the jeep, opened the glove compartment, and reached for the postcards. They were gone. A moment of panic ensued, and the staff members envisaged a rash of international incidents, one for each card Shriver had signed. Shriver was philosophical about the disappearance of the cards, but for months after the loss, the Peace Corps officials who knew about the situation felt as though they were sitting on explosives. The cards never reappeared. One staff member is convinced that a volunteer familiar with Shriver's practice took them to play a practical joke and then decided it would be wise to let the affair remain a mystery.

There have also been incidents that grew out of all proportion to their importance. In late 1967, for example, a nationally distributed photograph of a Peace Corps trainee on his way to a training site in Micronesia generated derisive editorials and considerable mail. One newspaper reader, in a letter to an editor, asked, "Has the Peace Corps flipped its lid?" Another wrote to the editor of the *Chicago Tribune*, "What a disgrace to this country to send a bum like that out to represent us." The flap was over the appearance of a young man boarding an airplane for Micronesia. He wore a straw hat, a plaid sports coat, and a shirt open at the collar. He was bearded. In his right hand he carried a briefcase; in his left, a record album and a guitar in a carrying case.

After the picture appeared in newspapers across the country, the Peace Corps received more than seventy letters, including congressional inquiries provoked by angry constituents. The letters voiced objections to "Peace Corps clothes and beards" and echoed the theme of the letter sent to the *Chicago Tribune*. The agency drafted an answer to each of them and in its response, quoted a member of the training staff who had worked with the volunteer under attack:

> He has managed to gain the highest score in the latest FSI (Foreign Service Institute) test—a 2-plus in the Kusaien language, he is the top participant in the economic development program here on Udot, he is loved by the people in his village, he has translated American songs into Kusaien—he will make an excellent volunteer.

At times a volunteer's identification with his hosts leads to excessive enthusiasm for a cause. One such incident occurred in a Central American country in 1967 when the U.S. Ambassador accompanied the President of the country to the inauguration of a health clinic in an urban slum. Outside the clinic, they were met by a picket line of protesters carrying placards that read, "A year of promises and mud, we want a street." Leading the dissenters was a Peace Corps volunteer, a forty-four-year-old woman who had managed a bicycle repair shop in the United States before joining the Corps. The Ambassador was dismayed to find the volunteer taking part in a local protest movement and scolded her. She replied that if his shoes had been wet twenty-four hours a day for a year, he might protest, too. The Ambassador expressed his displeasure to Vaughn, who immediately contacted the President of the country. Vaughn was assured that the actions of the volunteer were fine. In fact, the President admired her spunk.

## Anti-American Attacks

Not all volunteers have been the targets of anti-American protests but a significant number have been cursed, insulted, and otherwise publicly ridiculed by members of dissident groups not in sympathy with U.S. involvement in their countries. Although no volunteer has lost his life because of civil disturbances or military uprisings, there have been a number of near tragedies brought on by demonstrations, bombings, and civil war. The vagaries of local as well as international politics have caused the Peace Corps to withdraw from six countries, and civil strife has resulted in reduced operations in another.

In a few countries, the Peace Corps itself has been the target of bombings, demonstrations, and charges of CIA affiliation. In Chile, left-wing organizations have long badgered the Peace Corps and twice its office in Santiago was bombarded with Molotov cocktails. In June, 1967, five makeshift fire bombs were thrown at the building, but none exploded. A month later, one of two bombs thrown did ignite on a first floor balcony but did no damage.

There was a more serious bombing in Brazil. In mid-morning on August 1, 1967, a young Brazilian employed by the Peace Corps saw a small package in front of the Peace Corps office in Rio de Janeiro. He inspected it and was putting it down when the package exploded. Two young female volunteers were injured, not seriously, and the young boy lost a hand. Brazilian President Arthur da Costa e Silva and the foreign ministry expressed their profound sorrow over the incident, and the Brazilian press expressed horror over the bombing and restated its strong support for the Peace Corps.

In mid-September, 1968, the Peace Corps presence provoked a demonstration in Colombia. About 150 students at the University of Valle in Cali moved into the university's school of sociology and threatened to remain there until the eighty-four Peace Corps volunteers training on the campus were dismissed. The volunteers had been taking courses designed to increase their understanding of Colombian culture and social problems, and the protesters complained that the university had been giving excessive attention and "wasting money and valuable teaching efforts" on them. The Peace

Corps worked out a redistribution of the professors' time and the protest faded away.

Allegations that the Peace Corps is an arm of the CIA or another intelligence group have become familiar in dozens of countries, and such charges were used to oust volunteers from the Indian state of Kerala, a long-time Communist Party stronghold. Volunteers working in agricultural programs there were asked to leave in July, 1967, although those working with local industries and small business groups were permitted to remain until their two-year tours ended in 1968.

In Turkey, sharp criticism has been leveled at the Peace Corps by the leftist press and by nationalistic and leftist members of Parliament, although charges of CIA connections are generally the only claims made. One of the critics of the Peace Corps is the Turkish Labor Party, an extreme left-wing organization. Its opponents were amused in 1967 when Turkish reporters discovered that Sadun Aren, a party theoretician and a member of Parliament, had rented his luxury flat in Ankara to the Peace Corps country director.

## THE ISSUE OF FREE SPEECH

In 1966, 1967, and 1969, Louis Harris and Associates conducted a survey for the Peace Corps to determine the attitudes of college seniors toward volunteer service. The sampling included 1,005 college seniors eligible to be volunteers. The results of the 1966 survey showed that only 3 per cent of those interviewed believed that the Peace Corps limited a volunteer's right to express himself freely. A year later, over 30 per cent of those interviewed believed their freedom of speech would be limited in the Peace Corps. The drastic change was primarily the result of an event that occurred in May, 1967.

At that time, thirteen volunteers working in Santiago, Chile, decided to take a public stand against the war in Vietnam. They circulated a petition that was signed by ninety-two volunteers in Chile, although some later withdrew their names. The organizers met with U.S. Ambassador Ralph Dungan on June 2 and then drafted a letter to be sent to headquarters in Washington explaining their views on the right to express their political beliefs. Ambassador Dungan personally delivered the letter to Vaughn. On June 7, Vaughn replied to the volunteers in Chile in a letter that redefined the agency's policy on free speech. He wrote:

> The Peace Corps was established as an apolitical organization, and it has been our firm belief that preservation of that character is essential to its effectiveness. This has meant that as an organization and as individuals, whether staff or Volunteers, we avoid any official or seemingly official involvement in political matters whether those of the host government or our own.
>
> You may, as individuals, express your opinions to the President, the Congress and the U.S. press if you completely avoid public identification of your Peace Corps connections.
>
> Letters to the U.S. press for possible publication cannot include your Peace Corps connection or, if a number of you wish to join in a petition, your foreign address, since the latter makes identification almost inevitable.
>
> These simple steps will allow full freedom of expression and will assure that your statements will be considered solely on the basis of their intrinsic merit rather than because of the here-extraneous circumstance of your Peace Corps service.

Vaughn added that the exploitation of Peace Corps status to focus attention on the words or actions of individuals or groups of volunteers was not acceptable because to do so jeopardized the Peace Corps's ability to achieve its purpose. He also implied that continued defiance of the policy would mean recall of those involved and suggested that volunteers unable to accept the policy restrictions resign.

A test of Vaughn's policy occurred within a month. Bruce Murray, a volunteer music teacher at the University of Concepción in Concepción, Chile, wrote a letter to *The New York*

*Times* protesting the U.S. bombing of North Vietnam and objecting to the Peace Corps restrictions outlined in Vaughn's letter. He identified himself as a Peace Corps volunteer. Shortly thereafter, Murray translated his letter into Spanish for publication in the Chilean newspaper *El Sur*. He did so, he later told the Associated Press, because of an article in the paper that gave a "false impression" of Peace Corps policy against public statements by volunteers. He wanted to prove that U.S. citizens did have the right to express their political opinions publicly. He undoubtedly was also subjected to some pressure from Chilean left-wing agitators, who had been claiming that volunteers were merely pawns of the U.S. Government. Murray, who had only until the following November to complete his tour, was recalled to Washington and dismissed from the Corps.

Following Murray's dismissal, the Peace Corps issued a statement through the director of Public Information, Thomas S. Page. In his statement, Page said:

> Politics and the Peace Corps don't mix. And it doesn't matter what the politics are. If a volunteer insists on getting into politics when he is overseas, then he should get out of the Peace Corps. This has been Peace Corps policy since 1961. And we couldn't make an exception in Bruce's favor even though he was otherwise doing a fine job as a Peace Corps volunteer. We can't allow anyone to convert the Peace Corps into a personal soapbox for the public expression of controversial individual views. We had no choice but to terminate Bruce's tour.

During an interview in Washington, Murray said, "I made very clear in my article that the opinions expressed in the letters were my own and that I wasn't speaking for the Peace Corps nor for any other volunteers. The Peace Corps has always stated that volunteers should not get involved in matters concerning host-country governments, but this was an issue involving my own government, not that of Chile." The Peace Corps replied that the war in Vietnam was "a major political issue" in Chile, and, thus, Murray had involved himself in local politics.

Murray's dismissal was given national coverage and provoked heavy protest from volunteers and former volunteers, whose letters began to appear in newspapers throughout the country. Three weeks after the incident, the Peace Corps issued a "clarification" of its stand. It re-emphasized the ban on volunteer involvement in host-country politics but said Corpsmen could criticize U.S. policies at home. An agency spokesman announced that volunteers are "free to write individual letters on public issues to newspapers in this country," and that they could identify themselves as members of the Peace Corps.

Despite this statement, the agency has not entirely recovered from the incident. Many staff members and volunteers believe the issue of free speech has had a more adverse effect on recruiting than any other event. The most recent of the Harris surveys seems to substantiate this view. Almost seven in ten students interviewed in 1969 were not sure that an individual could speak freely while serving in the Peace Corps.

## DRUGS

The Peace Corps has taken a no-nonsense stand on drug usage among volunteers. Officials do not attempt to moralize on the subject, but they emphasize firmly that many host countries have more stringent laws governing the use of drugs than does the United States. The penalty in one African country, for example, for persons simply found in a room with an individual smoking marijuana is a minimum of ten years in prison at hard labor. Volunteers are warned that they are subject to host-country laws while they serve overseas and that there is no place in the Peace Corps for drug users. They are told that nothing will lead more quickly to a lawsuit, an early termination of service, or a damaged reputation of the Peace Corps than this practice.

Up to this time, known usage of hard drugs and the more

dangerous hallucinogenic drugs such as LSD is almost non-existent. There have been some publicized instances of volunteers growing and smoking marijuana, and in every case, the practice has led to instant dismissal. In general, agency officials claim that drug abuse has not been a problem. Privately, volunteers and former volunteers admit that there has been a fair amount of experimentation with marijuana, especially in those countries where laws regarding its use are lax or where supplies are plentiful.

## THE SELECTIVE SERVICE

In the past three years, the selective service has become a problem for the Peace Corps. Not only have more than one hundred volunteers had their tours cut short by the draft, but attitudes among college students toward government service have changed drastically. Until Vaughn announced in December, 1967, that he would personally intervene on behalf of all volunteers seeking draft deferments while on active service, the Peace Corps did little more than advise a male volunteer of selective service laws and procedures and confirm his active volunteer status to his local draft board. Now the agency helps those who are drafted carry their request for deferment to the Presidential Appeal Board, the court of last resort for draft reclassification. At present, nearly 5 per cent of male volunteers have draft problems and about 1 per cent terminate their service early for draft reasons. "It is a rather ridiculous situation," said one staff member, "to call up these kids, who are committed to helping others and to the cause of peace, to be trained to wage war and maybe even give their lives in some damn jungle among people who, under other circumstances, probably would have volunteers working with them."

Recently, Blatchford proposed that Peace Corps service be lengthened to three years—two years of service overseas and one year in a joint Peace Corps-VISTA program at home—and the volunteer be given draft exemption. The recent Harris survey indicates that a program which substitutes Peace Corps service for military service would be popular. According to the report, there is

> a strong and increasing support among all groups for service in the Peace Corps as a substitute for an individual's military obligation. . . . "postponing service in the military until the Vietnam war is over" as a "very important" reason for joining the Peace Corps is up from 8 per cent in 1967 to 15 per cent today for all male seniors. For men seriously considering the Peace Corps, the increase is from 8 per cent to 20 per cent.
>
> While the draft both increases and decreases interest in the Peace Corps, the data in this section strongly suggests [sic] that the current draft situation's effect is mainly to encourage interest in the Peace Corps. . . . Its impact, however, can only be felt in individuals who have a natural desire to help improve the lot of his [sic] fellow man, and in these individuals it acts as a secondary motivating force. The person who is interested in the Peace Corps solely to avoid military service is probably quite rare.

Most of the problems the Peace Corps has faced are not easily resolved. Volunteers and overseas staff will always live in a goldfish bowl. There will be conflicts with groups and individuals antagonistic to the United States as long as volunteers go overseas to countries that permit varied opinion. And the issue of how freely a volunteer should be able to speak will not be settled easily, if at all. The Peace Corps has lived with these problems since its creation. No doubt, it will live with them a good while longer.

# XIV

## The Returned Volunteer

In anticipation of the problems returning volunteers would face, President Kennedy set up a career planning board at the time the Peace Corps was created. He understood the potential contributions volunteers could make to American life and wanted to draw them into public service and teaching careers. The initial legislation submitted to Congress contained a provision for the permanent establishment of the board, which was to advise and consult with the President on the development of programs designed to provide career assistance to returning volunteers. The original board members served a short tenure, however, for the provision was not included in the legislation passed by Congress. The Senate Foreign Relations Committee's report on the Peace Corps bill stated the reason:

> The committee did not think the need for such a board existed at the present time; and it also believd that if Peace Corps volunteers are able individuals and do a good job, they will be capable of planning their own careers, and might, in fact, even resent the implication that they are not.

The House Foreign Affairs Committee disagreed with the Senate. The House bill included a provision for the permanent creation of the board, but during the conference committee proceedings on the Peace Corps bill, the House managers agreed to the Senate version.

When the first volunteers began to return in 1963, however, it became apparent that they needed advice and assistance in working out their immediate career plans. Not only had they been working in locations that offered little contact with educational institutions or potential employers, but a significant number of them had changed their career plans completely as a result of their work overseas. Thus, in 1963, the Peace Corps set up the Career Information Service, initially funded by the Carnegie Corporation and administered by the American Council on Education. In 1964, Congress passed an amendment to the Peace Corps Act that permitted the agency to administer the program and gave it official status. Congress restricted counseling services to one year following a volunteer's completion of service. The Career Information Service has since been renamed the Division of Returned Volunteer Services (RVS).

The RVS contacts a volunteer a full year before his tour ends with a career planning kit and monthly issues of the *Greensheet*, a compilation of current employment and educational opportunities and other information to help with career planning. The RVS also provides information on overseas testing procedures for the Federal Service Entrance Examination, the joint Foreign Service-U.S. Information Agency examination, and tests normally required for university admission. A library of career materials is maintained in every headquarters office overseas, and the RVS supplies, on request, special reports on career fields, applications for study grants, and information on specific fields of study. At the completion of his tour, the volunteer begins to receive copies of the *Hotline*, a weekly listing of immediate job openings. The RVS believes that its most important service is the personalized help it gives volunteers. The division receives nearly seven hundred letters a month, each of which is answered individually.

## COMPLETION OF SERVICE CONFERENCE

Until 1969, volunteers completing their tours attended a Completion of Service Conference (COSC) to review and discuss their experiences. It was usually the last time these volunteers, who trained and arrived in the host country together, met as a group. The conference consisted of five sessions covering two and a half days. In the first session, volunteers filled out a questionnaire, the results of which were used in ensuing discussions on volunteer assignments, the Peace Corps, the host country, and going home. To encourage frank comments, volunteers did not sign the questionnaires and members of the local Peace Corps staff did not attend the sessions. The answers to the questionnaires and the discussion comments were extremely candid, and volunteers were often harsh critics of the staff, the programs, and themselves. During the conference, they aired complaints about everything from a lack of staff and host-country support to insufficient transportation. They also revealed that most of them would join the Peace Corps if they had it to do over again and would serve in the same host country, and that they felt they had made a positive contribution to the country's development.

For many volunteers, the conference was important because it allowed them to voice their complaints and suggestions and to put their Peace Corps experiences in a perspective. For the Peace Corps, the conference was a source of information about overseas operations and volunteer attitudes and experiences, and the information gathered at each meeting was put into a report for the Peace Corps staff in Washington and in the host country.

Completion of Service Conferences have now become optional and are held only if a majority of each volunteer group requests one. The agency believes that they have outlived their usefulness since attitudes have become predictable and few suggestions to improve operations are being gained. Not all staff members agree with this change. According to one of them:

The COSC is for the volunteer, not the Peace Corps. If the Peace Corps gains useful information from these conferences, that's fine. But we can't bring the volunteer back from two years in a foreign culture without giving him a chance to talk about it, to share his experiences with others who will understand the same kind of experiences. For some, re-entry is rough enough even with the COSC.

## THE RE-ENTRY CRISIS

For most volunteers, returning home is a matter of shifting mental gears—of trying to think American again after twenty months or more of thinking Nigerian, or Brazilian, or Iranian. Volunteers have worked overseas with a minimum of supervision and have relied on initiative and sensitivity to get along with co-workers and to get a job done. They have become knowledgeable about the ways of living and working in a foreign culture and, often unconsciously, have adopted many of the local customs. When the time to leave for home approaches, most volunteers discover that they have absorbed more of their hosts' culture than they realized and they become acutely aware of how out of touch they are with what is going on in the United States. Returning home is often a painful and difficult experience.

When the first volunteers returned in the summer of 1963, *Life* magazine ran a feature article on their readjustment problems and coined the phrase "re-entry crisis" to describe their state. *Life* was one of the first magazines to give the phenomenon national attention. "In fact," recalls a volunteer who served with her husband in Malaysia, "the *Life* article traveled so far that when we left Malaysia in 1965, one of my students said with concern, 'I hope your re-entry crisis will not be difficult.'"

The problems of re-entry do not dissolve with the greetings of family and friends. They last at least several months and may continue for years. The crisis comes from discovering flaws in the United States that the volunteer may not have recognized before he left. As a result of his service, a volunteer's values, priorities, and goals have changed, and the

United States appears materialistic, intensely competitive, and filled with inequalities and hypocrisy. Things that matter seem to be ignored; things that do not matter are talked about and fretted over constantly. The volunteer no longer knows how to fit into life in the United States, or even if he wants to. A volunteer who served in a village high in the Peruvian Andes summed up this feeling:

I was really desperate to get home after two years. I actually left a month early because I had saved up some leave time. I just wanted to get home. I knew as soon as I landed in Miami that I had made a mistake. I found I couldn't remember much about the incredibly fast pace that Americans live. I returned to a consumer-goods society that caused reverse culture-shock. I couldn't get over the tremendous amount of money in circulation. The affluence made me feel like a stranger. Living with Peruvian Indians for two years had changed me with a permanence that, for a time, kept me at loose ends.

First I went to work in a shipyard. I found Americans to be much more insular and uninformed than I had suspected. I wanted to talk about my experiences. Typically, those I talked with asked a lot of questions in rapid order and seemed interested. They listened for about three minutes or so and then turned me off. It was tough to readjust to this, because I came back feeling that I had just done the most important job of my life. I guess I expected to be treated as a hero or at least as an important citizen. Past the initial expression of interest, no one seemed to care what I had done or with whom I had worked.

Not everyone has major re-entry problems. One volunteer who worked in the Dominican Republic described his immediate feelings on his return home in a letter to friends still there. "The only adjustment I had to make was to my clothing after I got up from kissing the runway in Miami." Another volunteer preparing to return home could see no reason why she would have trouble going back to a society that she had left only temporarily:

We brought our background with us. We traded a little bit of it in return for some of the ways of the Dominicans, and I hope we're both a little better for it. After everything is said about our involvement, our commitment, and our contributions, we'd be less than honest if we didn't admit that what keeps us going is the thought that we'll be going back home eventually. We're going to escape hopelessness.

## WHAT DO RETURNED VOLUNTEERS DO?

In late 1968, the Peace Corps could boast of a significant statistic. Twenty-five thousand volunteers had returned to the United States—more than twice the number then in training or service overseas. By 1970, that figure will have doubled.

Peace Corps staff members, national leaders, and volunteers themselves have talked of the special qualities and potential of volunteers. At a conference of returned PCV's held in Washington, D.C., in March, 1965, Bill D. Moyers, then special assistant to the President, challenged the more than one thousand participants to live up to that potential:

> You are special citizens. You are special citizens because you are volunteers, and a volunteer is a person who, in a free, democratic society, decides to serve that society—who by a conscious act of his or her free will has left the ranks of the bystanders and spectators to become a participant. A volunteer is a person with a large ego—and he should be. He is a person with a split personality, wondering on the one hand if he really can make a difference and knowing on the other hand that he must make a difference.
>
> You are special. And when you come back from abroad, if you don't think yourself special, you will simply disappear into the bog of affluent living—you won't make a difference—and your contributions, as well as your opportunities as a former and continuing Peace Corps volunteer, will be lost.

In their immediate career plans, most volunteers reflect the commitment Moyers outlined. Nearly 38 per cent return to school, not a surprising statistic since almost half of all volunteers change career plans during their two years of service. Of those not returning to school, over 31 per cent go into teaching, 29 per cent work for government agencies, 19 per cent work for business organizations, nearly 10 per cent go to nonprofit organizations, and slightly more than 10 per cent become housewives, go into military service, or enter professions classified by the Peace Corps simply as "other."

Shortly after Blatchford was appointed Director, he asked a group of staff members to suggest ways to provide a continuing involvement of returned volunteers in the Peace Corps and to make available more opportunities for their service to American society. One staff member explained the agency's increased interest in returning volunteers:

> I think a lot of us have been wondering why such a high percentage of our returned volunteers go back to school. Maybe it's because they've changed their career directions, and maybe it's because they've had no career guidance to begin with. We're not helping to make full use of their potential as community action people. If they are to be a force for change back home, they need more counseling and more help than we've been giving them.

To carry out Blatchford's plans, the agency announced that the RVS would set up regional operations through the regional offices of Volunteer Placement "to extend beyond the East Coast its field of close contact with prospective employees, graduate schools, and other organizations interested in bringing returned volunteers into their ranks." Blatchford also intends to ask Congress to extend the one-year period after service during which a returned volunteer can receive counseling.

In addition, a limited number of returned volunteers who wish to spend a month observing urban conditions in the United States will be offered the opportunity to do so through a program the Office of Voluntary Action calls Transitional

Experience. Experimental sessions will be set up in 1970 to "provide the returned volunteer with some basic concept of the challenges to a typical American city and to allow him to examine various private, government and community-generated programs which attempt to deal with the problems of the city."

Another innovation to encourage volunteers to continue community action work at home is a proposed Peace Corps Development Fund that would make money available to returned volunteers who are interested in helping develop social action, education, and other community-oriented programs. A foundation independent of the Peace Corps would administer the fund but would utilize the fund-raising capabilities of the agency's National Advisory Council. Operating procedures and funding principles will be established through consultation with returned volunteers.

Some groups bypass the Peace Corps and take their own initiative in reaching former volunteers. In 1967, for example, Governor George Romney created the Michigan Peace Corps Council as an affiliate of the State Human Resources Council. Objectives of the council are to advance better understanding of foreign cultures by Michigan citizens, to give assistance to returned Peace Corps volunteers in Michigan, and to encourage volunteers still in service to live in the state when their tours end.

EDUCATION

Of those volunteers who continue their education after Peace Corps service, approximately 75 per cent enter graduate school, and over 40 per cent of those in graduate programs study social sciences or education. Volunteers usually enroll in school immediately after their return to the United States, and a majority apply for admission while still overseas. A number of colleges and universities recognize the educational value of a volunteer's training and overseas experience and give graduate or undergraduate credits for Peace Corps service. More than sixty colleges and universities have established scholarships, assistantships, or fellowships exclusively for former volunteers.

In 1968, Vaughn announced that a loan fund of $.5 million had been made available to returned volunteers who want to continue their education. The fund was started with $48,000 raised several years ago by members of the Peace Corps National Advisory Council to assist trainees entering advance training programs. When the advance training programs were discontinued, the money was invested with the United Student Aid Funds, through which the funds are available. Former volunteers may borrow up to $7,500 and are eligible to borrow money for as long as two years after completion of Peace Corps service, or four years if they enter military service or are employed by the Peace Corps.

## TEACHING

The teaching field attracts 20 per cent of all returned volunteers and about 31 per cent of those who take jobs immediately after their tours. These statistics are significant since not even one-sixth of all volunteers intended to teach prior to Peace Corps service. Recent agency figures show that 42 per cent of those who teach do so at the secondary level, 23 per cent teach in elementary schools, 15 per cent teach in colleges and universities, and 10 per cent choose the Teacher Corps or special education. Another 10 per cent become college administrators. Recognition of the returned volunteer's potential as a teacher is spreading, and states and municipalities continue to launch drives to attract PCV teachers. Returned volunteers have proved especially effective in urban schools. Robert Blackburn, director of Philadelphia's Office of Integration and Intergroup Education, expressed the views of many officials when he stated in testimony before a House committee, "We regard [returned volunteers] as the single best source of top-flight educators available to us anywhere."

Three states have made special efforts to attract volunteer teachers. Michigan, California, and New York have appointed officers at the state level specifically to recruit returned volunteers for teaching or public-service careers. Other states have assigned the task to educators as a partial responsibility of their offices. Nearly every state now makes some attempt to recruit former volunteers to be teachers, and most give credit toward certification or a higher starting salary for Peace Corps service.

Cities have aggressively campaigned for volunteer teachers, too. In 1967, Philadelphia launched a mail campaign to recruit volunteers still in service to teach in the city's ghetto areas. Officials signed 175 PCV's to teaching contracts, sight unseen and without interviews. At the end of the school year in 1969, there were more than two hundred former volunteers teaching in Philadelphia's schools. In the summer of 1968, two of the District of Columbia's school officials went to Tunisia, Ghana, Ethiopia, Korea, and the Philippines to recruit volunteers to teach in the District's schools. They returned with contracts or applications from 146 volunteers.

GOVERNMENT SERVICE

There is a natural attraction between public agencies and Peace Corps volunteers, and more than a third of employed returned volunteers work for federal, state, or local governments or for nonprofit organizations that complement public service agencies. The jobs they hold are heavily concentrated in community action projects, Head Start, the Job Corps, VISTA, and other antipoverty programs.

To attract returned volunteers to federal service, President Kennedy issued an executive order that permits them to take the Federal Service Entrance Examination on a noncompetitive basis. All that is required for federal employment is satisfactory completion of Peace Corps service and a passing grade on the examination. This privilege expires one year after a volunteer's completion of service. In addition, the Peace Corps Act provides that, for the purpose of full-time federal employment after Peace Corps service, volunteers are considered to have been receiving a salary at the level of a GS-9 or an FSR-7. The period of satisfactory Peace Corps service is credited toward federal service seniority and retirement.

Public agencies absorb approximately 17 per cent of all returned volunteers. Of this total, slightly more than 80 per cent work for the federal government, 12 per cent for local governments, and 7 per cent for state governments.

The Peace Corps itself is the most obvious federal agency to which volunteers apply and today not a single department or section of the agency is without them. In October, 1969, there were 415 returned volunteers working for the Peace Corps world-wide. The State Department, the Agency for International Development, and the U.S. Information Agency seek volunteers and frequently contact them before the completion of their service. At the end of 1968, nearly 230 former volunteers had worked or were working for AID; 26, for the U.S. Information Agency; and 100, with the Foreign Service. Former volunteers were also at work in the Bureau of Indian Affairs, the Office of Education, and the Office of Economic Opportunity.

## BUSINESS

In an effort to attract returned volunteers to management positions, the American Management Association has set up a management internship program for which it has actively recruited returned volunteers. In October, 1968, about 150 former PCV's entered the program. This drive by a leading management group is the first deliberate attempt to interest returned volunteers in a career with private enterprise, although individual businesses and industries submit announcements of job opportunities regularly to volunteers through the *Greensheet*. About 12 per cent of all returned volunteers work in business.

## INTERNATIONAL AND NONPROFIT AGENCIES

International and nonprofit organizations employ about 7 per cent of all returned volunteers. In early 1969, 19 former volunteers were working for the United Nations and affiliated agencies, 35 were employed by CARE, and 43 were working for foreign governments. Among nonprofit organizations, 185 former Peace Corpsmen worked in family care and health programs, 284 were employed by social service agencies, 44 worked for private educational organizations, 70 were on the staffs of nonprofit overseas groups, and 6 worked for labor unions.

A few returned volunteers have begun organizations of their own. Roger Landrum, a former volunteer in Nigeria, is a co-founder of Teachers Incorporated, a nonprofit organization with headquarters in New York City that prepares teachers for assignments in ghetto schools. Volunteer Training Specialists, Inc. (VTSI) was founded in May, 1967, by twelve former Peace Corps volunteers, seven of whom worked in the first land resettlement program in Kenya. It has participated, under contract, in the agency's training programs conducted for land resettlement and agricultural projects in Kenya and has recently taken part in three training programs to prepare teachers for assignments in East Africa.

The largest and best-known organization to be spun off from the Peace Corps is TransCentury Corporation, a technical assistance organization with offices in Washington, D.C., founded by Warren W. Wiggins, former Peace Corps deputy director. The firm, which has employed about two hundred former volunteers, contracts with government agencies and private foundations to supply middle-level manpower for antipoverty programs and to conduct research and evaluation studies in low-income communities. In May, 1969, Blatchford asked Wiggins and his group to help in a study aimed at improving Peace Corps programing.

## A CONFERENCE OF RETURNED VOLUNTEERS

On January 26, 1965, President Lyndon B. Johnson wrote to Vice-President Hubert Humphrey asking him to accept the chairmanship of the National Advisory Council of the Peace Corps. In the letter, the President asked Humphrey to "convene soon a Conference of Returned Peace Corps Volunteers on or about March 1, the fourth anniversary of the establishment of the Peace Corps." The President wrote that it was time

> to assemble a representative group of [returned volunteers] to discuss their role in our national life, at home and abroad. I want you to bring them together with leaders of American education, of business and labor, of community action programs, of federal, state and local government. In serious workshop sessions, they should consider the opportunities for further service by the returning Volunteer in all parts of our public life—in the War on Poverty and in the Foreign Service, in our work to promote human rights at home and in our overseas AID programs, in our school classrooms and in our universities, in our unions and in private enterprise.

The conference, held March 5–7, 1965, at the Department of State in Washington, D.C., was organized by returned volunteers and staff members in forty days. Expenses for the entire meeting were provided in advance by large corporations and nonprofit organizations. More than one thousand returned volunteers, four times as many as had been expected, met with 250 special participants—congressmen, teachers, university presidents and professors, representatives from the press and television, executives from advertising and public relations agencies, labor union officials, management consultants, business and industry executives, social-service workers, and government officials. They discussed such topics as: What kind of citizen is the returned volunteer? Where is his overseas experience most relevant? What new directions does he want for America at home and abroad? How can what has been called "this new national resource" best be used? Workshop sessions dealt with the local community, primary and secondary education, foreign students in America, government service, colleges and universities, international service, labor, and business and industry.

In his letter to President Johnson accompanying the report of the conference proceedings, Vice-President Humphrey wrote, in part:

> The Conference was a dialogue between generations—something urgently needed, but as infrequent as it is important and exciting. . . . What emerged most impressively was the potential of the volunteers, and their desire to act, to serve, to take part in the tasks which lie ahead for this nation and the world. They were concerned, not only for the quality of American life and our social institutions, but how they, as individuals, could make a difference. What they articulated was a stronger concept of citizenship which encompasses public service as a more universal responsibility. . . . Proposals ranged from the creation of internships in community action programs to the establishment of new middle-level positions in the Agency for International Development; from new programs in experimental education to the formation of citizens groups to initiate projects under the Economic Opportunity Act.

The recommendations of the returned volunteers were thoughtful and wide-ranging. Repeatedly, they insisted that they wanted no special privileges. They argued that there was a need for additional opportunities for international service because, as the conference report stated, "There is so little in between the Peace Corps volunteer at the bottom and the expert advisers at the top. Americans who are adept at cross-cultural communication could provide some of the middle-level skills needed and supplement the present programs." They suggested the establishment of special programs that would combine community service and graduate study. Others recommended giving a number of days each month to voluntary community service. A proposal for an exchange Peace Corps that would bring foreign volunteers to the United States became a reality with the Volunteers to America program. Another proposal suggested that the Peace Corps "see itself as a university with a teaching and learning faculty of 10,000 or 20,000 volunteers and staff." Closer relationships between the Peace Corps and U.S. colleges and universities were recommended, "including the granting of academic credit in both the undergraduate and graduate curricula for Peace Corps service." That suggestion, too, has become a reality on a number of campuses.

Although the conference of returned volunteers has not been reconvened and most volunteers consistently reject the idea of a formal PCV organization, individually and in small groups they have not let up on the pressure for constructive change. By 1970, the number of former volunteers will total nearly 50,000. It does not take clairvoyance to predict that these individuals will make their presence felt.

# XV

# New Directions

During the first weeks after his appointment as Peace Corps
Director, Joseph Blatchford took a self-imposed crash course
on the agency and its operations. He read program evaluations, reports from completion of service conferences, and
special reports prepared at his request. Staff members briefed
him on new programs, special problems, and proposals for
changes in policy then under consideration. Immediately
after the Senate confirmed his appointment in April, 1969, he
assigned staff members to ten task force committees to explore such subjects as the Volunteers to America program, a
national voluntary service program, recruitment of blue-collar workers and minority groups, binationalism and improved
overseas programing, extended services for returned volunteers, and the role of the Peace Corps in promoting volunteerism in America. He also made a 3-week trip to Kenya,
Libya, and Iran to visit volunteers and staff and to talk with
national leaders about the Peace Corps. In statements to the
press and on Capitol Hill, and in briefing sessions within the
agency in the summer and fall, he began to elaborate on the
new directions he envisions for the agency.

Blatchford has proposed that the Peace Corps respond
more directly to the immediate needs of host countries by
initiating more technical assistance programs. To do so, the
agency will have to recruit more skilled volunteers. In an
interview in July, 1969, Blatchford discussed this proposal:

During my recent trip to Africa, national leaders said to me,

"Mr. Blatchford, we love your young, enthusiastic Americans who are so full of commitment, but we need more than youthful enthusiasm. We also need technical assistance and help in problem solving that comes only from experience." I agree with those leaders. We have to find a way to recruit the people these officials have described and send them overseas. I would insist that the life-style of the volunteer remain the same. But a mid-career professional living among host-country nationals with his family would, in my view, have more impact than the young, single American with an unlimited capacity to adapt to new and strange living conditions.

Blatchford went on to say that he hoped to lift restrictions that prevent a volunteer from taking dependents overseas and to raise the living and readjustment allowances to encourage more professional and skilled men from business and industry to join the Peace Corps. Until the Peace Corps Act can be modified to permit this, the agency will use the provisions for volunteer leaders to cover this new kind of volunteer.

Blatchford would also like the Peace Corps to encourage industry, business, and labor to grant short-term "sabbatical" leaves of at least three months to specialists who would go abroad to work on special problems in host countries. Under such a program, the salaries of technicians or professional volunteers would be paid by their employers, and the Peace Corps would arrange and pay for their travel, locate housing for them, and provide any support needed on the job. Those entering the program would have to agree to live like other Peace Corps volunteers, outside U.S. compounds and without special privileges.

In line with Blatchford's insistence that the Peace Corps respond more directly to a country's priorities, he also hopes to encourage more binationalism in the agency's programs. He believes that there are problems in the Peace Corps's dependence on host-government agencies, especially in community development programs, when the agencies themselves have no stake in the volunteers' work. Most of the countries recognize the importance of community development, but many do not have the government machinery to carry on or provide support for such programs. Blatchford believes that binationalism is one way to establish new channels through which community change may come about, for the programs would then become host programs as well as Peace Corps programs, and host agencies would have a vested interest in their success. To make binationalism work, according to Blatchford, "we've got to find these qualified host nationals, and if we can't find them, we've got to train them, and if we can't train them in one year, we should take five. But we must find ways to solve the problems of adequate structures and host-national participation."

In addition to expanding the kind of volunteer assistance provided to host countries, Blatchford also hopes to encourage the expansion of volunteer programs. He believes the Peace Corps can act as a catalyst for such expansion, both at home and overseas. To encourage volunteerism at home, Blatchford has suggested the creation of a National Service Corps that would permit combined service with the Peace Corps and a domestic agency such as VISTA. The three-year program would replace military service. In an interview in July, 1969, Blatchford discussed the plan. "We must broaden our base of volunteerism—of becoming involved—in American society. A National Service Corps could be the real beginning. I would like to see volunteering become a way of life for all Americans, not just those with the Peace Corps or VISTA or the Job Corps."

Blatchford also hopes to expand the Volunteers to America program, which he has called an "Exchange Peace Corps." In July, 1969, he told the House Foreign Affairs Committee:

> One way by which we can demonstrate our respect for the pride and independence of other nations is our support and enlargement of an Exchange Peace Corps. . . . just as we send Americans abroad to begin self-help projects, and just as we value their contribution upon return, so we should bring to the United States people who want to do two things—first,

help us meet our manpower needs, and, second, help their own country develop national service corps to meet their manpower needs. . . .

The Peace Corps has received requests for literally hundreds of people such an exchange would make available. The superintendent of schools in Philadelphia is seeking twenty Latin Americans to work with young Spanish-speaking students. Baltimore has set aside $500,000 for the same purpose and has asked the Peace Corps for help. Other opportunities exist in industry and in local, state and federal government. . . .

An Exchange Peace Corps provides more than an opportunity to replace Americans, or even to move other countries toward national voluntary service, great as those benefits may be. It provides an opportunity for a great country to step back from the concept of "foreign aid" with its inevitable client relationship between nations and to focus on the universal nature of social, health, and educational problems. To acknowledge America's problems no longer takes magnanimity, but to ask others to help solve them, as we seek to help others, could have real value in the foreign policy of this country.

Blatchford also hopes to encourage host countries to create their own domestic volunteer programs, with the Peace Corps providing technical assistance and professional guidance. This, he believes, will be stimulated by the Volunteers to America program, because participants will return to their countries better prepared to organize and run these programs.

In July, 1969, the leaders of voluntary groups from West Germany, France, Switzerland, the Netherlands, and England met with Blatchford and other Peace Corps staff members to discuss the development of multinational volunteer programs. The movement toward an international voluntary development corps is not new, but it has not been implemented, because there has been no structure for its administration, and national leaders have been reluctant to channel it through the United Nations. Blatchford hopes that the Peace Corps, through the International Secretariat for Volunteer Service, will play a leading role in creating an independent organization to coordinate such programs.

Blatchford's enthusiasm for volunteerism has even carried over into his plans for the Washington staff. One task force was asked to explore how members of the federal establishment, especially Peace Corps staff members, can be of service to the nation's capital. Blatchford explained his reasoning in an interview in July, 1969:

> Here we have the greatest concentration of expertise in voluntary service in the world and every evening we fight the rush hour traffic back to our homes in the suburbs while Washington's ghettos cry for help. I have talked with the city's officials about this proposal, and the response has been highly enthusiastic to say the least. I don't think we should sit here and preach volunteerism and not practice it a little bit ourselves.

The Peace Corps's Office of Voluntary Action has already begun to coordinate such a program with the city government.

Blatchford sees his own role with the Peace Corps as that of planner and strategist for achieving the goals he has set for himself and the agency. With his deputy director supervising the day-to-day operations, he will be free to strengthen the lines of communication with Congress and executive agencies, make public appearances on behalf of the Peace Corps and meet with leaders of other nations, assist in recruiting volunteers, make good use of a revitalized Peace Corps National Advisory Council, and maintain close contact with leaders in education, industry, and labor, who will be asked to help provide guidance as the Peace Corps travels in new directions. Blatchford's philosophy for leading the Peace Corps during the next few years seems to be embodied in the following excerpts from the statement he made when he appeared on Capitol Hill in July, 1969, to ask for appropriations for fiscal 1970:

> What perspective I do have on the Peace Corps has been gained

during ten years of pursuing similar goals in the private sector. During those years I have lived like a Peace Corps volunteer in the slum dwellings of Venezuela's poor, directed self-help projects in education, housing and small business, worked to involve private enterprise and government in the urban problems of Latin America and, in general, tried to look at development in the way it is seen by the vast majority of the world's people: from the bottom up. . . . I believe in the American tradition of service and voluntary solution to community problems, whether in a single neighborhood or in the world community. I believe that lasting development must be rooted in people and their attitudes based on self-help, not giveaway, and involve all of a country's people, not just a few.

# Appendix A

# Summary of Volunteers, by Country and Program, May 1, 1969

LATIN AMERICA

| Country & Program | In Training | In Country |
|---|---|---|
| **Bolivia** | | |
| Agriculture | | 89 |
| TB Control | 4 | 37 |
| Vocational Education/Rural Community Development | | 31 |
| University Education | | 8 |
| Mining | | 30 |
| Community Development | | 44 |
| **Brazil** | | |
| Urban Community Development | | 96 |
| Rural Community Development | | 221 |
| Agriculture/Cooperatives | | 108 |
| Rural Electrification | | 5 |
| Health | 50 | 30 |
| Social Action | 20 | — |
| **British Honduras** | | |
| Education | | 35 |
| **Chile** | | |
| Cooperatives | | 1 |
| Rural Community Development | | 2 |
| University Education | | 39 |
| Forestry/Community Development | | 103 |
| Municipal Planning | | 37 |
| Fisheries | | 22 |

| Country & Program | In Training | In Country |
|---|---|---|
| **Colombia** | | |
| Agricultural Extension | 30 | 1 |
| Agriculture/Nutrition | | 35 |
| Teacher Training | | 29 |
| Rural Community Development | | 269 |
| Urban Community Development | | 26 |
| Educational TV | | 49 |
| Small Business Management | | 51 |
| Physical Education | | 14 |
| Secondary Education | | 54 |
| Project Peace Pipe | | 5 |
| **Costa Rica** | | |
| Credit Unions | | 1 |
| University Education | | 1 |
| Community Development/Agriculture | | 38 |
| Rural Community Development | | 30 |
| Physical Education/Teacher Training | | 10 |
| Fisheries | | 7 |
| **Dominican Republic** | | |
| Teacher Training | | 49 |
| Community Development | | 78 |
| University Education | | 6 |
| **Eastern Caribbean Islands \*** | | |
| Cooperatives/Education/Nursing | | 6 |
| Education | | 113 |
| Nursing/Nurses Training | 1 | 18 |
| **Ecuador** | | |
| Arts & Crafts | | 5 |
| Agricultural Extension | | 77 |
| Rural Electrification | | 18 |
| Youth Development | | 23 |
| Leadership Training | | 17 |
| Rural Community Development | | 73 |

\* Eastern Caribbean Islands includes Antigua, Barbados, Dominica, Grenada, Montserrat, St. Kitts, Nevis, Anguilla, St. Lucia, and St. Vincent.

| Country & Program | In Training | In Country |
|---|---|---|
| **El Salvador** | | |
| Rural Community Development | | 43 |
| Community Development/Agriculture | | 34 |
| Education | | 4 |
| Nursing | | 7 |
| Fisheries | | 11 |
| **Guatemala** | | |
| Rural Community Development | | 43 |
| Nursing | | 8 |
| Cooperatives | 3 | 49 |
| Fisheries | 1 | 6 |
| Municipal Management | | 5 |
| **Guyana** | | |
| Education | | 44 |
| **Honduras** | | |
| Rural Community Development | | 54 |
| Education | | 41 |
| Nurses | | 6 |
| Community Development/Cooperatives | | 31 |
| Fisheries | | 11 |
| Community Development/Nurses Training | 53 | — |
| **Jamaica** | | |
| Education | | 116 |
| **Nicaragua** | | |
| Agriculture | | 17 |
| Fisheries | | 9 |
| Nutrition | | 7 |
| University Education | | 2 |
| **Panama** | | |
| Community Development/Vocational Education | | 98 |
| Fisheries | | 10 |
| Agriculture/Cooperatives | 22 | — |

| Country & Program | In Training | In Country |
|---|---|---|
| **Paraguay** | | |
| Agricultural Extension | | 55 |
| Education | | 11 |
| **Peru** | | |
| Rural Community Development/ Agriculture | | 61 |
| Urban Community Development | | 22 |
| Small Business Management | | 26 |
| Cooperatives | | 42 |
| Education | | 18 |
| **Uruguay** | | |
| Educational TV | | 5 |
| Professional Services | 9 | |
| **Venezuela** | | |
| Rural Cooperatives | | 76 |
| Municipal Management | | 38 |
| Physical Education/Youth Training | | 73 |
| Community Development/Cooperatives | | 45 |
| Agrarian Reform | | 20 |
| Secretarial | | 2 |
| Rural Health | 34 | — |
| Total | 227 | 3,191 |

## AFRICA

| Country & Program | In Training | In Country |
|---|---|---|
| **Botswana** | | |
| Law/Public Administration | | 8 |
| Education | | 3 |
| Teacher Training | | 44 |
| Community Development/Cooperatives | | 16 |
| **Cameroon** | | |
| Secondary Education | | 32 |
| Health | | 12 |
| Agriculture | | 6 |

| Country & Program | In Training | In Country |
|---|---|---|
| **Chad** | | |
| Health | | 14 |
| Wells/Irrigation | | 8 |
| TEFL | | 19 |
| Health | 5 | — |
| **Dahomey** | | |
| Rural Community Development | | 26 |
| Agriculture/Wells | 13 | — |
| **Ethiopia** | | |
| Community Development/Health | | 1 |
| Education | | 165 |
| TEFL | | 63 |
| Rural Community Development | | 30 |
| Urban Community Development | | 85 |
| Educational TV | | 89 |
| Agricultural Extension | 35 | — |
| Public Health | 17 | — |
| Agriculture | | 9 |
| **Gambia** | | |
| Community Development | | 14 |
| **Ghana** | | |
| Rural Community Development | | 24 |
| Teacher Training | | 55 |
| Geology | | 3 |
| Secondary Education | | 103 |
| Cooperatives | | 14 |
| Theater Development | 4 | — |
| **Guinea** | | |
| Equipment Repair | 28 | — |
| **Ivory Coast** | | |
| Home Economics | | 12 |
| School Gardens | | 5 |
| Secondary Education | | 5 |
| Small Business Administration | | 12 |
| Health | | 11 |

| Country & Program | In Training | In Country |
|---|---|---|
| Vocational Education | | 13 |
| TEFL | | 32 |
| Rural Housing | | 14 |
| Health Education | 5 | — |
| **Kenya** | | |
| Secondary Education | | 200 |
| Agriculture | | 44 |
| Land Resettlement | | 30 |
| Nurses Training | | 9 |
| **Lesotho** | | |
| Rural Community Development | | 15 |
| Health | | 7 |
| Education | | 37 |
| **Liberia** | | |
| Education | | 289 |
| Public Administration | | 25 |
| Teacher Training | | 22 |
| Health | 22 | — |
| **Malawi** | | |
| Education | | 71 |
| Agriculture/Rural Community Development | | 25 |
| Health | | 46 |
| **Niger** | | |
| Agriculture | | 34 |
| Health | | 6 |
| Rural Community Development/Health | | 21 |
| TEFL | | 10 |
| Health Education | 34 | — |
| Environmental Improvement/Well Digging | 13 | — |
| **Nigeria** | | |
| Elementary Education | | 21 |
| Secondary Education | | 11 |
| Teacher Training | | 70 |

| Country & Program | In Training | In Country |
|---|---|---|
| Agriculture/Rural Community Development | | 2 |
| **Senegal** | | |
| Social Work | | 74 |
| TEFL | | 32 |
| Community Development | | 4 |
| Agriculture | | 15 |
| **Sierra Leone** | | |
| Elementary Education | | 65 |
| Secondary Education | | 139 |
| Community Development | | 60 |
| **Somalia** | | |
| Elementary Education | 45 | 41 |
| Agriculture | | 15 |
| **Swaziland** | | |
| Education | 1 | 29 |
| Rural Development | 10 | — |
| Small Business Administration | | 6 |
| **Tanzania** | | |
| Soil Survey | | 8 |
| **Togo** | | |
| TEFL | | 33 |
| Health | | 26 |
| Rural Community Development | | 10 |
| Agriculture | | 21 |
| **Uganda** | | |
| Secondary Education | | 80 |
| Health | | 20 |
| **Upper Volta** | | |
| Rural Community Development/Health | | 51 |
| TEFL | | 1 |
| Total | 232 | 2,672 |

## North Africa, the Near East, and South Asia

| Country & Program | In Training | In Country |
|---|---|---|
| **Afghanistan** | | |
| Education | | 136 |
| Smallpox Vaccination | 3 | 18 |
| Omnibus * | | 16 |
| TEFL | 47 | — |
| **Ceylon** | | |
| Agricultural Extension/Community Development | | 34 |
| **India** | | |
| Agriculture | 44 | 231 |
| Rural Community Development | | 36 |
| Health | | 31 |
| Nutrition | | 25 |
| Family Planning | | 63 |
| Consumer Cooperatives | | 23 |
| TEFL/Technical Training | 23 | 24 |
| Teacher Training | | 10 |
| Tubewells/Irrigation | 16 | 32 |
| Science Teachers Workshop | 20 | 21 |
| Vegetable Gardens/Home Economics | | 38 |
| Irrigation | 1 | 18 |
| Small Industry Management | | 16 |
| **Iran** | | |
| Agriculture | | 47 |
| TEFL | | 137 |
| Municipal Engineers | | 40 |
| Nursing | | 12 |
| **Libya** | | |
| TEFL | | 175 |
| **Morocco** | | |
| Agriculture/Community Development | 2 | 76 |

* The Peace Corps uses the omnibus designation to indicate a program with volunteers in a variety of assignments, such as architecture, law, public administration, and accounting.

| Country & Program | In Training | In Country |
|---|---|---|
| TEFL | | 40 |
| Rural Public Works | | 6 |
| **Nepal** | | |
| Agriculture | | 20 |
| Agriculture/Forestry | | 62 |
| Education | | 19 |
| Teacher Training | | 45 |
| Vocational Education | | 21 |
| Rural Construction | | 30 |
| **Tunisia** | | |
| TEFL | | 155 |
| Architecture | | 33 |
| Family Planning/Health | | 8 |
| **Turkey** | | |
| Education | | 98 |
| TEFL | | 119 |
| Child Care | | 15 |
| Secretarial | 1 | — |
| Total | 157 | 1,930 |

EAST ASIA AND THE PACIFIC

| Country & Program | In Training | In Country |
|---|---|---|
| **Fiji** | | |
| Education | | 140 |
| Agriculture | 22 | — |
| **Malaysia** | | |
| Education | | 367 |
| Health | | 42 |
| Rural Community Development | | 22 |
| Industrial Arts | | 25 |
| TB Eradication | | 24 |
| Agriculture/Fisheries | | 26 |
| Agriculture/Education | 15 | — |

| Country & Program | In Training | In Country |
|---|---|---|
| **Micronesia** | | |
| TEFL/Communications | | 306 |
| Health/Economic Development | | 118 |
| Omnibus | | 55 |
| Vista (Head Start) | | 17 |
| **Philippines** | | |
| Education | 16 | 634 |
| University Education/Teacher Training | 14 | 42 |
| Malaria Eradication | 16 | 17 |
| Bicol Development | | 19 |
| Food Production | 29 | — |
| **Korea** | | |
| Education | 2 | 119 |
| Health | | 71 |
| TEFL | | 76 |
| **Thailand** | | |
| English Teaching | 65 | 60 |
| Rural Community Development | | 26 |
| Health | | 71 |
| Physical Education | | 16 |
| Education | | 34 |
| Malaria Eradication | | 16 |
| Food Production | 41 | — |
| **Tonga** | | |
| Health | | 34 |
| Education/Agriculture | | 58 |
| Education | 30 | — |
| **Western Samoa** | | |
| Health/Public Works | | 57 |
| Education/Agriculture | | 49 |
| Education | | 12 |
| Total | 250 | 2,553 |

# Appendix B

# Executive Order 10924: Establishment and Administration of the Peace Corps in the Department of State

By virtue of the authority vested in me by the Mutual Security Act of 1954, 68 Stat. 832, as amended (22 U.S.C. 1750 et seq.), and as President of the United States, it is hereby ordered as follows:

Section 1. *Establishment of the Peace Corps.*—The Secretary of State shall establish an agency in the Department of State which shall be known as the Peace Corps. The Peace Corps shall be headed by a Director.

Section 2. *Functions of the Peace Corps.*—(*a*) The Peace Corps shall be responsible for the training and service abroad of men and women of the United States in new programs of assistance to nations and areas of the world, and in conjunction with or in support of existing economic assistance programs of the United States and of the United Nations and other international organizations.

(*b*) The Secretary of State shall delegate, or cause to be delegated, to the Director of the Peace Corps such of the functions under the Mutual Security Act of 1954, as amended, vested in the President and delegated to the Secretary, or vested in the Secretary, as the Secretary shall deem necessary for the accomplishment of the purposes of the Peace Corps.

Section 3. *Financing of the Peace Corps.*—The Secretary of State shall provide for the financing of the Peace Corps with funds available to the Secretary for the performance of functions under the Mutual Security Act of 1954, as amended.

Section 4. *Relation to Executive Order No. 10893.*—This order shall not be deemed to supersede or derogate from any provision of Executive Order No. 10893 of November 8, 1960, as amended, and any delegation made by or pursuant to this order shall, unless otherwise specifically provided therein, be deemed to be in addition to any delegation made by or pursuant to that order.

JOHN F. KENNEDY

*The White House,*
*March 1, 1961*

# Appendix C

# The Peace Corps Act

*Be it enacted by the Senate and House of Representatives of the United States of America in Congress assembled,*

## TITLE I—THE PEACE CORPS

### SHORT TITLE

SECTION 1. This Act may be cited as the "Peace Corps Act".

### DECLARATION OF PURPOSE

SEC. 2. The Congress of the United States declares that it is the policy of the United States and the purpose of this Act to promote world peace and friendship through a Peace Corps, which shall make available to interested countries and areas men and women of the United States qualified for service abroad and willing to serve, under conditions of hardship if necessary, to help the peoples of such countries and areas in meeting their needs for trained manpower, and to help promote a better understanding of the American people on the part of the peoples served and a better understanding of other peoples on the part of the American people.

### AUTHORIZATION

SEC. 3. (a) The President is authorized to carry out programs in furtherance of the purposes of this Act, on such terms and conditions as he may determine.

(b) There is hereby authorized to be appropriated to the President for the fiscal year 1969 not to exceed $112,800,000 to carry out the purposes of this Act: *Provided, however,* That not to exceed $500,000 of funds made available hereunder for fiscal year 1967 shall be obligated under contracts or agreements to carry out research: *Provided further,* That no such contracts or agreements shall be executed unless the research in question relates to the basic responsibilities of the Peace Corps. Unobligated balances of funds made available hereunder are hereby authorized to be continued available for the general purposes for which appropriated and may at any time be consolidated with appropriations hereunder.

### DIRECTOR OF THE PEACE CORPS AND DELEGATION OF FUNCTIONS

SEC. 4. (a) The President may appoint, by and with the advice and consent of the Senate, a Director of the Peace Corps and a Deputy Director of the Peace Corps.

(b) The President may exercise any functions vested in him by this Act through such agency or officer of the United States Government as he shall direct. The head of any such agency or any such officer may promulgate such rules and regulations as he may deem necessary or appropriate to carry out such functions, and may delegate to any of his subordinates authority to perform any of such functions.

(c) (1) Nothing contained in this Act shall be construed to infringe upon the powers or functions of the Secretary of State.

(2) The President shall prescribe appropriate procedures to assure coordination of Peace Corps activities with other activities of the United States Government in each country, under the leadership of the chief of the United States diplomatic mission.

(3) Under the direction of the President, the Secretary of State shall be responsible for the continuous supervision and general direction of the programs authorized by this Act, to the end that such programs are effectively integrated both at home and abroad and the foreign policy of the United States is best served thereby.

(d) Except with the approval of the Secretary of State, the Peace Corps shall not be assigned to perform services which could more usefully be performed by other available agencies of the United States Government in the country concerned.

### PEACE CORPS VOLUNTEERS

SEC. 5. (a) The President may enroll in the Peace Corps for service abroad qualified citizens and nationals of the United States (referred to in this Act as "volunteers"). The terms and conditions of the enrollment, training, compensation, hours of work, benefits, leave, termination, and all other terms and conditions of the service of volunteers shall be exclusively those set forth in this Act and those consistent therewith which the President may prescribe; and, except as provided in this Act, volunteers shall not be deemed officers or employees or otherwise in the service or employment of, or holding office under, the United States for any purpose. In carrying out this subsection no political test shall be required or taken into consideration, nor shall there be any discrimination against any person on account of race, creed, or color.

(b) Volunteers shall be provided with such living, travel, and leave allowances, and such housing, transportation, supplies, equipment, subsistence, and clothing as the President may determine to be necessary for their maintenance and to insure their health and their capacity to serve effectively. Supplies or equipment provided volunteers to insure their capacity to serve effectively may be transferred to the government or to other entities of the country or area with which they have been serving, when no longer necessary for such purpose, and when such transfers would further the purposes of this Act. Transportation and travel allowances may also be provided, in such circumstances as the President may determine, for applicants for enrollment to or from places of training and places of enrollment, and for former volunteers from places of termination to their homes in the United States.

(c) Volunteers shall be entitled to receive a readjustment allowance at a rate not to exceed $75 for each month of satisfactory service as determined by the President. The readjustment allowance of each volunteer shall be payable on his return to the United States: *Provided, however,* That, under such circumstances as the President may determine, the accrued readjustment allowance, or any part thereof, may be paid to the volunteer, members of his family or others, during the period of his service, or prior to his return to the United States. In the event of the volunteer's death during the period of his service, the amount of any unpaid readjustment allowance shall be paid in accordance with the provisions of the Act of August 3, 1950, chapter 518, section 1

(5 U.S.C. 61f). For purposes of the Internal Revenue Code of 1954 (26 U.S.C.), a volunteer shall be deemed to be paid and to receive each amount of a readjustment allowance to which he is entitled after December 31, 1964, when such amount is transferred from funds made available under this Act to the fund from which such readjustment allowance is payable.

(d) Volunteers shall be deemed to be employees of the United States Government for the purposes of the Federal Employees' Compensation Act (39 Stat. 742), as amended: *Provided, however,* That entitlement to disability compensation payments under that Act shall commence on the day after the date of termination of service. For the purposes of that Act—

(1) volunteers shall be deemed to be receiving monthly pay at the lowest rate provided for grade 7 of the general schedule established by the Classification Act of 1949, as amended, and volunteer leaders (referred to in section 6 of this Act) shall be deemed to be receiving monthly pay at the lowest rate provided for grade 11 of such general schedule; and

(2) any injury suffered by a volunteer during any time when he is located abroad shall be deemed to have been sustained while in the performance of his duty and any disease contracted during such time shall be deemed to have been proximately caused by his employment, unless such injury or disease is caused by willful misconduct of the volunteer or by the volunteer's intention to bring about the injury or death of himself or of another, or unless intoxication of the injured volunteer is the proximate cause of the injury or death.

(e) Volunteers shall receive such health care during their service, applicants for enrollment shall receive such health examinations preparatory to their service, applicants for enrollment who have accepted an invitation to begin a period of training under section 8(a) of this Act shall receive such immunization and dental care preparatory to their service, and former volunteers shall receive such health examinations within six months after termination of their service, as the President may deem necessary or appropriate. Subject to such conditions as the President may prescribe, such health care may be provided in any facility of any agency of the United States Government, and in such cases the appropriation for maintaining and operating such facility shall be reimbursed from appropriations available under this Act.

(f) (1) Any period of satisfactory service of a volunteer under this Act shall be credited in connection with subsequent employment in the same manner as a like period of civilian employment by the United States Government—

(A) for the purposes of the Civil Service Retirement Act, as amended (5 U.S.C. 2251 et seq.), section 852 (a) (1) of the Foreign Service Act of 1946, as amended (22 U.S.C. 1092(a) (1), and every other Act establishing a retirement system for civilian employees of any United States Government agency; and

(B) except as otherwise determined by the President, for the purposes of determining seniority, reduction in force, and layoff rights, leave entitlement, and other rights and privileges based upon length of service under the laws administered by the Civil Service Commission, the Foreign Service Act of 1946, and every other Act establishing or governing terms and conditions of service of civilian employees of the United States Government: *Provided,* That service of a volunteer shall not be credited toward completion of any probationary or trial period or completion of any service requirement for career appointment.

(2) For the purposes of paragraph (1) (A) of this subsection, volunteers and volunteer leaders shall be deemed to be receiving compensation during their service at the respective rates of readjustment allowances payable under sections 5(c) and 6(1) of this Act.

(g) The President may detail or assign volunteers or otherwise make them available to any entity referred to in paragraph (1) of section 10(a) on such terms and conditions as he may determine: *Provided,* That not to exceed two hundred volunteers may be assigned to carry out secretarial or clerical duties on the staffs of the Peace Corps representatives abroad: *Provided, however,* That any volunteer so detailed or assigned shall continue to be entitled to the allowances, benefits and privileges of volunteers authorized under or pursuant to this Act.

(h) Volunteers shall be deemed employees of the United States Government for the purposes of the Federal Tort Claims Act and any other Federal tort liability statute, the Federal Voting Assistance Act of 1955 (5 U.S.C. 2171 et seq.), the Act of June 4, 1954, chapter 264, section 4 (5 U.S.C. 73b–5), the Act of December 23, 1944, chapter 716, section 1, as amended (31 U.S.C. 492a), and section 1 of the Act of June 4, 1920 (41 Stat. 750), as amended (22 U.S.C. 214).

(i) The service of a volunteer may be terminated at any time at the pleasure of the President.

(j) Upon enrollment in the Peace Corps, every volunteer shall take the oath prescribed for persons appointed to any office of honor or profit by section 1757 of the Revised Statutes of the United States, as amended (5 U.S.C. 16), and shall swear (or affirm) that he does not advocate the overthrow of our constitutional form of government in the United States, and that he is not a member of an organization that advocates the overthrow of our constitutional form of government in the United States, knowing that such organization so advocates.

(k) In order to assure that the skills and experience which former volunteers have derived from their training and their service abroad are best utilized in the national interest, the President may, in cooperation with agencies of the United States, private employers, educational institutions and other entities of the United States, undertake programs under which volunteers would be counseled with respect to opportunities for further education and employment.

(l) Notwithstanding any other provision of law, counsel may be employed and counsel fees, court costs, bail, and other expenses incident to the defense of volunteers may be paid in foreign judicial or administrative proceedings to which volunteers have been made parties.

### PEACE CORPS VOLUNTEER LEADERS

SEC. 6. The President may enroll in the Peace Corps qualified citizens or nationals of the United States whose services are required for supervisory or other special duties or responsibilities in connection with programs under this Act (referred to in this Act as "volunteer leaders"). The ratio of the total number of volunteer leaders to the total number of volunteers in service at any one time shall not exceed one to twenty-five. Except as otherwise provided in this Act, all of the provisions of this Act applicable to volunteers shall be applicable to volunteer leaders, and the term "volunteers" shall include "volunteer leaders": *Provided, however,* That—

(1) volunteer leaders shall be entitled to receive a readjustment allowance at a rate not to exceed $125 for each month of satisfactory service as determined by the President;

(2) spouses and minor children of volunteer leaders may receive such living, travel, and leave allowances, and such housing, transportation, subsistence, and essential special items of clothing, as the President may determine, but the authority contained in this paragraph shall be exercised only under exceptional circumstances;

(3) spouses and minor children of volunteer leaders accompanying them, and a married volunteer's child if born during the volunteer service, may receive such health care as the President may determine and upon such terms as he may determine, including health care in any facility referred to in section 5(e) of this Act, subject to such conditions as the President may prescribe and subject to reimbursement of appropriations as provided in section 5(e); and

(4) spouses and minor children of volunteer leaders accompanying them may receive such orientation, language, and other training necessary to accomplish the purposes of this Act as the President may determine.

### PEACE CORPS EMPLOYEES

SEC. 7. (a) (1) For the purpose of performing functions under this Act outside the United States, the President may employ or assign persons, or authorize the employment or assignment of officers or employees of agencies of the United States Government, who shall receive compensation at any of the rates provided for persons appointed to the Foreign Service Reserve and Staff under the Foreign Service Act of 1946, as amended (22 U.S.C. 801 et seq.), together with allowances and benefits thereunder; and persons so employed or assigned shall be entitled, except to the extent that the President may specify otherwise in cases in which the period of the employment or assignment exceeds thirty months, to the same benefits as are provided by section 528 of that Act for persons appointed to the Foreign Service Reserve, and the provisions of section 1005 of that Act shall apply in the case of such persons, except that policymaking officials shall not be subject to that part of section 1005 which prohibits political tests;

(2) The President may utilize such authority contained in the Foreign Service Act of 1946, as amended, relating to Foreign Service Reserve officers, Foreign Service staff officers and employees, alien clerks and employees, and other United States Government officers and employees apart from Foreign Service officers as he deems necessary to carry out functions under this Act; except that (A) no Foreign Service Reserve or staff appointment or assignment under this paragraph shall be for a period of more than five years unless the Director of the Peace Corps, under special circumstances, personally approves an extension of not more than one year on an individual basis; and (B) no person whose Foreign Service Reserve or staff appointment or assignment under this paragraph has been terminated shall be reappointed or reassigned under this paragraph before the expiration of a period of time equal to his preceding tour of duty. Such provisions of that Act as the President deems appropriate shall apply to persons appointed or assigned under this paragraph, including in all cases, the provisions of section 528 of that Act: *Provided, however,* That the President may by regulation make exceptions to the application of section 528 in cases in which the period of the appointment or assignment exceeds thirty months: *Provided further,* That Foreign Service Reserve officers appointed or assigned pursuant to this paragraph shall receive within-class salary increases in accordance with such regulations as the President may prescribe: *Provided further,* That under such regulations as the President may prescribe persons who are to perform duties of a more routine nature than are generally performed by Foreign Service staff officers and employees of class 10 may be appointed to an unenumerated class of Foreign Service staff officers and employees ranking below class 10 and be paid basic compensation at rates lower than those of class 10; and

(3) The President may specify what additional compensation authorized by section 207 of the Independent Offices Appropriation Act, 1949, as amended (5 U.S.C. 118h), and which of the

allowances and differentials authorized by title II of the Overseas Differentials and Allowances Act (5 U.S.C. 3031 et seq.) may be granted to any person employed, appointed or assigned under this subsection (a) and may determine the rates thereof not to exceed those otherwise granted to employees under those Acts.

(b) The President is authorized to prescribe by regulation standards or other criteria for maintaining adequate performance levels for persons appointed or assigned for the purpose of performing functions under this Act outside the United States pursuant to subsection (a) (2) of this section and section 527(c) (2) of the Mutual Security Act of 1954, as amended, and may, notwithstanding any other law, separate persons who fail to meet such standards or other criteria, and also may grant such persons severance benefits of one month's salary for each year of service, but not to exceed one year's salary at the then current salary rate of such persons.

(c) In each country or area in which volunteers serve abroad, the President may appoint an employee or a volunteer as a Peace Corps representative to have direction of other employees of the Peace Corps abroad and to oversee the activities carried on under this Act in such country or area. Unless a representative is a volunteer, the compensation, allowances and benefits, and other terms and conditions of service of each such representative, shall be the same as those of a person appointed or assigned pursuant to paragraph (1) or (2) of subsection (a) of this section, except that any such representative may, notwithstanding any provision of law, be removed by the President in his discretion.

## VOLUNTEER TRAINING

SEC. 8. (a) The President shall make provision for such training as he deems appropriate for each applicant for enrollment as a volunteer and each enrolled volunteer. All of the provisions of this Act applicable respectively to volunteers and volunteer leaders shall be applicable to applicants for enrollment as such during any period of training occurring prior to enrollment, and the respective terms "volunteers" and "volunteer leaders" shall include such applicants during any such period of training.

(b) The President may also make provision, on the basis of advances of funds or reimbursement to the United States, for training for citizens of the United States, other than those referred to in subsection (a) of this section, who have been selected for service abroad in programs not carried out under authority of this Act which are similar to those authorized by this Act. The provisions of section 9 of this Act shall apply, on a similar advance of funds or a reimbursement basis, with respect to persons while within the United States for training under authority of this subsection. Advances or reimbursements received under this subsection may be credited to the current applicable appropriation, fund, or account and shall be available for the purposes for which such appropriation, fund, or account is authorized to be used.

(c) Training hereinabove provided for shall include instruction in the philosophy, strategy, tactics, and menace of communism.

### PARTICIPATION OF FOREIGN NATIONALS

SEC. 9. In order to provide for assistance by foreign nationals in the training of volunteers, and to permit effective implementation of Peace Corps projects with due regard for the desirability of cost-sharing arrangements, where appropriate, the President may make provision for transportation, housing, subsistence, or per diem in lieu thereof, and health care or health and accident insurance for foreign nationals engaged in activities authorized by this Act while they are away from their homes, without regard to the provisions of any other law: *Provided, however,* That per diem in lieu of subsistence furnished to such persons shall not be at rates higher than those prescribed by the Secretary of State pursuant to section 12 of Public Law 84–885 (70 Stat. 890). Such persons, and persons coming to the United States under contract pursuant [to] section 10(a) (4), may be admitted to the United States, if otherwise qualified, as nonimmigrants under section 101(a) (15) of the Immigration and Nationality Act (8 U.S.C. 1101(a) (15)) for such time and under such conditions as may be prescribed by regulations promulgated by the Secretary of State and the Attorney General. A person admitted under this section who fails to maintain the status under which he was admitted or who fails to depart from the United States at the expiration of the time for which he was admitted, or who engages in activities of a political nature detrimental to the interests of the United States, or in activities not consistent with the security of the United States, shall, upon the warrant of the Attorney General, be taken into custody and promptly deported pursuant to sections 241, 242, and 243 of the Immigration and Nationality Act. Deportation proceedings under this section shall be summary and the findings of the Attorney General as to matters of fact shall be conclusive.

## GENERAL POWERS AND AUTHORITIES

SEC. 10. (a) In furtherance of the purposes of this Act, the President may—

(1) enter into, perform, and modify contracts and agreements and otherwise cooperate with any agency of the United States Government or of any State or any subdivision thereof, other governments and departments and agencies thereof, and educational institutions, voluntary agencies, farm organizations, labor unions, and other organizations, individuals and firms;

(2) assign volunteers in special cases to temporary duty with international organizations and agencies when the Secretary of State determines that such assignment would serve the purposes of this Act: *Provided,* That not more than one hundred and twenty-five Peace Corps volunteers or volunteer leaders shall be assigned to international organizations as described in this section;

(3) accept in the name of the Peace Corps and employ or transfer in furtherance of the purposes of this Act (A) voluntary services notwithstanding the provisions of 31 U.S.C. 665(b), and (B) any money or property (real, personal or mixed, tangible or intangible) received by gift, devise, bequest, or otherwise; and

(4) contract with individuals for personal services abroad, and with aliens (abroad or within the United States) for personal services within the United States: *Provided,* That no such person shall be deemed an officer or employee or otherwise in the service or employment of the United States Government for any purpose.

(b) Notwithstanding any other provision of law, whenever the President determines that it will further the purposes of this Act, the President, under such regulations as he may prescribe, may settle and pay, in an amount not exceeding $10,000, any claim against the United States, for loss of or damage to real or personal property (including loss of occupancy or use thereof) belonging to, or for personal injury or death of, any person not a citizen or resident of the United States, where such claim arises abroad out of the act or omission of any Peace Corps employee or out of the act or omission of any volunteer, but only if such claim is presented in writing within one year after it accrues. Any amount paid in settlement of any claim under this subsection shall be accepted by the claimant in full satisfaction thereof and shall bar any further action or proceeding thereon.

(c) Subject to any future action of the Congress, a contract or agreement which entails commitments for the expenditure of funds available for the purposes of this Act, including commitments for the purpose of paying or providing for allowances and other benefits of volunteers authorized by sections 5 and 6 of this Act, may extend at any time for not more than thirty-six months.

(d) Whenever the President determines it to be in furtherance of the purposes of this Act, functions authorized by this Act may be performed without regard to such provisions of law (other than the Renegotiation Act of 1951, as amended) regulating the making, performance, amendment, or modification of contracts and the expenditure of Government funds as the President may specify.

(e) The President may allocate or transfer to any agency of the United States Government any funds available for carrying out the purposes of this Act including any advance received by the United States from any country or international organization under authority of this Act, but not to exceed 20 per centum in the aggregate of such funds may be allocated or transferred to agencies other than the Peace Corps. Such funds shall be available for obligation and expenditure for the purposes of this Act in accordance with authority granted in this Act or under authority governing the activities of the agencies of the United States Government to which such funds are allocated or transferred.

(f) Any officer of the United States Government carrying out functions under this Act may utilize the services and facilities of, or procure commodities from, any agency of the United States Government as the President shall direct, or with the consent of the head of such agency, and funds allocated pursuant to this subsection to any such agency may be established in separate appropriation accounts on the books of the Treasury.

(g) In the case of any commodity, service, or facility procured from any agency of the United States Government under this Act, reimbursement or payment shall be made to such agency from funds available under this Act. Such reimbursement or payment shall be at replacement cost, or, if required by law, at actual cost, or at any other price authorized by law and agreed to by the owning or disposing agency. The amount of any such reimbursement or payment shall be credited to current applicable appropriations, funds, or accounts from which there may be procured replacements of similar commodities, services, or facilities, except that where such appropriations, funds, or accounts are not reimbursable except by reason of this subsection, and when the owning or disposing agency determines that such replacement is not necessary, any funds received in payment therefor shall be covered into the Treasury as miscellaneous receipts.

## REPORTS

SEC. 11. The President shall transmit to the Congress, at least once in each fiscal year, a report on operations under this Act.

### PEACE CORPS NATIONAL ADVISORY COUNCIL

SEC. 12. (a) The President may appoint to membership in a board to be known as the Peace Corps National Advisory Council twenty-five persons who are broadly representative of educational institutions, voluntary agencies, farm organizations, and labor unions, and other public and private organizations and groups as well as individuals interested in the programs and objectives of the Peace Corps, to advise and consult with the President with regard to policies and programs designed to further the purposes of this Act.

(b) Members of the Council shall serve at the pleasure of the President and meet at his call. They shall receive no compensation for their services, but members who are not officers or employees of the United States Government may each receive out of funds made available for the purposes of this Act a per diem allowance of $50 for each day, not to exceed twenty days in any fiscal year in the case of any such member, spent away from his home or regular place of business for the purpose of attendance at meetings or conferences and in necessary travel, and while so engaged may be paid actual travel expenses and per diem in lieu of subsistence and other expenses, at the applicable rate prescribed by the Standardized Government Travel Regulations, as amended from time to time.

### EXPERTS AND CONSULTANTS

SEC. 13. (a) Experts and consultants or organizations thereof may, as authorized by section 15 of the Act of August 2, 1946, as amended (5 U.S.C. 55a), be employed by the President for the performance of functions under this Act, and individuals so employed may be compensated at rates not in excess of $75 per diem, and while away from their homes or regular places of business, they may be paid actual travel expenses and per diem in lieu of subsistence and other expenses at the applicable rate prescribed in the Standardized Government Travel Regulations, as amended from time to time, while so employed: *Provided,* That contracts for such employment may be renewed annually.

(b) Service of an individual as a member of the Council authorized to be established by section 12 of this Act or as an expert or consultant under subsection (a) of this section shall not be considered as employment or holding of office or position bringing such individual within the provisions of section 13 of the Civil Service Retirement Act, as amended (5 U.S.C. 2263), section 872 of the Foreign Service Act of 1946, as amended, or any other law limiting the reemployment of retired officers or employees or governing the simultaneous receipt of compensation and retired pay or annuities, subject to section 201 of the Dual Compensation Act.

### DETAIL OF PERSONNEL TO FOREIGN GOVERNMENTS AND INTERNATIONAL ORGANIZATIONS

SEC. 14. (a) In furtherance of the purposes of this Act, the head of any agency of the United States Government is authorized to detail, assign, or otherwise make available any officer or employee of his agency (1) to serve with, or as a member of, the international staff of any international organization, or (2) to any office or position to which no compensation is attached with any foreign government or agency thereof: *Provided,* That such acceptance of such office or position shall in no case involve the taking of an oath of allegiance to another government.

(b) Any such officer or employee, while so detailed or assigned, shall be considered, for the purpose of preserving his allowances, privileges, rights, seniority, and other benefits as such, an officer or employee of the United States Government and of the agency of the United States Government from which detailed or assigned, and he shall continue to receive compensation, allowances, and benefits from funds authorized by this Act. He may also receive, under such regulations as the President may prescribe, representation allowances similar to those allowed under section 901 of the Foreign Service Act of 1946 (22 U.S.C. 1131). The authorization of such allowances and other benefits, and the payment thereof out of any appropriations available therefor, shall be considered as meeting all of the requirements of section 1765 of the Revised Statutes (5 U.S.C. 70).

(c) Details or assignments may be made under this section—

(1) without reimbursement to the United States Government, by the international organization or foreign government;

(2) upon agreement by the international organization or foreign government to reimburse the United States Government for compensation, travel expenses, and allowances, or any part thereof, payable to such officer or employee during the period of assignment or detail in accordance with subsection (b) of this section; and such reimbursement shall be credited to the appropriation, fund, or account utilized for paying such compensation, travel expenses, or allowances, or to the appropriation, fund, or account currently available for such purpose; or

(3) upon an advance of funds, property or services to the United States Government accepted with the approval of the President for specified uses in furtherance of the purposes of this Act; and funds so advanced may be established as a separate fund in the Treasury of the United States Government, to be available for the specified uses, and to be used for reimbursement of appropriations or direct expenditure subject to the provisions of this Act, any unexpended balance of such

account to be returned to the foreign government or international organization.

UTILIZATION OF FUNDS

SEC. 15. (a) Funds made available for the purposes of this Act may be used for compensation, allowances and travel of employees, including Foreign Service personnel whose services are utilized primarily for the purposes of this Act, for printing and binding without regard to the provisions of any other law, and for expenditures outside the United States for the procurement of supplies and services and for other administrative and operating purposes (other than compensation of employees) without regard to such laws and regulations governing the obligation and expenditure of Government funds as may be necessary to accomplish the purposes of this Act.

(b) Funds made available for the purposes of this Act may be used to pay expenses in connection with travel abroad of employees and, to the extent otherwise authorized by this Act, of volunteers, including travel expenses of dependents (including expenses during necessary stopovers while engaged in such travel), and transportation of personal effects, household goods, and automobiles when any part of such travel or transportation begins in one fiscal year pursuant to travel orders issued in that fiscal year, notwithstanding the fact that such travel or transportation may not be completed during the same fiscal year, and cost of transporting to and from a place of storage, and the cost of storing automobiles of employees when it is in the public interest or more economical to authorize storage.

(c) Funds available under this Act may be used to pay costs of training employees employed or assigned pursuant to section 7(a) (2) of this Act (through interchange or otherwise) at any State or local unit of government, public or private nonprofit institution, trade, labor, agricultural, or scientific association or organization, or commercial firm; and the provisions of Public Law 84–918 (7 U.S.C. 1881 et seq.) may be used to carry out the foregoing authority notwithstanding that interchange of personnel may not be involved or that the training may not take place at the institutions specified in that Act. Any payments or contributions in connection therewith may, as deemed appropriate by the head of the agency of the United States Government authorizing such training, be made by private or public sources and be accepted by any trainee, or may be accepted by and credited to the current applicable appropriation of such agency: *Provided, however,* That any such payments to an employee in the nature of compensation shall be in lieu, or in reduction, of compensation received from the United States Government.

(d) Funds available for the purposes of this Act shall be available for—

(1) rent of buildings and space in buildings in the United States, and for repair, alteration, and improvement of such leased properties;

(2) expenses of attendance at meetings concerned with the purposes of this Act, including (notwithstanding the provisions of section 9 of Public Law 60–328 (31 U.S.C. 673)) expenses in connection with meetings of persons whose employment is authorized by section 13(a) of this Act;

(3) rental and hire of aircraft;

(4) purchase and hire of passenger motor vehicles: *Provided,* That, except as may otherwise be provided in an appropriation or other Act, passenger motor vehicles for administrative purposes abroad may be purchased for replacement only, and such vehicles may be exchanged or sold and replaced by an equal number of such vehicles, and the cost, including exchange allowance, of each such replacement shall not exceed $2,500 in the case of an automobile for any Peace Corps country representative appointed under section 7(c): *Provided further,* That passenger motor vehicles may be purchased for use in the United States only as may be specifically provided in an appropriation or other Act;

(5) entertainment (not to exceed $5,000 in any fiscal year except as may otherwise be provided in an appropriation or other Act);

(6) exchange of funds without regard to section 3561 of the Revised Statutes (31 U.S.C. 543) and loss by exchange;

(7) expenditures (not to exceed $5,000 in any fiscal year except as may be otherwise provided in an appropriation or other Act) not otherwise authorized by law to meet unforeseen emergencies or contingencies arising in the Peace Corps: *Pro-*

*vided,* That a certificate of the amount only of each such expenditure and that such expenditure was necessary to meet an unforeseen emergency or contingency, made by the Director of the Peace Corps or his designee, shall be deemed a sufficient voucher for the amount therein specified;

(8) insurance of official motor vehicles acquired for use abroad;

(9) rent or lease abroad for not to exceed five years of offices, health facilities, buildings, grounds, and living quarters, and payments therefor in advance; maintenance, furnishings, necessary repairs, improvements, and alterations to properties owned or rented by the United States Government or made available for its use abroad; and costs of fuel, water, and utilities for such properties;

(10) expenses of preparing and transporting to their former homes, or, with respect to foreign participants engaged in activities under this Act, to their former homes or places of burial, and of care and disposition of, the remains of persons or members of the families of persons who may die while such persons are away from their homes participating in activities under this Act;

(11) use in accordance with authorities of the Foreign Service Act of 1946, as amended (22 U.S.C. 801 et seq.), not otherwise provided for; and

(12) ice and drinking water for use abroad.

#### APPOINTMENT OF PERSONS SERVING UNDER PRIOR LAW

SEC. 16. * * * [Repealed—1966]

#### USE OF FOREIGN CURRENCIES

SEC. 17. Whenever possible, expenditures incurred in carrying out functions under this Act shall be paid for in such currency of the country or area where the expense is incurred as may be available to the United States.

#### APPLICABILITY OF MUTUAL DEFENSE ASSISTANCE CONTROL ACT

SEC. 18. The Mutual Defense Assistance Control Act of 1951 (22 U.S.C. 1611 et seq.) shall apply with respect to functions carried out under this Act except in cases where the President shall determine that such application would be detrimental to the interests of the United States.

## EXCLUSIVE RIGHT TO SEAL AND NAME

SEC. 19. (a) The President may adopt, alter, and use an official seal or emblem of the Peace Corps of such design as he shall determine which shall be judicially noticed.

(b) (1) The use of the official seal or emblem and the use of the name "Peace Corps" shall be restricted exclusively to designate programs authorized under this Act.

(2) Whoever, whether an individual, partnership, corporation, or association, uses the seal for which provision is made in this section, or any sign, insignia, or symbol in colorable imitation thereof, or the words "Peace Corps" or any combination of these or other words or characters in colorable imitation thereof, other than to designate programs authorized under this Act, shall be fined not more than $500 or imprisoned not more than six months, or both. A violation of this subsection may be enjoined at the suit of the Attorney General, United States attorneys, or other persons duly authorized to represent the United States.

## MORATORIUM ON STUDENT LOANS

SEC. 20. * * * [Repealed—1966]

## AMENDMENT TO CIVIL SERVICE RETIREMENT ACT

SEC. 21. * * * [Repealed—1966]

## SECURITY INVESTIGATIONS

SEC. 22. All persons employed or assigned to duties under this Act shall be investigated to insure that the employment or assignment is consistent with the national interest in accordance with standards and procedures established by the President. If an investigation made pursuant to this section develops any data reflecting that the person who is the subject of the investigation is of questionable loyalty or is a questionable security risk, the investigating agency shall refer the matter to the Federal Bureau of Investigation for the conduct of a full field investigation. The results of that full field investigation shall be furnished to the initial investigating agency, and to the agency by which the subject person is employed, for information and appropriate action. Volunteers shall be deemed employees of the United States Government for the purpose of this section.

### UNIVERSAL MILITARY TRAINING AND SERVICE ACT

SEC. 23. Notwithstanding the provisions of any other law or regulation, service in the Peace Corps as a volunteer shall not in any way exempt such volunteer from the performance of any obligations or duties under the provisions of the Universal Military Training and Service Act.

### FOREIGN LANGUAGE PROFICIENCY

SEC. 24. No person shall be assigned to duty as a volunteer under this Act in any foreign country or area unless at the time of such assignment he possesses such reasonable proficiency as his assignment requires in speaking the language of the country or area to which he is assigned.

### DEFINITIONS

SEC. 25. (a) The term "abroad" means any area outside the United States.

(b) The term "United States" means the several States and the District of Columbia.

(c) The term "function" includes any duty, obligation, right, power, authority, responsibility, privilege, discretion, activity, and program.

(d) The term "health care" includes all appropriate examinations, preventive, curative, and restorative health and medical care, and supplementary services when necessary.

(e) For the purposes of this or any other Act, the period of any individual's service as a volunteer under this Act shall include—

(i) except for the purposes of section 5(f) of this Act, any period of training under section 8(a) prior to enrollment as a volunteer under this Act; and

(ii) the period between enrollment as a volunteer and the termination of service as such volunteer by the President or by death or resignation.

(f) The term "United States Government agency" includes any

department, board, wholly or partly owned corporation, or instrumentality, commission, or establishment of the United States Government.

(g) The word "transportation" in sections 5(b) and 6(2) includes transportation of not to exceed three hundred pounds per person of unaccompanied necessary personal and household effects.

#### CONSTRUCTION

SEC. 26. If any provision of this Act or the application of any provision to any circumstances or persons shall be held invalid, the validity of the remainder of this Act and the applicability of such provision to other circumstances or persons shall not be affected thereby.

#### EFFECTIVE DATE

SEC. 27. This Act shall take effect on the date of its enactment.

## TITLE II—AMENDMENT OF INTERNAL REVENUE CODE AND SOCIAL SECURITY ACT

#### TAXATION OF ALLOWANCES

SEC. 201. * * * [Repealed—1966]

#### SOCIAL SECURITY COVERAGE

SEC. 202. * * * [Repealed—1966]

## TITLE III—ENCOURAGEMENT OF VOLUNTARY SERVICE PROGRAMS

SEC. 301. (a) The Congress declares that it is the policy of the United States and a further purpose of this Act to encourage countries and areas to establish programs under which their citizens and nationals would volunteer to serve in order to help meet the needs of less developed countries or areas for trained manpower, and to encourage less developed countries or areas to establish programs under which their citizens and nationals would volunteer to serve in order to meet their needs for trained manpower.

(b) Not more than $300,000 may be used to carry out the

purposes of this title in fiscal year 1964. Activities carried out by the President in furtherance of the purposes of this title shall be limited to the furnishing of knowledge and skills relating to the selection, training, and programing of volunteer manpower. None of the funds available to carry out the purposes of this Act which are used in furtherance of the purposes of this title may be contributed to any international organization or to any foreign government or agency thereof; nor may such funds be used to pay the costs of developing or operating volunteer programs of such organization, government, or agency, or to pay any other costs of such organization, government, or agency.

(c) Such activities shall not compromise the national character of the Peace Corps.

# Bibliography

## BOOKS

ALBERTSON, MAURICE L., and others. *New Frontiers For American Youth: Perspective on the Peace Corps.* Washington, D.C.: Public Affairs Press, 1961.

FOX, ERNEST; NICOLAU, GEORGE; and WOFFORD, HARRIS, eds. *Citizen in a Time of Change: The Returned Peace Corps Volunteer.* Report of the Conference for Returned Volunteers held in Washington, D.C., March 5–7, 1965. Washington, D.C.: The Peace Corps, 1965.

FUCHS, LAWRENCE H. *"Those Peculiar Americans": The Peace Corps and American National Character.* New York: Meredith Press, 1967.

HAYES, SAMUEL P. *An International Peace Corps: The Promise and Problems.* Washington, D.C.: Public Affairs Institute, 1961.

HOOPES, ROY. *The Complete Peace Corps Guide.* New York: Dial Press, 1961.

————, ed. *The Peace Corps Experience.* New York: Clarkson N. Potter, 1968.

LEDERER, WILLIAM J. and BURDICK, EUGENE. *The Ugly American.* New York: W. W. Norton & Co., 1958.

LISTON, ROBERT A. *Sargent Shriver: A Candid Portrait.* New York: Farrar, Straus and Co., 1964.

SCHLESINGER, ARTHUR M., JR. *A Thousand Days: John F. Kennedy in the White House.* Boston: Houghton Mifflin, 1965.

SORENSON, THEODORE C. *Kennedy.* New York: Harper & Row, 1965.

TEXTOR, ROBERT B. *Cultural Frontiers of the Peace Corps.* Cambridge: M.I.T. Press, 1966.

WHITE, THEODORE H. *The Making of the President 1960.* New York: Atheneum, 1962.

WINGENBACH, CHARLES E. *The Peace Corps: Who, How, and Where.* New York: John Day, 1961.

267

ARTICLES

CLEVELAND, HARLAN. "Internationalizing the Concept of the Peace Corps." *Department of State Bulletin,* April 17, 1961, pp. 551–2.
RUSK, DEAN. "The President." *Foreign Affairs,* April 1960, pp. 353–369.
SHRIVER, SARGENT, and others. "Ambassadors of Good Will, The Peace Corps." *National Geographic,* September 1964, pp. 297–345.
VAUGHN, JACK. "The Peace Corps: Now We Are Seven." *Saturday Review,* January 6, 1968, p. 21.

JOURNALS

*The Annals of The American Academy of Political and Social Science,* May, 1966. The entire issue is devoted to the Peace Corps and includes thirteen articles that range from a historical introduction to an examination of new directions.

GOVERNMENT DOCUMENTS

KENNEDY, JOHN F. *Public Papers of the Presidents of the United States.* Washington: Government Printing Office, 1962.
Peace Corps. *Annual Report.* Washington: Government Printing Office, annual.
U.S. House. Foreign Affairs Committee. *Mutual Security Act of 1960.* Report (No. 1464) on H.R. 11510, 86th Cong., 2d Sess. Washington: Government Printing Office, 1960.
———. *Mutual Security Act of 1960.* Conference Report (No. 1593) to accompany H.R. 11510, 86th Cong., 2d Sess. Washington: Government Printing Office, 1960.
———. *The Peace Corps.* Hearings on H.R. 7500, 87th Cong., 1st Sess. Washington: Government Printing Office, 1961.
———. *Peace Corps Act.* Conference Report (No. 1239) to accompany H.R. 7500, 87th Cong., 1st Sess. Washington: Government Printing Office, 1961.
———. *Peace Corps Act.* Report (No. 1115) on H.R. 7500, 87th Cong., 1st Sess. Washington: Government Printing Office, 1961.
———. *Peace Corps Act Amendment of 1967.* Hearings on S. 1031, 90th Cong., 1st Sess. Washington: Government Printing Office, 1967.
———. *Peace Corps Act Amendment of 1968.* Hearings on H.R. 15087, 90th Cong., 2d Sess. Washington: Government Printing Office, 1968.
———. *Peace Corps Act Amendments.* Hearings on H.R. 10404, 87th Cong., 2d Sess. Washington: Government Printing Office, 1962.
———. *Section-by-Section Analysis of Bill to Amend the Peace Corps Act.* 87th Cong., 2d Sess. Washington: Government Printing Office, 1962.

U.S. House. Subcommittee on Foreign Operations Appropriations. *Foreign Operations Appropriations for 1963.* Hearings, 87th Cong., 2d Sess. Washington: Government Printing Office, 1962.

————. *Foreign Operations Appropriations for 1965.* Hearings, 88th Cong., 2d Sess. Washington: Government Printing Office, 1964.

U.S. Senate. *A Bill To Establish a Peace Corps.* Introduced by Senator Hubert H. Humphrey, 86th Cong., 2d Sess. Washington: Government Printing Office, 1960.

U.S. Senate. Committee on Appropriations. *Foreign Assistance and Related Agencies' Appropriations for 1963.* Hearings on H.R. 13175, 87th Cong., 2d Sess. Washington: Government Printing Office, 1962.

U.S. Senate. Committee on Foreign Relations. *The Peace Corps.* Hearings on S. 2000, 87th Cong., 1st Sess. Washington: Government Printing Office, 1961.

————. *The Peace Corps.* Report (No. 706) on S. 2000, 87th Cong., 1st Sess. Washington: Government Printing Office, 1961.

————. *Peace Corps Act Amendment of 1968.* Hearings on S. 2914, 90th Cong., 2d Sess. Washington: Government Printing Office, 1968.

————. *Peace Corps Act Amendments.* Hearings on S. 2935, 87th Cong., 2d Sess. Washington: Government Printing Office, 1962.

————. *Peace Corps Act Amendments.* Report (No. 1325) to accompany S. 2935, 87th Cong., 2d Sess. Washington: Government Printing Office, 1962.

————. *Peace Corps Act Amendments, 1969.* Hearings on S. 2041, 91st Cong., 1st Sess. Washington: Government Printing Office, 1969.

U.S. Senate. Subcommittee on Freedom of Communications. *The Speeches of Senator John F. Kennedy, Presidential Campaign of 1960* (Part I); *The Speeches of Vice President Richard M. Nixon, Presidential Campaign of 1960* (Part II). 87th Cong., 1st Sess. Washington: Government Printing Office, 1961.

## UNPUBLISHED MATERIAL

CASE, ANDREW L. "The Launching of the Peace Corps: An Analysis of the Interplay of Bureaucratic and Charismatic Forces." Master's thesis, School of Government, Business, and International Affairs, George Washington University, 1963.

CLINTON, J. JARRETT, and WOODSON, ROBERT D. "Hepatitis Among Peace Corps Volunteers: Effectiveness of Immune Serum Globulin in its Prevention." From the National Communicable Disease Center, Public Health Service, U.S. Department of Health, Education and Welfare, Atlanta, Georgia, and the Office of Medical Programs, Peace Corps, Washington, D.C., 1969. Mimeographed.

"College Seniors and the Peace Corps—1969." Survey conducted for the Peace Corps by Louis Harris and Associates in May, 1969. Multilithed.

JONES, DEBORAH. "The Making of a Volunteer: A Review of Peace Corps Training, Summer 1968." Special report from the Office of Evaluation, December 1968. Multilithed.

"Strengthening Headquarters Organization." Report of recommendations on the organization of the Peace Corps in Washington by McKinsey & Company, August 1969. Multilithed.

## PEACE CORPS PUBLICATIONS

The Peace Corps issues numerous brochures that describe specific activities of the agency and its volunteers. The publications listed below are just a few of the many available by request.

*An Adventure in Medicine: The Peace Corps Staff Physician.*
*Agriculture: The Fight to Feed a Hungry World.*
*Architects, City Planners, and Engineers: The Professional Puts Technology To Work for Human Development.*
*Community Development: From Village to City. Charting the Course of Human Progress.*
*Health Work: A Crucial Struggle to Control Disease in Developing Nations.*
*Language, Skill, and Service: The Education of a Volunteer.*
*Peace Corps: How Minorities View It.*
*Returned Volunteers: Applying Experience Abroad to Problems and Potential at Home.*
*Teaching: Education Lays the Foundation for Human and Economic Development.*
*The Peace Corps Reader.*
*Two's Company: Married Couples in the Peace Corps.*
*You Can't Send a Girl There!*

# Index